In Love and Struggle

GENDER AND CULTURE

GENDER AND CULTURE
A Series of Columbia University Press
Nancy K. Miller and Victoria Rosner, Series Editors

A complete list of books in this series can be found on pages 313–315.

In Love and Struggle

Letters in Contemporary Feminism

MARGARETTA JOLLY

Columbia University Press　*New York*

Columbia University Press
Publishers Since 1893
New York   Chichester, West Sussex

Copyright © 2008 Columbia University Press
All rights reserved

Library of Congress Cataloging-in-Publication Data
Jolly, Margaretta.
  In love and struggle : letters in contemporary feminism / Margaretta
Jolly.
     p. cm.—(Gender and culture)
  Includes bibliographical references and index.
  ISBN 978-0-231-13792-8 (cloth : alk. paper)—ISBN 978-0-231-51075-2
(e-book)
     1. Feminists—Correspondence.   2. Feminists—Social networks.
3. Feminism—Great Britain—History—20th century.   4. Feminism—United
States—History—20th century.   5. Letter writing—History—20th century.
6. Letters—Women authors—History and criticism.
7. Electronic mail messages—Social aspects.   I. Title.   II. Series.

HQ1154.J573 2007
305.42092'2—dc22   2007028475

Columbia University Press books are printed on permanent and durable acid-free paper.
This book is printed on paper with recycled content.
Printed in the United States of America
c 10 9 8 7 6 5 4 3 2 1

References to Internet Web sites (URLs) were accurate at the time of writing. Neither the
author nor Columbia University Press is responsible for URLs that may have expired or
changed since the manuscript was prepared.

For Susie Jolly, sister, friend, inspiration

Contents

The Feminist World of Love and Ritual

3 JANUARY, 1977

Dear Lise,

I am going to try but I am not sure of this. I don't think I know how to write without being intimate, without exposing myself and my real feelings about what is going on around me and I am not as charitable as I appear. Also the nature of our relationship is not clear. How do I speak the truths to you that at the same time I speak to myself? Write to me more about what you want to happen and do not be disappointed if it doesn't. Perhaps we could decide on a general subject and exchange our meditations on it.[1]

Writing a letter is often a delicate task. It is especially so when we negotiate expectations of intimacy. My contention is that these expectations were exciting and important in the women's movements of the 1970s and 1980s and that this extraordinary political moment produced extraordinary correspondences. Women saw their relationships with one another as newly significant, and their letters say so. But this book will also reveal how troubling the desire for intimacy can be. "How do I speak the truths to you that at the same time I speak to myself?" Joan Nestle, founding member of The Lesbian Herstory Archives, asked her correspondent, Lise, in the letter that opens this chapter. But Nestle seems to be asking herself as well. Honesty between women, as well as friendship, was a cherished ideal in the era of consciousness-raising and political confession. Yet how far could we really trust one another? What happened if we felt less "charitable" than we appeared, than we wanted to be, most especially to other women in need? What happened if we did not like one another or, just as difficult, if we desired one another unevenly? "Write me more about what you want to happen and do not be disappointed if it doesn't."

This book provides the first cultural history of British and American second-wave feminism from the point of view of its intimate archives: the letters sent between women activists and writers. This was a period of revolution in many women's lives, and the effervescence and depth of feeling has often been described. But the letters of the period give a unique insight. They track a relationship history—and they also suggest feminism's ideals about personal relationship itself as a belief system. Correspondences among activists, lovers, academics, families survive as a powerful record of women's unprecedented willingness to prioritize the relationships among themselves, particularly in contrast to those with men. At the same time, they reveal women's new demands of one another and the disappointments that often followed.

Letters are a staple of any political movement, and I hope this book will enable a sensitive appreciation of this fact. My interest, however, is not so much to canvass the many thousands of correspondences that lie behind the great campaigns of the era but to theorize a range of writings from the key contexts of the feminist relationship, with a primarily literary eye. The crucial place of lesbian relationships and, more generally, passionate friendships in feminist communities, for example, was expressed in a wave of love-letter writing, as well as in the archiving and publishing of lesbians' letters from earlier eras. Seductions and skirmishes, these texts now read as self-conscious declarations of independence from heterosexual as well as patriarchal roles. But angry breakup letters are equally significant measures of feminist relations. The question of how and whether political alliance or personal friendship was possible between black and white, lesbian and straight, Jewish and Gentile, differently abled women emerges in the characteristically feminist genre of open letter of petition or complaint. Mother-daughter correspondences also reveal a formative scene of second-wave relation: family life. The relationships they describe span hope, confusion, and rage, as writers attempt to politicize the domestic, the maternal, and the duties of family letter writing itself. Of course, the women's movement was also all about community relations. Anyone who has ever taken part in a campaign will know that whom you know and how you know them means everything in terms of whether you turn up for the march, get the newsletter distributed, host the meeting. All this, too, is documented in letters, for the movement was on the move, and networking was crucial to its sustenance.

How should we interpret this world of romantic appeals, angrily given gifts, and personalized polemics? And what light does it shed upon letter writing as a literary and social, as well as political practice? Answering these questions in the course of this book, I propose three guiding arguments.

The first is that letters and letter forms constitute a significant literature of the second-wave women's movement, though one that has received no academic attention to date. All letters embody complex social codes; we only have to think of the struggle to compose a job application or condolence card to know this. But the correspondents I investigate in this book often seem to view letter writing explicitly as a form of women's art, certainly as a creative process. It needs to be explored alongside the striking number of feminist epistolary novels, poems, essays, and "open letters." Some of the texts I look at are by women who were already established professional writers: Mary Meigs, Alice Walker, Gillian Hanscombe, Suniti Namjoshi, Audre Lorde, and the "Three Marias," for example. But as often, they are by women who seem to be dipping their toes into writing, inspired by the idea of a political community of readers or fellow activists. The exuberant open letters to and from the women at Seneca Women's Encampment for Peace and Justice, or the love letters that lesbians volunteered to publish in Kay Turner's 1996 anthology, *Between Us: A Legacy of Lesbian Love Letters*, are the work of amateurs. As homegrown as the feminist press and media are, such ephemera is much more than merely historical source material. Like other life-writing forms, these letters tell us about the individual's sense of self-expression, about rhetoric and the pleasure of writing. .

My second argument moves from the aesthetic interests of such material to focus directly on what it says about the construction of feminist relationships in this period. Letters reveal a powerful assumption of both identity and mutual care between women. They are part of a *culture of relationship* that was contemporaneously being theorized as special to women's values and communities. I theorize this in terms of the feminist philosophy-of-care ethics. This ethics crystallized the idea of the relational self as a feminist ideal, defining "the moral subject as a self-in-relation—an individual who values and enjoys intimacy, whose identity is in significant measure defined through her interpersonal ties, and whose concerns are interdependent with those of other people" (Meyers, "Agency," 375). Many of these letter writers implicitly appear to value and enjoy intimacy in just these moral terms, assuming responsibility in caring for others, avoiding harm, and, essentially,

keeping relationships going. Yet just as obvious is the fact that feminist relationships proved ill-equipped to deal with evidence of indifference or even
hostility between women. Indeed, letters show more poignantly than autobiography or even novels of the period the struggle to realize ideals of sisterhood from within and the puzzle of how to create genuine coalition and
community across political gulfs of race or class or sheer differences of temperament. In investigating how letters constructed relationships, I shift
from thinking about individuals who enjoyed the letter as a kind of proto–
art form to how letter writing was a trope for the idea of the women's
"web," an invisible, yet primal bond between women that was, at the same
time, deeply romanticized.

My third argument is philosophical and confronts the nature of feminism as a social movement. If we accept that letters and letter writing reflect
feminist assumptions about ethical relationship, we have to deal with their
equally eloquent expression of failures of those ideals. As a kind of discourse
about as well as within feminism, epistolary texts provoke us to wonder how
an ethics of care, at least in the instinctive form of these letters, is compatible
with political process. This very difficult question becomes the end point of
the book. At the same time, it would not be fair to ask it without looking at
what has happened since the second wave. I thus end by considering the
"third wave" of feminism alongside its own communication practices, particularly since the advent of e-mail.

Yours in Sisterhood . . ,

17 JANUARY, 1977

Dear Joan,
Yes—between us only. And no holding back. It won't be soon that we're
comfortable or even able to be so open. But we can do it—with practice. And I
hope we'll be each other's ideal reader. Do you know what I mean? One woman
encourages something different in you than another woman encourages? Well,
I'd wish for us that we would facilitate much for each other, that we would both
want to share a great range of perceptions. (Groan—I'm writing like walking in
mud. Forgive me.) O.K. Maybe twice in my life I had an intense exchange with

a woman by mail. I was never happier—because my experiences were set off when I shared them with another. (Joan, I can't wait until this is free. We both have to write what we can throw away—O.K.? I wrote four sentences and started over. Now I don't want to make a third start. I'm giving myself permission to leave tacky stuff. Since this is my practice, to get going, and between us only). So. I fell in love yesterday. A woman on the plane, my seat mate. . . .

I do know I have to work at friendship—meaning, friendship is existential; meaning that like karate you don't have it apart from the practice of it. Know what, I'm not having trouble writing now. Since I decided to flow free there's no more jargon-filled sentences. Yep, I think this will be fun. Let's do it, Joan—fill all the golden sheaths with dancing words.

25 JANUARY, 1977

We might experiment with how we want to say something but that will be for our joy of trying—not because the margins of the page demand a form. Also it implies that disciplined pieces give birth to disciplined thinking, a thought being punished or a thought punishing? And discussing though it may be free form is to me the most exciting way to capture the beauty of a thought.

We must try to escape from our terrible self consciousness which is not really us but the embedded voice that asks who do you think you are? One thing—I don't [think] regularly writing will give either of us a new self and I don't think we really need one. We just might discover what kind of voice we really have and what in our years of living has become part of us. I hope by ideal reader you will include questioning what doesn't ring true and so will I.[2]

This response from Lise to Joan Nestle, whose letter I quote at the beginning of this chapter, epitomizes the arguments I will make about letter writing as a literary practice in the women's movement. Fired and alarmed by a dream of women's friendship, these two activists test out words on a pad of yellow foolscap, post them into the sensitive space between them, hoping to nurture a new voice, if not a new self. Checkered with differences of time, temperament, status, they wonder about intimacy in a romance with writing as well as with women. It is a political, idealistic, therapeutic experiment, but also as literary as second-wave feminism itself. As such, it needs cultural explanation.

We still have few words to describe or understand the cultural value of private, ephemeral letters like these, which I found, with no further explanation of what happened to Joan and Lise's correspondence, in the Lesbian Herstory Archives in Brooklyn. It is one aim of this book to begin to provide this lexicon by uniting literary analysis of the form with socio-anthropological and philosophical theories of women's relationships in the 1970s and 1980s. Humbly dependent upon the post office for their audience, letters are probably the most common form of creative writing and historically the form least subject to monopoly by a particular sex or class (Altman, "Women's Letters," 101). At the same time, a correspondence such as Joan and Lise's reminds us what is distinctive about letter writing *as writing*: its oddness compared to other ways of relating.

What is the art of letter writing? And what makes one kind of letter an art form, another merely a communication? Literary critics are still deeply unsure, although the question has been debated ever since the first handbooks on the art in ancient Greece. Letters, provoked in the first instance by the wish to communicate across distance, flaunt the functionality of writing in a way that proves indigestible for much aesthetic theory. Only where functionality ends, it seems, can art begin. Yet what other kind of writing can yield this level of readerly fulfillment—for the original addressee? And doesn't all writing, including the most traditionally "literary," have a social function of some sort?

Romantic conceptions of writing as the medium of intimacy, spontaneity, and presence still dominate popular conceptions of the letter, and indeed the e-mail; we will see how strong they were in the women's movement. But modern epistolary critics stress that private letters are pervaded by social, linguistic, and literary codes. Structuralist and poststructuralist theorists emphasize the reader's construction of a text's meaning over its author's intention, often allied to deconstructive suspicions about the stability of meaning in general. Jacques Lacan famously drew on Edgar Allen Poe's story "The Purloined Letter" as an allegory for the compulsive ways in which language holds us in a symbolic order ("The Purloined Poe"). The philosopher Jacques Derrida influentially responded that, just as a letter can always *fail* to arrive at its destination or, indeed, can arrive after its sender has died, language is defined by the possibility of misinterpretation or indeterminacy ("The Purveyor of Truth"). Barbara Johnson in turn postulated that the letter's destination is *wherever* it is read ("The Frame of Reference").

(Think about e-mail's habit of getting misinterpreted, forwarded, copied to the very person who should not have seen it . . .) Despite their differences, such critics are united in using the letter to turn conventional literary assumptions on their head; for them, the author, and even writing's powerful presence and promise of immortality, is illusory (Royle, "What Is Deconstruction?" 6–7). Simultaneously, analyzing the letter becomes a wonderful opportunity to show how even apparently functional or highly individual passionate outpourings actually reflect elaborate "systèmes épistolaires" (Bray, "Quelques aspects").

Throughout this book, I also hope to recognize the art of private letters. But I consider it a mistake to insist that letters are written as deliberate aesthetic exercises any more than they are merely symptoms of social and linguistic codes to which the individual writer or relationship is irrelevant. In fact, creativity often evolves *within* personal or local relationships; literary effect, if not ambition, can combine with basic intentions to please, anger, or educate. On one level this is common sense: you adopt a polite tone when writing to the bank manager, a respectful one to your granny, a self-righteous whine to your former lover. Less obvious is the persona you discover when maintaining a long-term correspondence without meeting in person, although lately people's experiences with e-mail relationships have widely publicized this aspect of letter writing. It is not necessary to say that letters are deliberate lies or conscious fictions, although we might want to be suspicious of the assumption that they are the spontaneous outpourings of the true self. Rather, I see in them a subtle interchange among fantasy, writing, and relationship. In fact, the ambiguity of the letter as a literary genre shows us there is something expressive, excessive about all writing. Equally, there is something irreducibly communicative and, at some level, referential. Contrary to deconstructive critics, then, I have sought paradigms that emphasize the possibility and even necessity of dialogue, while also recognizing its fragility across time, place, and code.

Although dialogic theorists after Bakhtin have provided me with a happy perspective, it is the detailed case studies of social literacy theorists, who interpret writing anthropologically, that I have found most useful in this regard. Janet Maybin's study of British correspondences with American prisoners on death row, for example, shows that letter writing allows prisoners to create life-sustaining virtual families and also to develop a sense of inner self and self-esteem. Equally, their pen friends find altruistic intentions blown away in engrossing relationships that help them through traumas of their own ("Death Row Penfriends"). Another example is Laura Ahearn's tracking of the sudden growth of letter writing between courting couples in 1990s rural Nepal. This originated in new national policies on teaching girls to write, along with the influx of global commercial cultures. Nepali village women now write and dream over romantic letters because they want to marry "for love," not because their parents found somebody suitable for them (*Invitations to Love*). In these examples, we see the way that letter writing, as a social practice defined through "the texts, the participants, the activities and the artefacts," and ultimately its historical context (Barton and Hall, "Introduction," 1), is far more than simply a means of communication.

I contend that the American and British women's movements operated a similarly complex "epistolary system." Comparable to the conceptions of letters as semipublic artifacts that have driven many cultures of familiar letter writing, feminists' political self-consciousness turned private forms of writing toward a fantasized women's community. They personalized public forms such as newsletters, academic essays, and political argument through epistolary framing. They consciously valued letters as "women's forms" of domestic art and feminist "coming out." Less consciously, this epistolary culture drew on ideas of self-realization, ironically often sharing much common ground with conventional ideologies of romantic love and self-help.

Through close readings of what these texts meant to their writers and readers themselves, I also hope to bring out a much more delicate, not always happy story about a movement's own love affair with the idea of women's love and care. The aesthetic value of these letters as relational forms inheres in the oddness and emotion of a whole culture of relationality. Ironically, although these political and often intellectual women pioneered the valuing of women's letters at the time, the real poetry their own letters offer is much less straightforward.

Joan Nestle told me she did not pursue this correspondence as she was not really very close to Lise.[3] And perhaps Lise knew this, hence her struggle to fill "the golden sheaths" with "dancing words." What touches me about these writings as much as their feminist commitment is their poignant demonstration of what these most determined women were unable to foresee and when they were unable to care, and this included their relationships with each other. Moving on from the question of literary value and effect, the second part of the book attempts to explain this in broader historical terms.

Letter Writing and the Ethics of Care

During the 1970s, feminist writers, academics, and activists explicitly began to connect the form of the letter with evolving ideas about women's writing, women's ways of doing politics, and women's ways of relating, although they made few comments upon their own letter-writing practices. An influential article on nineteenth-century white, middle-class American women's "private letters and diaries," published in 1975 by Caroll Smith-Rosenberg, exemplifies this ("The Female World of Love," 368). Valuing what no one had before, Smith-Rosenberg sees in these intensive epistolary networks a "female world of love and ritual." Challenging existing assumptions that women were merely oppressed by Victorian gender segregation, the letters show that women were involved in loving, indeed passionate relationships with one another throughout their lives. For them, these relationships were clearly compatible with the conventions of heterosexual marriage and motherhood that often took them away from the mothers, sisters, and friends they were writing to. Smith-Rosenberg argues that these letters show a female homosocial world in which primary relationships among women were socially valued and respected, and that perhaps the twentieth century ironically lost in its undoing of gender segregation and supposed heterosexual liberation.

Just as much as Smith-Rosenberg's perceptions tell the story of a particular nineteenth-century American culture, they also reveal something about the *feminist* world of love and ritual that was emerging at the time of the epistolary networks I examine in this book. What was it like to think you were discovering—or rediscovering—a world where women could be passionate about other women, not just in adolescence but forever? In which those relationships could regain cultural prominence and organizing power? This was a moment when a female-centered world was being deliberately reconstructed. The culture of letter writing explored the fun of women's "difference" from men, as part of a politics no longer satisfied with the formalization of equality.

The tone varied, of course. In many ways this was most appealing to women who had an archaic memory of such a culture but for whom it was felt to have been lost: the very white middle-class heterosexual protestants of whom Smith-Rosenberg was writing. For African American women and women from groups for whom men had never been powerful patriarchs, this was often a less romantic discovery. Gender separatism could not make sense for those experiencing racism or any other exploitation that so clearly defined men as part of the oppressed. Separatism also probably had less appeal for women from societies or cultures where gender segregation was still current, such as some immigrant communities. Lesbianism as a political practice could emphasize the gulf between black and white women's interests, as well as between old and "new" lesbians (Kanneh, "Sisters Under the Skin"). But by the late 1970s and early 1980s, when black feminism exploded, the romance of black women for black women was creating its own epistolary subcultures, along with emerging solidarities among other minority groups: Jewish, Chicana, women with disabilities, and the like.[4] As Audre Lorde put it in 1984, "We have to consciously study how to be tender with each other until it becomes a habit because what was native has been stolen from us, the love of Black women for each other" (Lorde, "Eye to Eye," 175). The letters and letter literature I have assembled show that all these groups believed that love among women was essential to their liberation, an erotic form of class consciousness that went way beyond traditional calls for brotherhood in men's class struggles. The letter was a textual looking glass through which women could pass to find themselves again in love with their own kind.

We can understand much of feminist epistolary culture by looking at the expectations that it dramatized about relationships in a social movement. In many ways, in the midst of a new articulation of women's *rights*, letters record an equally powerful, though less articulated demand for attention to women's *needs*. Needs are not the same as rights. Unquantifiable in the same way, they do not translate as easily into programs for legislation, demands, or mission statements. But needs intuitively express each individual's particular position, and thus the differences and inequalities between people. Needs go beyond the conventionally political into the realm of the psychological and the physical.

The difference between needs and rights, and the importance of respecting them both, was articulated at the time by a group of feminist psychologists and philosophers, notably Carol Gilligan, Nel Noddings. and Sara Ruddick (Gilligan, *In a Different Voice*; Noddings, *Caring: A Feminine Ap-*

proach to Ethics and Moral Education; Ruddick and Daniels, *Working It Out*; Ruddick, *Maternal Thinking*, "Maternal Thinking"). They suggested that feminist—and feminine—values supported a moral philosophy that went beyond conventional adjudication of competing interests through a law of justice. They formulated this as an "ethics of care." For them, mothers in their experience of child rearing, nurses, teachers in their role as nurturers, or simply women and girls in their everyday social roles as mediators and carers, all demonstrate a set of moral values, not simply instinct or servitude. They argued that these values of "care" are important to any good society, since trusting, practical, noneconomically driven, holistic relationships sustain the public as well as the private sphere. Just as a person is not divided into "a public or a working person and a private person," collective enterprises have "shared, relational" dimensions. This seemed particularly true of the idealistic "communities" of feminists themselves, which were all about developing relationships of "trust and concern" in concrete, particular, family-ish ways, rather than the abstract theories of socialist communitarian philosophers (Held, *Feminist Morality*, 187–88). Seventeenth-century aristocrat Madame de Sévigné puts it more cheekily, replying to her daughter's letter about reading Decartes' then-revolutionary propositions about the individual self:

> Ainsi, ma bonne, *je pense, donc je suis;* je pense avec tendresse, donc je vous aime; je pense uniquement a vous de cette manière, donc je vous aime uniquement. [Thus, my dear, *I think, therefore I am*; I think tenderly, therefore I love you; I think about only you this way, therefore I love only you.]
> (quoted in Farrell, *Yours in Sisterhood*, 260; my translation)

Although Sévigné was hardly feminist, the more than a thousand romantic letters to her daughter aptly demonstrate a philosophy where thought proves not individual existence but the capacity for individual love.

These thinkers have unsurprisingly garnered intense criticism from other feminists. Although Gilligan and others always argued that it was crucial that women learned to care for themselves as well as others, validating women's "caring" can risk updating the white Victorian "angel in the house" or the African American "mamma," perpetuating and entrenching existing gender roles as well as falsely universalizing gender patterns specific to class and race. I do not pretend to give a full account of these debates in this book. What I wish to show is that even as feminists worried about any political platform of difference, their letters, including open epistolary manifestos, make it clear that they *continued to expect care from one another*. That it was good and right for feminists to nurture one another in addition to negotiating, that the movement should heal and self-help as well as lobby, that love and desire could inspire change, indeed, that difference itself was no obstacle to but the raison d'être of alliance: all reflect fundamental elements of an ethics of care.

I do not argue that feminists were always or even often successful in enacting such an ethics, in responding to one another's often intense neediness—indeed, writers were often motivated to write precisely because they didn't feel able to work it out in person. Even with the best intentions, it is tricky to maintain care across distance, as today's debate over whether Internet communities can ever substitute for face-to-face relationships reminds us. Letters, like the get-well card or even the phone call, can be ambiguous substitutions for the kind of giving that an ethics of care classically celebrates, the physical response to another whose need you can clearly see. Put another way, just as relationships of care can be intensified in letters, so letters can amplify the special painfulness of care's failure. And this, too, was very much an experience at the heart of the movement.

The Limits of Care:
Letters and the Life Cycle of a Social Movement

It is no coincidence that the early elaborations of care ethics emerged in the late 1970s, when women's "difference" from men was most simply celebrated. But as we shall see, letters equally dramatize the limits of care, in their very particularity, embeddedness, and reflexivity, the sense that "one under the guidance of an ethic of caring is tempted to retreat to a manageable world" (Noddings, "Caring," 18). They can show how public life—especially in the personalized form of feminist groups—can ironically be scuppered by the insistence upon meeting the other as one who cares, for "when this reaching out destroys or drastically reduces her actual caring, she retreats and renews her contract with those who address her" (18). Such retreat can even become a flight from the call to care in ways that may explain a return to the stiffer terms of justice precisely because care was felt to be too much to give. This is one way to understand the shift away from the idea of "sisterhood," to the rhetoric of "coalition." The perception of women's internal differences provoked a much more thoroughgoing critique of personal politics in general, with a lot of disillusionment along the way.

The nineteenth-century letters that Smith-Rosenberg unearthed show women tender, dependent, affectionate, lonely for one another. The *feminist* epistolary world of love and ritual is, in many ways, more complicated and contradictory. Alongside the passion was a new level of anger and disappointment. In part, this is because loyalties between women and men, the heterosexual and the homosocial, were put in competition; in part, because the question of alliance across lines such as race or class was so volatile. But more generally, and paradoxically, the politicization of women's relationships began to eat away at the principles of care itself. There is something of a bad faith in *demanding* to be cared for. Isn't it the nature of care to be unquantifiable even, at its best, to be freely given as a gift? The contradiction between women's need for care and justice is in fact the heart of these letters, and the heart, perhaps, of what is fascinating about feminist relationships. It is what makes these relationships so palpably idealistic, so strangely erotic in the kind of intimacy they stimulate. At the same time, this contradiction draws on the nature of letter writing itself, for the letter is a gift that always exacts a return, a reaching out that always interpellates a reply. This is true even in the most functional of missives to the bank. How much more so in the intricate semaphores these women were sending?

This book's framing argument, then, is not that we need to develop more care ethics or that letter writing is a powerful aspect of political networking or even that political letter writing is aesthetically interesting, although I agree with all these things. Rather, I am outlining a literary history of feminist letter writing as a social practice very particular to its time and place. The *form* of these letters, their *symbolic function* and *reception*, as much as their content, is crucial to their meaning. These written relationships express an emerging network and in turn play their part in constructing a gender-class consciousness. But they are also texts that negotiate less obvious identifications and desires, needs and demands. In this, they tell us about unconscious aspects of group making and group excluding. Feminist letters make not just a virtual but an imagined community in that sense. They act as unconscious expressions of women's *expectation* of care, or even demand for it, rather than an ethics of care as response to another's need.

Care becomes seen as a right, and the letter's ambiguous status as gift embodies this ethical ambiguity.

This book, then, offers a historical perspective on both feminist ethics and feminist letters. The women's movement was partially successful in developing new ways of doing politics and new values. We see this today in the political recognition of nurture and the institutionalization of care; in the need for forgiveness and recognition in situations of trauma; and, differently, in the debate over networking on the Internet. But these letters also show tensions between the values of autonomy and of care. These underlie more obvious tensions between women's sense of identity and their assertions of difference from one another. We see the second wave going through a period of separation and exclusiveness, as any political movement does, but also how this period was distinguished by its intense emphasis on nurturing and desiring relationships *internally*. In other words, the ethics of care was both part of the movement's culture, such that a woman with chronic fatigue could expect recognition of her needs as part of her rights and a mother unable to attend a demonstration could be viewed as doing her part as a reproductive worker. Yet this ethics could be incompatible with the practicalities of political lobbying, on the one hand, and with one's wish for a private life, on the other. How to respond when the woman with chronic fatigue writes a furious letter to you saying she feels unsupported? When she publishes this exchange in an open letter in a collection of writings by women with M.E.? What does the mother think when, after all, the campaign organizers post a petition for help at the office or the rally? The attempt to reconcile care and rights was a challenge that went beyond the much more commonly discussed problems that came with identity politics. The very belief in relationality, and its ethics, wavered as feminists struggled to sustain its practice. Perhaps nowhere was this more obvious than in decisions to exclude men—decisions also recorded in letters between feminist women and men, and, more often, implicitly in the new literature of women-centered correspondence.

Reading Other People's Letters

Feminist letters then are poignant texts—always straining towards an ideal yet shouting about the real, deeply romantic, and yet horribly ordinary in the failure of romance. In many ways, this book is about the embarrassing

condition of politics and the particular way that feminism struggled to reconcile means with ends. Because of this, it has been a sensitive book to
write. Delving into feminism's relationship history is no easier than delving
into the history of any middle-aged or older person, as the small amount of
my own autobiography I have allowed into the story has made me acutely
aware. Remembering my passionate, embarrassing, twenty-something correspondences with women friends and lovers, I have also had to confront a
contradiction in my own ethical framework, trying to be caring yet also
truthful, scrupulous yet also scholarly and accessible. I make no claim,
therefore, that the small numbers of letters and letter genres I discuss can
represent the movement. They are, frankly, those I have been able to access
in feminist publications, Internet appeals, and archives, and they tend also
to be those always intended for a public readership. In the book's concluding chapters, I give a fuller account of my research methods and reflect upon
the challenges of epistolary research generally, and I make a plea for further-
ing the feminist archive. However, even with what is available at present,
there is much we can enjoy.

The order of the chapters roughly reflects a chronology of letters through
the late 1970s and 1980s to the advent of feminist email activism in the 1990s
and 2000s. But the book is centered on case studies from the early 1980s, for
my wish is rather to show not so much the history of each individual relationship or group but rather how *genres* of letter mediate a central ideology
about feminist care, which was strongest at this time.

I begin with a discussion of women's love letters. These are lesbian letters, and most of them originated in private correspondences. I show, however, that they can also be read as a literature of early feminism, sometimes
intended as such, when these texts were circulated or published as versions
of "coming out" letters. These missives also carry a sense of excitement
about letter writing itself as a creative form in this context, but there is already the hint of new conventions of both relationship and writing that
made it difficult to write about the failure of lesbian relationship. This first
chapter also addresses the way this perpetuated an old association of women
with personal letter writing, even as feminists removed the practice from its
conventional associations with heterosexual ritual and role.

Chapter 2, "Feminist Epistolary Romance," continues to explore feminists' attraction to the genre of the letter as a symbol of a "women-centered"
world in which women's relationships with one another were the priority.

I look at some well-known epistolary novels of the time, including the Three Marias' *New Portuguese Letters*, Dacia Maraini's *Letters to Marina*, Alice Walker's *The Color Purple*, and Gillian Hanscombe's *Between Friends* in this light, even though they are very often equally preoccupied with asserting the differences among women. Feminists were in love with the letter itself as a form that seemed so resonant of women's private memories, codes, and networks. The second half of the chapter explores the way that feminist academics contributed to this romance by unearthing forgotten letters from women of the past. Indeed, many academics personalized their own professional writing by writing it as a "letter" to a hoped-for feminist reader.

I titled chapter 3 "Velvet Boxing Gloves" because I was struck by how well-padded were the blows, how carefully and artfully women fought one another in feminist publications—and even private letters. This chapter looks at the literature that comes out of disappointed love and a sense of betrayal, in epistolary novels, criticism, and, above all, the open letter. Writing "in sisterhood" seemed so often in this period to mean writing in anger, but I suggest that in these well-known debates over "difference," what was so evocative was the continuing expectation of care and intimacy. The chapter ends by reading some private letters between two lovers who interpreted the end of their affair in characteristically political terms, and I argue that, ironically, this bittersweet mix lends them an unintended poetry.

I introduce the second section of chapter 4, "The Ethics of Care: Writing the Contracts of Sisterhood," with a survey of how critics have theorized the letter as a genre of particular interest to women over the last three decades. This arose from a general discourse about the female self as "relational," rather than the isolated and autonomous entity presumed to characterize male writings and values. Personal letters seemed especially animated by this theory since they so obviously represent the self in relationship and because of their historical association with women's duties in the family and local community. Yet, equally unsurprising, this simple equation of gender and genre has been subsequently unpacked, particularly in new work that explores the way that masculinity is also relational. What *has* endured is the notion that letter writing is defined by its ethical concerns, as are autobiography and other life-writing forms. It is here that I elaborate a definition of "care ethics," briefly described above. This ethics is not usually associated with writing—although Tom Couser has done so in relation to writing about and by people with disabilities in *Vulnerable Subjects*—but I propose that it is very close to the concerns expressed in these letters. I do not claim that care ethics are an essential explanation for all letters, let alone all life writing. Indeed, as this chapter explains, it is more likely that this philosophy and feminist epistolary practices are so close because they evolved at the same political and cultural moment. They both express a time when feminists wished to recover the value of women's support for one another and their values of relationship and care more generally. As I have already demonstrated, however, this was much more of an ideal than a reality.

The next three chapters take us further into this reality by exploring two classic scenes of care ethics through the perspective of letters. Chapter 5 is based upon Karen Payne's popular anthology *Between Ourselves: Letters Between Mothers and Daughters, 1750–1982*, published in 1983 and featuring intense correspondences between women in the second wave. Payne's hope was that these personal exchanges would speak of feminist values without preaching to a general public. The letters often support this hope, but the gritty ethical work of connection comes at a high emotional price. My close reading of one long correspondence between "Teresa and Kate," exploring issues of abortion, suicide, alcoholism, divorce, and living one's own life, makes this plain.

Chapters 6 and 7 tell a similar tale. Through letters between women peace activists, I trace the high idealism and imagination of the "women's web," which unfolded in the peace movement of the early 1980s. In particular, I describe letter writing as part of what turned the women's peace camp outside Greenham Common Royal Air Base in England into a virtual community, with sister camps and supporters around the world, notably at Seneca Women's Encampment for Peace and Justice in upstate New York. Personalized newsletters, campaign letters, and chain letters of invitation to protest were more than merely practical sources of information; they were symbols of the kind of egalitarian, dispersed, and tolerant community cherished by care ethicists. Chapter 7, however, once again tests this vision by considering letters that record internal dissent and confusion about who could and could not be in the community. I build here upon Louise Krasniewicz's anthropology of the Seneca encampment to think about letter writing as part of the rituals of defensive group making. Should we be writing to the government instead of one another? This is the question with which I end the chapter, acknowledging the difficult balance between sustaining a social movement and achieving its aims of social change at large. Yet in the frustrations we all have with petitioning our governments and other powers that be, I conclude this section with sympathy for activists who, like myself, get fed up and turn to making alternative lives with like-minded strugglers.

Part 3, "The Right to Be Cared For: Letters and the Life Cycle of a Social Movement," addresses the philosophical challenges posed by this journey through feminism's "relationship history" in letters. Chapter 8, "Care Versus Autonomy: The Problem of (Loving) Men," focuses on the difficulty of preserving the values of care when you are also trying to develop your autonomy, a tension that I identify as the motor of much of the correspondence examined in this book. I formulate this through the particular and obvious question of women's relationship to men. I recount my own memories of deciding to "put women first" before narrating three other "letter-stories" that trace a similar move away from sexual relationships with men for political reasons. In the story of "S," this resulted in the especially poignant moment of writing a "last letter" to her erstwhile boyfriend before moving to a women-only farm in Scotland.

Chapter 9 further focuses the question over how to bring an ethics of care into a social movement whose aim must necessitate some forms of separation, even exclusion, at least at some periods. I suggest that the philosophical "solution" to the problem has been in the notion that one should begin by taking responsibility for caring for oneself and, in this way, avoid demanding too much of others while finding autonomy. Yet I also argue that feminism encouraged women to feel that they had a "right" to be cared for. Letters reveal this because they are so often disguised expressions of need, dependency, and desire, even when they are written as declarations of independence. Recent feminist philosophy about what an ideal citizenship should comprise brings together care ethics with more traditional ideas about law, justice, and people's rights. I briefly consider this apparently inevitable destination for those hoping to found alternative forms of community. My main interest, however, is how letters continue to raise the question of what we owe one another emotionally as well as politically. This is the way, then, that I approach the question of how more recent activists see their politics, in a reading of some open letters between second wavers and third wavers, including Phyllis Chesler, Ntozake Shange, Gloria Steinem, Eisa Davis, and Amy Richards.

It would be impossible to consider feminist communication today without addressing e-mail, and this is the subject of chapters 10 and 11. After giving an overview of the contradictory gender and sexual politics in popular and literary e-mail literatures, I summarize Manuel Castells's notion of "the network society" as a new political era (in *The Rise of the Network Society*). Although I am skeptical of the new round of idealized "virtual communities," including those proposed by communicative ethicists after Jürgen Habermas, I suggest that there is much to hope for in feminists' recent, more sophisticated attempts to network, lobby, and relate in writing. I offer a detailed reading of one e-mail forum, "Women on the Net," which self-consciously attempted to create dialogues between Northern and Southern, activists and academics, including men. It exemplifies the continuing debates over women's differences, but also that feminist ideas of emotional citizenship have something specific to offer an age of politics by mail.

The two chapters that constitute the final section, "The Afterlife of Letters," confront the meaning of letters as especially potent forms of memory. From the perspective of today's global activism and postfeminist pop culture, the second wave may seem already a world away, politically and technologically. Yet rummaging in its barely opened archive is an exercise in more than nostalgia, for, as I argue in chapter 12, letters are ambivalent substitutions for physical relationships. Indeed, the burned letter is an archetypal motif of revenge, cleansing, and commemoration because letters continue to pulsate with bodily traces. This has a particular meaning for women because, like letters, we have been objects of sexual exchange and fetishization.

Should we always save and publish letters, then? And what do we do about saving e-mail? In chapter 13, I explore the balancing act between telling the truth and preserving trust that haunts anyone working with letters. I contextualize feminists' decisions about epistolary legacies in the context of general debates over privacy and compare their ethics of care to the ideas of others who have tried to outline an ethical policy for life writing. I do appreciate that women of my generation or older might wish to burn, rather than to publish, the record of an amazing political youth. Yet I conclude that, for all the dangers, the legacy of movement relationships is one to save.

The book's conclusion remains politically cheerful about feminism's goals. In the letters and letter fictions of feminists through the second wave and in the fantastic diversity of e-mail networking today, we perceive the literature of an emerging gender-class, finally recording that relationships among women are as crucial, indeed as romantic, as those with men. Yet this unsung literature also testifies to the muddle of political methods that attempt to meet everyone's needs at once, even if they are a predictable part of the life cycle of a social movement. The pain of feeling uncared for and, indeed, of deciding not to care form the plot of these letters, as much as the romance of erotic identity. I hope that they will contribute to our respect for feminism as a maker of community and do justice to letter writing as a writing practice just as interesting and just as troublesome as the relationships it sustained.

PART ONE

Yours in Sisterhood . . .

CHAPTER ONE

Love Letters to a New Me

On my way home the tears began to fall. Not because I am madly in love with her—I am not mad enough to let myself fall in love with anyone any more before they have begun to fall in love with me—but because I am so lonely and I do so want a lover and I like C very much and think we could have a nice time together. I have got my fingers burnt so many times that I am really reluctant to make the first move with anybody, yet in a way perhaps I ought to, just to put myself out of my misery. . . . A phone call seems very brazen and my success rate with letters has not been spectacular, but I do seem incapable of bringing things to a head in personal conversation. So I shall have to think more . . .

—Lorna Hardy, "Exposure"

S eduction is, by nature, a literary challenge. Those who write to a lover wrestle with words' inadequacy, exaggerating the awareness in all letter writing of physical absence. At the same time, of all genres, love letters most obviously demonstrate writing's ability to arouse, to prolong, and even, especially in paper form, to fetishize desire. In fiction, love letters dramatize a character's duplicity or the uncertainty of union. But anyone who has written or received a love letter or e-mail instinctively knows something of the unreliability of writing. Lorna Hardy's fear that a written proposal would not have much success with "C" is easy to understand.

Yet this woman's misery presents us with a plot that has been relatively unexplored in literary terms. Hardy (a pseudonym), was a young teacher in the early 1980s. She was brainy, feminist, but socially unconfident and had embraced lesbianism in her early twenties, imagining "complete freedom for sexual and emotional adventures" ("Exposure," 85). Her problem was that she discovered she was as unable to attract women as she had been men. She had political friends and lesbian and antiracist involvements; she wrote poetry; at work she worried about coming out: but she was punishingly lonely. Literary tradition has enshrined the scenario of a woman writing un-requited love letters to a man unfeelingly elsewhere. But what about the un-requited love for a woman who is in the throes of so-called women's liberation? What about the difficulties of love when it is attached to sexual identity?

Love letters of those who desire their own sex have only been cryptically part of any public canon. This reflects both the stigmatization and the rela-tively recent identification of gay and lesbian sexuality. It is heartening to see scholars beginning to challenge this neglect with anthologies and critical studies of gay letters. Several have claimed that the need to be covert in ho-mophobic societies has ironically produced especially artful writing (Hal-lett, *Lesbian Lives*; Jones, *The Love of Friends*; Lister and Liddington, *Female Fortune*; Turner, *Baby Precious Always Shines*). No one, however, has explored the ambiguities of love-letter writing between women in the 1970s and 1980s. This chapter begins the task. I will argue that, in contrast to earlier periods, writers during this time are clear about naming their desires and excited about writing them down, as well. In the context of private relation-ships, women play at being muse to each other, artists of their own sexual stories. Sometimes this can be highly experimental, but even when quite ev-eryday, it dramatically reverses the history of epistolary fiction, which has positioned women as love's losers, as the dupes and dependents of men. At the same time, this exploration reveals new subtexts and silences. The over-lap between coming out and seduction presupposes sexual pride and experi-ence, whose absence could be difficult to admit; it interweaves the lace of desire with the ponderousness self-consciousness of exemplary relationship. These letters register women's new claims to sexual autonomy at the mo-ment when gay and women's liberation met. Yet, oddly, they can obscure the ironies, silliness, and disappointment of love.

Women's Liberation Is a Lesbian Plot

Love letters may seem to be the most private form of writing, but they have played their part in defining lesbian experience. Although not as directly so as "coming out" letters, the intimacy of correspondence has been an important space in which to explore and assert new selves and desires. What is remarkable about women's love letters to each other after the explosion of sexual liberation in the late 1960s is how explicit and self-conscious they are about identity as much as desire. If coming out to parents or colleagues engendered agonized or defiant announcement, writing to a would-be or already snookered lover was proud in a different way.[1] This change in tone grew out of the combined forces of gay and women's liberation, after the repressive years of the mid-twentieth century, even as these two movements clashed and struggled over what the politics of lesbian desire should mean.

Consider the following exchange between Bertha Harris and Noel Phyllis Birkby. Harris, the novelist best known for *Lover* (1976), was introduced to the architect Birkby by Kate Millett, in a consciousness-raising group in 1974. Though Harris, like Birkby, had long had relationships with women, Harris chose to send an "audio letter" to avoid the "protectiveness" of traditional letter writing. No more beating around the bushes. The crackling tape begins with Harris saying that if she could "do it with voice" on tape, she could "do it with voice" in person. Comically taping while both smoking and driving noisily to her university in Chapel Hill "for literary chit chat," she muses on her frighteningly "real" and "intense" feelings for a woman she has just met:

> Did I make you up in my mind? . . . I don't even know you, but I *do* know you. . . . But I would like to know you more than I do already. This sensation of making you up. . . . The complete coalition between wish and reality. . . . But I'm just going to assume that you can take it, that it's ok to do this with you. And that you'll stop me from doing it when you want me to. Thank you for perfect freedom![2]

Anyone writing to a new lover may wonder about how far she is simply "making her up." But this cheeky "tape-letter" resonates with a wider sense of experiment, in which "wish" and "reality" could magically coalesce. Harris's stylized stream of consciousness in a roaring car literally animates her assertion of "perfect freedom." Birkby—who replied on the other side of the cassette—was charmed. Weighty with sighs and pauses as she searches for words to express the "rapport" and "fusion" between them, she confesses she is glad she can't remember kissing Harris because it feels "already too much."

Birkby and Harris's sense of pride and pleasure in the epistolary form suggests the moment of lesbian pride and new feminism that contextualized their meeting. And indeed, Birkby's coming out fuelled other experiments with love letters in different artistic forms. She produced long, dreamlike erotic missives to the filmmaker Barbara Hammer, who, in turn, sent her dramatic photographic self-portraits, sometimes written upon, as forms of visual correspondence that were also playful statements of her identity. Some time during the same period, she also shot a five-minute autobiographical film titled "Love Letter" that clearly poses the form as a cathartic means to a new self. It begins by panning down a slide of herself to show a life-size outline drawing of her body. This drawing includes a fried egg that is simultaneously crying and smiling inside the head, while "a new head" is inscribed around the outside. Another shot of bell-bottomed legs has one leg saying pain, the other, love. It ends with a graphic of Birkby imprinted over the slide of another woman.[3] Hammer's own later correspondence with Florrie Burke, who has been her partner since 1988, also playfully mixed visual with verbal in what seems to be as much autobiography as address. A photocollage of Hammer's face shows another woman's face inset over one of the eyes. A typed address to "Darling mine" over the image reminds her, "My hand reaches out to you, especially when you don't feel so well." Hammer annotates it with the explanation "separation inspires me and to keep the connection, I create missives of spontaneous love that often have spelling and punctuation mishaps but are filled with energy like a romantic lover who overlooks defects in her object of desire but lusts after her all the same" (quoted in Kay Turner, *Between Us*, 155). Hammer frankly compares the letter to the lover: it is her own perversely spontaneous "missives" about which she has romantic delusions and lusts.

A somewhat different intersection of creativity and politics describes the exchange between Joan Nestle and her lover, activist Lee Hudson, who use metaphors of geography and climate "to speak of our passion and fear of drifting apart" in a correspondence from 1989. Lee writes from the "Arctic" and Joan from the "Amazon" even though both of them were actually in New York (quoted in Kay Turner, *Between Us*, 153). These letters give the flavor of lesbian relationships as powerful, even power-driven, after that decade's debates over the politics of women's sex and whether the women's movement had desexualized it. This is very clear in Lee's description of an imaginary icy fishing expedition in one letter, which is evidently a flirta-

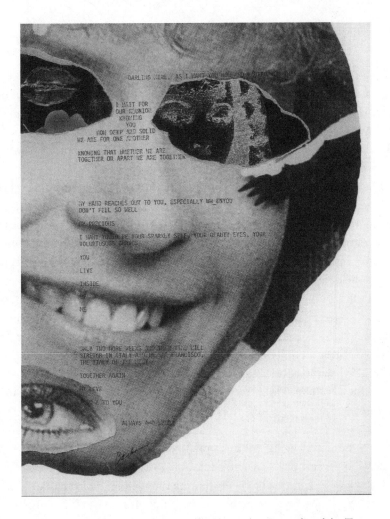

Barbara Hammer, letter photocollage to Florrie Burke. Reproduced in Turner, ed., *Between Us*.

tious attempt to "catch" Joan too. Her chase is guided by "Najo," an obviously technically competent and savvy woman, who shows her how to "cut a hole in the ice with powered auger—not the nostalgic saw many envision." This careful image suggests Hudson's determination not to appropriate another's land even in imagination, yet also suggests another kind of romanticism in populating the world with butch dykes. Najo's hunting technique is suggestively erotic as well: "Najo flips a perfect circle of ice, thick and frosty, onto the surface nearby with her tonged pole like a large white discus hurled from a giant shoulder" (*Between Us*, 45). Najo's expertise, furthermore, is matched by the image of Joan as a pike, a fish known for its power and cunning. Hudson is obviously also happily fishing for words in this fanciful letter: "Buried deep beneath the ice caps are a beautiful little-known species of pike. To catch them is an art—much like a writer casting about for words to reveal the soul and heart to the lover" (*Between Us*, 45).

The self-conscious inventiveness of these missives to a degree reflects the fact they are all written by professional writers and artists of some sort. But, despite their differences in origin, I suggest they all share a sense that lesbian relationships were a measure of women's erotic autonomy. The women's movement had popularized the hope that lesbian relationships could escape the determinations of heterosexuality, and even as lesbians like Nestle led the argument that lesbians' and women's struggles could not be conflated, such letters frame lesbianism as what Katie King has called feminism's "magical sign" (King, *Theory in Its Feminist Travels*, 124–37). We see this played out even in quite ordinary, private letters. A letter from Sue, written in 1975, for example, offers a typescript of lesbian feminist fantasies, declaring, "One day not too long ago I fell in love with a woman. I didn't try to or anything—it just happened":

> So here I am, hanging out in a brand new scene—seeing, feeling, knowing new things. First time I went to an all-woman dance the most impressive thing I felt was the gentle loving energy flowing throughout. Women were dancing, laughing, liking, loving together. It's beautiful, this women-loving-women.
>
> (quoted in Kay Turner, *Between Us*, 90)

"Sue," who later went by the name "Acorn" and then "Flame," explicitly adopts the newly minted language of women's identification even as she explains that she "didn't try" to fall in love. The novelty facilitates her sense of "beauty" in the scene, and she seems to need to explain the all-woman dance to her lover, perhaps to herself as well. Beauty brings politics with it. Significantly, the letter ends with the discovery of anger about a new sense of minority status: "In spite of all the positive feelings growing within me, there is outrage sprouting" (90).

Love letters thus turn out to be less private or, at least, less "spontaneous" than we might expect. Alongside new pride, they register new expectations and social minefields, including the very difficulties that ideals of women's love could engender. We see this in Kay Turner's anthology, *Between Us: A Legacy of Lesbian Love Letters*, which provides the only overview of letters from the period to date. On the one hand, Turner foregrounds the "humorous depictions of pot-smoking and pussy-power" characteristic of the 1970s and the personal struggles with the "sex wars" of the 1980s (*Between Us*, 19). On the other hand, Turner proposes that letter writing itself is the privileged expression of a "feminine code of entrustment":

> Certain of the themes might be found in any love correspondence: passionate outpourings, yearnings for reunion, jealousies, and so on. Other themes, I think, carry a characteristic lesbian sensibility about loving. . . . The sense of a chosen intimacy—deeply compelling and hard won—is invested with a desire to inhabit a certain way of loving that affirms a unique intersection of the erotic and the ethical. Themes that appear and reappear in the letters articulate a feminine code of entrustment that includes choosing love for itself, not for what it will bring in terms of status; a commitment to a non-hierarchical, reciprocal relationship; alliance and friendship as part of loving; a strong desire for the beloved's personal self-fulfillment; honesty and respect as determining qualities of love; sex as the expression of intimacy; a feeling of trust, and a dedication to the effort required to express a precision of feeling.
>
> (*Between Us*, 20)

Turner proposes a connection between lesbian relationship and feminist ideals of egalitarian love, even if she tries to avoid saying that lesbianism is *essentially* different from other sexualities. In this, she reflects a feminist hope that goodness will enable desire, that desire will bring goodness. Letters symbolize not just writing *about* women but women writing *to* each other; it takes careful work to find the right words for "feeling." Women, in this vision, are one another's best lovers as well as correspondents.

The following two examples show how this "feminine code of entrustment," and its emphasis on written self-expression, could become its own convention while facilitating a new identification as "woman-identified" lesbian. Eileen Bonner wrote daily to her first woman lover in the context of leaving her marriage and coming out. This was partly because the relationship was clandestine: in the early 1980s she was married with a child and working as a nurse. The sense of a new self in writing emerges from her comment to me that "the letters I wrote to my lover were my first tentative

steps into feminism for me. She was my feminist mentor, as it were, and often directed my reading of poetry, books and listening of music that had a
strong feminist flavor and exclusively by and for women."[4] Bonner closes her
letter with a heart drawn in the shape of kisses, annotated with the words—
"as you say inadequate." But this is matched by new aspirations to write: "I
am just sitting here wishing I could write my own poetry so there was
something that was really mine to give to just you. Still I can't be good at
everything can I?"[5] Bonner did begin writing poetry and taking self-
portraits for her lover. Interestingly, today she has combined an arts degree
as a mature student with working in social services.

Another woman, S, showed me a book-length letter, written and decorated by her and her lover in turn. The following, dated 10 September 1982,
gives a sense of the tone:

> S, hello friend, spirit sister— . . . I *loved* getting your letter. What a treat, to get
> your words, warmth and support. I'm up on the roof, as evening falls over a
> murky city—and the jays screech in the trees . . . Yes, writing is a wonderful
> way to get to know each other—I think it's only just hitting me, that you're not
> around the corner, that you really do exist out there in space, that you share so
> many of the same ideals as I do . . . and that we are both *equally* sharing our
> energy! A treasure, a thrill, a feeling of flying . . . like one of those funfair
> swing roundabouts, where the chairs swing out in a wide circle . . . And, dear
> stranger, how can I tell you—on that bit of plastic [phone], devoid of your
> physical, warm, presence that I love you—that it feels so natural to love you.
> You sing inside my heart! . . . Do you know—you're such a good letter-writer,
> what a joy to follow the threads over the pages! . . . Your letter has filled me
> with bubbling giggles—with your rabbiting and twittering, as you call it: and
> thank you so much for the painting . . . Getting to know someone like you
> means treading carefully, and listening carefully. Yes, I want to be careful with
> you. How to find words for the shining light in my heart? . . . Maybe I don't
> need them—but I wrap myself tenderly around you—heart to heart.[6]

"In the early 1980s not many women I knew had a phone in their home—so
for me it was endless letter writing," S told me.[7] Letters were practical connections. Yet this example suggests a distinctive form of intimacy that lent
itself easily to the new ideals of spiritual as well as erotic connection. Although this letter writer seems to have been provoked by literal separation,

she suggests that "writing" is "a wonderful way to get to know each other" and especially apt for lesbian courtship. Authentic in the way that saying "I love you" on a "plastic" phone was apparently not, she seems to align it with the shared but invisible energy that transcends the everyday cityscape along with the birds in the trees and the "feeling of flying" she projects between them. This language of natural women's love is as much of its time as the effusive handwriting on purple stationary decorated with spirals and trees.

The new conventions of lesbian address are perhaps most starkly illustrated in the letter M. T. Silvia wrote to a woman she had fallen for at the Southern Women's Music Festival in 1989, inviting her to a "Love and Lust Letter Writing Workshop":

> Several factors need to be considered when thinking about entering the exciting and titillating world of LLLW. May I suggest that to begin, you sit in a circle with yourself, take a long deep breath, pause for a moment and ask yourself, "Am I in love and lust with anyone?" This is very critical, for if the answer is no, then there is no reason to proceed and you may now disregard the rest of this letter. But, if you are fortunate enough to answer YES, then let's go on.
>
> (quoted in Kay Turner, *Between Us*, 70)

Silvia's joke is the sign of confidence not necessarily in this particular relationship (the woman she was pursuing already had a girlfriend), but in expressing women's mutual desire in writing. At the same time, her mockery of the idea of a handbook suggests her sense that lesbians had their own rules of seduction to break, probably involving refusing to sit in a circle. Indeed, a real lesbian letter-writing workshop was organized in 1989 by writers and lovers Gillian Hanscombe and Suniti Namjoshi in southwestern England (Dawson, *The Virago Book*, 3). Hanscombe and Namjoshi's workshop was also playful, no doubt, but it had a political agenda in supporting the literature of lesbian relationship. Hanscombe and Namjoshi had themselves fallen in love through correspondence, bridging Toronto and London after they met at a conference in London in 1984. That same year, they developed a collection of epistolary poetry out of their letters, *Flesh and Paper*, published by a small lesbian press in 1989. They introduce this poetic dialogue by proposing that, because "words invent the world," lesbians need to speak publicly and authoritatively but also *to one another*, in order to invent "who we are" on lesbian terms. Hanscombe and Namjoshi's claim of equal relationships between themselves as writers, but between them and their lesbian readers, perhaps explains their decision not to identify which of them has written which poem. Yet they are polemical about lesbian identification—here dramatically across differences of race, culture, and religion as well as country. Though the poems begin with a coy pun on the dishevelment of new love—"let us compose ourselves, two grown women"—they conclude politically, in the face of a censoring world, that "we can compose ourselves; / but it's our bodies, not our passports, / fit so uncommonly well" (Namjoshi and Hanscombe, *Flesh and Paper*, 9, 63).

By the end of the 1980s, lesbians in Britain and North America had enjoyed an unprecedented era of public recognition. Their letters had indirectly played a part in this—which role would become much more direct after those letters were published. Yet new codes of moral as well as erotic authority, including those that pitched love-letter writing as itself important for lesbians, could be double-edged. How, in this era of love triumphant, to compose a letter to a woman you fear does not desire you, or whom you do not really desire but you need anyway? Would Lorna Hardy, with whose sad diary account I began this chapter, have been better able to write to the indifferent "C" had she attended Hanscombe and Namjoshi's workshop? The awkward burden of representation that lesbian pride could engender is suggested in one woman's announcement to a lover who has obviously left her: "I release you into the great sea of love from whence you first came to me." She closes her letter with the assurance that "we have done some very good work together my darling comrade. The entire world has been uplifted by our love" (quoted in Kay Turner, *Between Us*, 86–87). Another reaches to Adrienne Rich's poem "Diving Into the Wreck" to try to explain why she had to leave: "Before we broke up, I felt oppressed at times. You wanted me to be with you all the time. I needed 'air,' or space as the diver in the poem needs to explore herself" (quoted in *Between Us*, 76). Letters in the epoch of lesbian feminism, then, remain as ambiguous as those of previous eras not because of a lack of language so much as the plethora of words that idealized women's romantic love.

Mary Meigs's novel about her relationship with a woman she only names as "R" provides a final example of the particular ironies that liberation could bring to an already ambiguous art. In 1992, aged seventy-five, she received a seductive fan letter from "an invisible woman, both impersonal and warmly personal," who had seen Meigs in the Canadian film *A Company of Strangers* (1990) when it was shown in her native Australia. The film told the story of a group of women stranded in the Canadian wilderness when their holiday bus breaks down. Finding they can survive together in this Edenic landscape, Meigs stood out as the butchest of them, a rangy seventy-four-year-old whom I remember clearly as the star of this low-budget feminist classic. Meigs thus began a correspondence across the continents, with the sixty-eight-year-old R, a correspondence that, "like amniotic fluid," rejuvenated both elderly women's literary as well as sexual ambitions (Meigs, *The Time Being*, 11). Meigs, a writer best known for *Lily Briscoe, A Self-Portrait*, made of the relationship an autobiographical novel, *The Time Being*. The novel was based on the letters, and Meigs also accepted the invitation of British feminist editor Jill Dawson to publish extracts from them in Dawson's *Virago Book of Love Letters*. Here she responds to receiving a first photograph of "R":

August 2, 1992: You evidently have a dimple just above the corner of your mouth, stage right which is really left? When you smile at me, a little light on your cheek and you're so radiantly beautiful! I wanted to send you a drawing to show the parts of my right-hand face that are still hyper-sensitive, perhaps always will be? So if I jump, in one of our long and lovely kissing séances you won't think it's your fault, my consummately careful darling. I wish we were in the middle of one right now, silently moving over each other's faces with resting-places, passionate ones, to linger at and in. I've lost my power over words and spent (after wandering around looking for raspberries and being bitten by bugs) a good part of the afternoon asleep on the sofa while the last Haydn trios were playing with slow movements written just for us. I've been thinking of *your* power over words, rather like a ballet mistress, and they are beautifully trained to follow your choreography so gracefully that they don't seem to have worked at it. I'm looking at your August 7th letter and your stern theory (based on my warnings, of course) of my tiny percentage of 'sex/physical and all that,' total control indeed. Our total control seems to have slipped a bit, doesn't it, and I wonder if I, for one, ever had it or was just basing my conception of it on past experience, for I had to learn what a mere photo of you can do to my corporeal soul. As for *your* soul, my love, when did the 'demonstrative R' go too far? And which of us is ahead of the other?

(quoted in Dawson, *The Virago Book*, 67)

Meigs suggests writing's insufficiency in the face of R's "inexhaustible power to arouse." She wishes they were able to kiss, speculates over a "mere photo," thinks about responding with a drawing of her own face's erotic and oversensitive grid. Yet as she rereads her as yet unmet lover's letter, she clearly aims to seduce in turn. In fact, her loss of "power over words" suggests a pleasurable losing of sexual control. Lovemaking as something only possible in the conditional tense of a hoped-for future meeting in the flesh turns wondrously present tense in the letter's illusion of synchronicity: "moving over each other's faces." The excitement of writing is matched by that of reading, projecting R's own, comparatively greater "power over words" as physically choreographed, balletic. The letter brings the union of physical and verbal to a climax in the image of Meigs's "corporeal soul."

Meigs offered her personal letters for publication in part to demonstrate her belief that not only lesbians but older women have a right to passion. But the illusions of love by correspondence led the relationship between Meigs and R to a bitter end shortly after they met and Meigs realized she was not willing to "yield up [her] solitary autonomy" (Meigs, *The Time Being* 11). Proudly able to write about her desires (in notable contrast to R), Meigs struggled to articulate the shame of its descent into an everyday clash of personalities. Meigs had hoped to write the story of their joint love together, planning early on with R to save their correspondence for it. But in the story of loss, yet relief, that Meigs found she had to tell on her own, we find a compelling realism about lesbian and women's love after "coming out."

How do you assess the value of a love letter? For the lover, it is surely whether it excites its addressee. I do not claim that these texts are aesthetically exceptional for a public reader. Yet it is striking to see how instrumental letters were in the invention of a new identity, rooted in ideas about being a woman and a lesbian. It is partly for this reason that they have found their way into the public domain. Further chapters will explore the stories that were harder to write or to publish and the new conflicts between autonomy and relationship that arose. But I want to end this chapter by asking whether lesbian lovers are typical of women who like writing and, more generally, who are attached to letters as the relics of relationships?

Why Do Women Like Personal Letters?

Whether women in general prefer love-letter writing more than men is a misleading question, depending on vast generalizations about literacy as much as sexual politics, just as is the misguided attempt to decide whether women are more "artful" as a whole in writing letters. In case anyone imagines that letter writing itself has been the particular province of women, let me be clear that this would be a nonsensical claim for a form so broad in scope and function. As Amanda Gilroy and W. M. Verhoeven explain, it is rather that an influential rhetoric persists in Western literary circles that "equates epistolary femininity and feminine epistolarity, a rhetoric that derives largely from a particular view of the eighteenth-century novel and its association with women" (Gilroy and Verhoeven, *Epistolary Histories*, 1). Immortalized in Jan Vermeer's portraits, white, bourgeois women became the face of personal letter writing in the seventeenth century, but this was more symbolic than any guide to practice. Women's letter writing had previously only been a sustained pursuit of European aristocrats and, to a degree, women in religious orders; celebrated letter collections were often in fact written by men. The stereotype of the woman letter writer was crystallized during the eighteenth century, again often by male writers like Samuel Richardson and Daniel Defoe. This reflected the expansion of a literate middle class with leisure time and increased opportunities for travel, combined with epistolary-conduct manuals for the upwardly mobile. We only need to think of the practically minded correspondence of Cornish laborers during the same period, or even the current fashion for romantic letter writing by young men as well as women in rural Nepal, to see how the gender relations of letter writing are as volatile as in any other social practice (Austin, "Letter Writing in a Cornish Community"; Ahearn, *Invitations to Love*).

However, it is true that in cultures that permit women to be literate, women have often been responsible for letter writing that relates to domestic affairs and to courtship. In the modern West, as well, women *are identified with* personal letters in a way that men are not (Barton and Hall, "Introduction," 7).[8] An interview with Pamela Newkirk about her anthology of African American love letters exemplifies the way this identification is popularly reinforced, as the reviewer notes "interestingly, most were written by men." "Isn't that strange?" Newkirk responds, laughing. "Part of that may have been that most of the letters are from the earliest periods (prior to 1900), when men were better-educated than women. . . . And it also may be because what was valued in many early collections were things that were collected by men." "Or perhaps women are more prone to saving the letters they receive than men," adds the reviewer (Behe, "Love Letter Collection"). More work needs to be done to investigate the material cultures of letters. Yet I suggest that women's identification with personal letters, which extends across classes, races, and cultures at different times, reflects more than the legacy of the Vermeer stereotype in domestic and sexual roles. For this reason, in many cultures where women have historically written less publicly than men, they have maintained profuse personal correspondences as well as becoming the guardians of family letters. In the context of Western history, this has positioned women as the writers of morale-boosting letters to men at war and sustained the women-centered kinship and friendship networks of a variety of societies from migrant Australia to middle-class American and British reformers of the nineteenth century (Clarke and Spender, *Life Lines,*; Smith-Rosenberg, "The Female World of Love"; Barton and Hall, *Letter Writing*).[9]

Today, distinctions between public and private spheres are becoming much more fluid, ironically in the very expansion of networked economies and the proliferation of highly individualized niche cultures. Fascinatingly, there does seem to be evidence that personal corresponding in e-mail and text messaging is being taken up by men previously uninterested in letter writing, though suggestions that this is facilitating more "emotional" self-expression remain impressionistic.[10] Yet the legacy of women's special identification with personal relationships and informal economies remains strong. Letter-writing surveys in the United Kingdom in the mid-1980s revealed that girls wrote twice as many personal letters as did boys (Barton and Hall, "Introduction," 7). More recently, the mobile phone company Vodaphone targeted its female customers in its "phone-photograph postcard" feature, typical of the marketing of mobile phones to women in terms of aesthetic and interactional appeal in contrast to the gadgetry and electronic game playing emphasized for male customers.[11] Similarly, both the U.K. and the U.S. Greeting Cards Associations count upon the women who buy two-thirds of the three and seven billion greeting cards sold in the United Kingdom and United States, respectively, each year to help expand the burgeoning "electronic card" market.[12]

Feminists have been the first to wrestle with the pernicious monoliths of both "woman" and "genre" that these marketing ploys suppose. And yet, second-wave writers, editors, academics, and activists in their own practice continued to tie the two together. As Susan Brownmiller joked to Gloria Steinem in a handwritten letter of 1974, "why are all feminist communiqués mimeographs of dear sister letters?"[13] Signing "in sisterhood" now seems quaint, but in the 1970s and 1980s it signaled a desire to share the "whole world of women's experience," as Mary Thom described the letters page of *Ms.* magazine (Thom, *Letters to Ms.*, xv). That vividly imagined world made reading Sylvia Plath's letters home to her mother a rite of communicative passage for young women themselves coming of age in 1976 (Plath and Plath, *Letters Home*). It made women's love letters to each other a thrill to discover, like the sly courtship of Virginia Woolf and Vita Sackville-West published in 1984 (Sackville-West et al., *Letters*). Epistolary essays and novels flourished in the new women's presses and publishers' lists; the correspondences of long-forgotten housewives, servants, migrants, sex workers, and suffragettes were suddenly precious to archivists and critics.[14] An influential academic study of women's epistolary literature published in 1988 called these letters "the female voice" (Goldsmith, *Writing the Female Voice: Essays on Epistolary Literature*). At the same time, Olga Kenyon praised "female letter-writing" in her anthology *Eight Hundred Years of Women's Letters*, for showing women's refusal to be "authorities" (xix).

Unearthing the textual subtleties of letters has felt particularly important to feminist critics. Women's social positioning as communicators, but not artists, is eerily subsumed by ideologies that position them as "natural" letter-writers. A wave of feminist critics has revealed how double-edged is the praise for the "untutored" expression of women like Mme. de Sévigné, Mary Wortley Montagu, Hester Thrale, Fanny Burney, and Jane Welsh Carlyle (Goldsmith, "Authority"; Farrell, *Yours in Sisterhood*; Jensen, *Writing Love*). The legacy continues even today: one Internet agency, introducing "beautiful Russian ladies," offers in its "letter writing tips" to would-be husbands, the reminder that "*La Bruyère, at the end of the 17th century, remarked that women succeed better than men in the epistolary form. So don't be surprised if your fair bride's letters are different from yours :).*"[15] Praise as a letter writer carries limited literary authority, especially as published female letter writers often remain anonymous—or turn out to be the subterfuge of male writers wanting to write about love. The "feminization" of the literary letter in the seventeenth

LIFE LINES

Australian women's letters and diaries 1788 to 1840

Edited by Patricia Clarke and Dale Spender

David Legge, cover of Clarke and Spender, *Life Lines*.

and eighteenth centuries had much more to do with the assertion of new class and national cultures than women's political interests (Favret, *Romantic Correspondence*). Working-class correspondents have suffered even more neglect than middle-class women because of the assumption that they write merely to communicate and not to express, or that they were not literate at all (Steedman, "A Woman Writing"; Austin, "Letter Writing").

For feminists it has therefore been tempting to insist upon art, authority, autonomy, even "intention" in letters, from Virginia Woolf's prescient praise of the seventeenth-century Dorothy Osborne, who, like Sévigné, wrote nothing else but personal letters, to Daria Donnelly's reclamation of the "poetry" in Emily Dickinson's correspondences and Janet Altman's emphasis on Sévigné's literary ambition (Woolf, "Dorothy Osborne's Letters"; Donnelly, "The Power to Die"; Altman, "Women's Letters"). But this insistence causes difficulties for critics who have wanted to reconcile such projects with social and deconstructive approaches to letters. Linda Kauffman typifies this double act in arguing that women's love letters are more about language than feeling. In her terms, the epistolary "discourse of desire" "questions mimesis, draws attention to the ambiguous implications of signature, and exposes the artifice involved in critical perceptions of gender" (*Discourses of Desire*, 21). Although Kauffman echoes the classical terms of letter writing as rhetoric, she interprets this to mean deconstruction rather than persuasion. A parallel perversity describes Peggy Kamuf's reading of the historical changes in the way the seventeenth-century *Lettres Portugaises* have been interpreted according to whether people believed they were written by a woman or a man. Kamuf concludes there is no such thing as "women's writing," anymore than an essential definition of "woman." While this is so, as Nancy K. Miller parries, readers react very differently to a tale of female masochism if they know it was written by an aristocratic French man rather than a poor Portuguese woman, just as it makes a difference if we believe a letter is factual or fictional (McAlpin, "Poststructuralist Feminism").

Such sentiments were intensified in lesbian love-letter writing as it absorbed the double imperatives of gay and women's liberation. For feminism opened up a romance with letters alongside the romance of women's desire, where writing to each other was a symbolic commitment to an idea as well as a relationship. This becomes more obvious when I turn from private love letters to consider the epistolary fiction and criticism of the time.

CHAPTER TWO

Feminist Epistolary Romance

MALKA SHELI, delicious lover,
With you, nothing is ever enough, I want you even when you're not
around . . . desire/your fingers . . . push me over the edge.

I am sliding downhill, all the way. I want to be fucked, desperate . . .
your coat flies out the door before I am awake. Without your body, heavy
on top of me, I am weightless.

You pour out LOVE, so I stand back to mistrust, then I fall into you.
Late at night, on the last train, spelling desire on our palms, people are
watching: we play hermanas latinas, we pass for whatever is necessary, we
pass for so much, in front of those eyes we speak no English. So we can
say "where we come from women hold hands and love each other."

We run in the street, we run behind our front doors, we eat olives,
fuck each other senseless, drowning in wetness, tongues drawing fruit
and juice inside our jewish mouths, a thousand tastes and memories.

      —Esther Y. Kahn, "Letters Long Distance to a Lover"

Beginning a story of feminist relationship with love letters may annoy
those who wish for feminism to be less about love and more about politics. Alice Echols, historian of the second wave, argued that "cultural feminism" dissipated the radical visions of early 1970s feminists in part through
"false universalism" and "the familiar terrain of romantic love" (*Daring to
Be Bad*, 256). There was always tension over whether "personalizing the political" was a travesty of feminism's "politicizing of the personal," and certainly, many feminisms developed directly in opposition to each other, most
prominently black feminism, or womanism, to white feminism in the 1970s.
But the public-private letters of activists show that romance was deeply part
of feminist as well as lesbian subjectivity. As movement veteran Ros Baxandall describes it, for her, "the women's liberation movement was love at first

sight" ("Catching the Fire," 210). Barbara Smith remembered the experience of the early years of the Combahee River Collective in the same way:

> The thrill of having people arriving, car load after car load of women who knew each other, but some who didn't know we were being brought together by five different women. We were just thrilled. There were so many colors, so many faces, so many bodies, from all over, and a chance to hear what was going on in different cities. [We were] standing around and looking at us all standing on that lawn, and realizing we are all women who are taking this big risk.
>
> (quoted in Harris, "'All of Who I Am'")

Not just the writing, but also the saving and publishing of these letters position love as a prized capture for women exploring what the world was like when defined primarily in relation to others like themselves.

Simpler than the political record, love letters are much like popular feminist novels of the time in focusing on the private, especially sexual transformation. Paulina Palmer, analyzing the products of the British feminist publishers Virago and The Women's Press in the 1980s, remarked on their curious preponderance of radical rather than socialist feminist themes (see *Contemporary Women's Fiction*). She concluded that their promotion of fiction about sexual abuse, such as Kathy Page's *Back in the First Person* or Pat Barker's *Union Street*, reflected the justice of that politics. Admittedly, Palmer may have underplayed the effect of genre itself: popular novels tend to deal with the private sphere. Similarly, feminist poetry was largely confessional in style because short lyric poetry in the West usually is, particularly for new writers. And letters will always be a genre of love, archetypally arch one minute, overblown the next, and as quickly resonant of misunderstanding and betrayal as they are of joy. Yet my contention is that women such as those cited above were self-consciously excited by the idea of reforming a genre deeply associated with women's sexual enthrallment to men. As Maroula Joannou and Imelda Whelehan have theorized, the blockbuster confessionals of Marge Piercy, Erica Jong, Marilyn French, Lisa Alther, Rita Mae Brown, and Fay Weldon—alongside love letters—make a new literature of "sexuality and reproduction, love and personal relationships, women's friendships and the role of the artist in changing our world-view" ("This

Book Changes Lives," 125). However, while "the consciousness-raising novels of the 1970s embody a highly personalized notion of the political, of the
embattled individual woman witnessing to the 'truth' and swelling the
ranks of the growing numbers of women who are determined to stand up
and be counted" (127), letters evidently provide an implicit solution to wom-
en's isolation in the very fact of their writing to one another. If letters between men and women are rooted in a division of labor in which woman
waits while man travels, feminist epistolarians interpret distance as patriarchal isolation and turn women into confidantes who rediscover how close
they really are.

Falling in Love with Letter Writing

Feminist writing is full of metaphorical love letters of one kind and another.
Carole Hanisch, one of the New York Radical Women who precipitated the
1968 protest at the Miss America Pageant in Atlantic City, remembers that
after the newspaper headlines, "we were deluged with letters, more than our
small group could possibly answer, many passionately saying, 'I've been
waiting all my life for something like this to come along'" (Hanisch, "Two
Letters," 200). It is no coincidence that feminist epistolary fiction was
launched through rewriting some famous heterosexual love letters in the
form of a correspondence between women writers. Written in 1971 and first
published in Portugal in April 1972, as second-wave feminism hit Europe
and North America, *Novas Cartas Portuguesas* (*New Portuguese Letters*), by
Maria Barreno, Maria Horta, and Maria Velho da Costa recast the
seventeenth-century French literary classic the *Lettres Portugaises* and with it
"the female letter of suffering and victimization" (Goldsmith, "Authority,"
viii). Supposedly written by a Portuguese nun Mariana Alcoforado to a
French chevalier who had abandoned her, the *Lettres* were actually the hoax
of le comte de Guilleragues, a hack writer of the time. Notwithstanding
their origin, they had long been canonized as archetypically feminine writing, brilliant in passion rather than art. Horta, Barreno, and Velho da Costa
politicized the nun's desperate, unrequited letters to show the continuity of
women's oppression in modern Portugal and to break the taboo over expressing women's (hetero)sexual desires. This also asserted the artfulness of
the woman letter writer, debating her role in a complex series of semific-

tional letters. "Having married out of passion, I was inflamed by it and blinded by it," confides one character, "Mónica M., on the Morning She Committed Suicide, to Dona Joana de Vasconcelos," "forgetting myself entirely, my hair lying loose on the pillow, simply waiting for my husband to take me, neither caring nor noticing whether he was taking me out of love or merely making use of me" (Barreno, Horta and Costa, *The Three Marias*, 207). This is followed by an open and anonymous letter of address to "my sisters," containing only the questions, "But what can literature do? Or rather: what can words do?" (210).

The political portrayal of such confidences between women was presented as an aspect of the book's authoring as well its subject. The three authors pooled their individual addresses anonymously with the proviso that nothing would be censored and that they could answer one another in further writings. In the published version, the fictional missives and poems of the cloistered nun and her relations are interspersed with anonymous letters among the authors in which they explore their different political and literary approaches. The book ends with a testament to the consciousness-raising that this dialogic process of writing involved:

> This is not the work of an isolated writer struggling with personal phantoms and problems of expression in order to communicate with an abstract Other, nor is it the summing-up of the production of three such writers working separately on the same theme. The book is the *written record* of a much broader, common, lived experience of creating a sisterhood through conflict, shared fun and sorrow, complicity and competition.
>
> (231)

Although they contend that "all of literature is a long letter," this form of exchange promotes a radical idea of women's autonomy: "the hand above the paper sets down ideas in a letter that we write, not so much for another as for our own nourishment" (13–14).

The "Three Marias" became landmarks of the second wave when they were arrested by the censorship committee of the ruling Portuguese Estado Novo dictatorship and sued for abusing the freedom of the press and outraging public morals and decency. "What distinguished *Novas Cartas Portuguesas* from other female erotic literature judged pornographic by a patriarchal regime" was "the way it exploited collective solidarity in both its literary format and its courtroom strategy. The three co-authors refused to identify the perpetrator of the anonymous passages on which the prosecution was based" (Owen, "Exiled in Its Own Land," 57). This scuppered the legal process while adding another layer to the novel's representation of women's alliance in letters. A further layer was added in 1973 when feminists began to organize internationally in support. In Paris, they processed to Notre Dame bearing effigies of the Three Marias and singing a revised version of the "Dies Irae"; Robin Morgan organized a Broadway benefit in New York; airline offices and Portuguese embassies were picketed; demonstrations were held in Europe, the United States, Brazil and Australia; the case was covered in *Time* magazine; and a statement was prepared for the United Nations Human Rights Commission (Kauffman, *Discourses of Desire*, 280). Following Antonio de Figueiredo's comments on "The Portuguese Context" in *Index on Censorship*'s coverage in 1974, British feminist Faith Gillespie countered that

> Often the press, for all its attention and goodwill toward 'The Three Marias,' tended to neglect, obscure or distort the question, overlooking the fact that women are responding on the basis of sexual politics, and not revealing that the significance of this widespread response lies in the determination of women to gain the power signified in the control of their own bodies and control of their own destinies. . . . 'It is not by accident that we are faced with an obscenity charge,' one of the authors told me, 'and not a political charge. A political charge carries dignity and some importance, but an obscenity charge is humiliating, degrading, and that is what the government wants to do to us. . . . Realising this, Senhor Rodrigues said, 'I think this book, instead of being tried as pornographic, could be tried as a political book.' Doubtless the State realises this also. But in terms of this book, merely to see that it is political is inadequate. When the women write of the wars in the Portuguese colonies, it is with a deep realisation of quite another political reality, the reality of the politics of the personal, in their own colonised condition.
>
> ("The Women's Liberation Context," 23)

Feminists campaigning outside of Portugal may have flattened out the writers' declared hesitation at speaking for poor women, immigrant women, and women in Portugal's African colonies. But this was typical of feminists' early attempt to articulate "quite another political reality." The letters were a passionate code for a new identification, repeated in the feminist organizations mobilized in the writers' defense (Morgan, *Going Too Far*, 207). Extracts of the book were read at the first French "women-only" event on 25 October 1973. In their introduction to the French edition, Monique Wittig and Evelyne Garrec suggest that the authors' use of letters to express women's desires permitted them to ask the "same questions that all women in struggle ask":

> Si aucune autre alternative ne nous est donnée que la guerre ouverte contre tout un système social que nous refusons à la base, dans lequel nous devrons détruire tout, nos propres maisons y compris si nécessaire, reculerons-nous? [If we are given no other alternative than open warfare against a social system that fundamentally excludes us, in which, if necessary, we should destroy everything including our houses, would we draw back?]
>
> (Wittig and Garrec, "Note pour l'edition francaise"; my translation).

The epistolary motif of a newly perceived intimacy between women is particularly striking when women's differences and other axes of exploitation and separation occasion a work's plot. This is most obvious in the other feminist epistolary classic, Alice Walker's 1982 novel *The Color Purple*. Better known in Britain and the United States and certainly more accessible, the novel makes clear that women's isolation from other women is created as much through racism as through patriarchy, and Walker's "womanist" revision of that fate is symbolized by Celie's turn from writing to a white patriarchal "God" to her black sister. As part of this, the letter is aligned with slave narrative and prayer to suggest the special trust and identity between black women (Williams, " 'Trying to Do Without God' "; Kauffman, *Special Delivery*). Yet *The Color Purple* draws on many of the traditional aspects of the genre as a woman's plea for love and spiritual redemption in the face of men's sexual abuse. In that way, letter writing is a useful aspect of Walker's advocacy of womanism not only as a black revision of white feminism but as "a home for the black feminine" ((Charles), "The Language of Womanism," 283). It is then no accident that Celie is finally put back in touch with her sister through the independent woman Shug, with whom she is also sexually liberated at last.

The Senegalese Mariama Bâ's novel *Une si longue lettre* (1980) (published in English as *So Long a Letter*) and Marjorie Agosâin and Emma Sepâul-veda-Pulvirenti's entwined *Amigas: Letters of Friendship and Exile* (2001) are similarly focused on the territory of women's sexual and domestic struggle against men and the intimacy that ensues among women, even as these authors draw this through specifically black African Muslim and Chilean women's solidarities. "Letters Long Distance to a Lover" by Esther Y. Kahn, quoted in the epigraph to this chapter, is in fact a sexual exploration of Jewish women's identity in the face of hostile "anglo-saxon rain" (74). As anthologized in the Sheba Collective's *Serious Pleasure: Lesbian Erotic Stories and Poetry* (1989), lesbian love is equally ethnic self-assertion: "Our passion is our culture," one letter ends, "Sweet kisses of the tongue, rimon, ani ohevotach at, Esther" (73). Similarly, the love letter defines a political alliance across the divides between black British and Asian women in Carmen Tunde's "An Open Letter," in the 1987 collection *Black Women Talk Poetry*:

> Dear Risparl,
> Jaswinder
> Hazel
> Perminder
> It hasn't been easy
> Loving you.

Evoking the different stereotypes they each battle with, the poem concludes:

> Afro-Asian unity?
> A stormy lesbian relationship,
> close and challenging.
> And yet
> I don't want to be in the
> minority again.
> Neither do you.
> What are we both afraid of?
>   (87, 91)

Letter writing as the form in which women's differences can be safely even, lovingly, explored is perhaps most extensively represented in Gillian Hanscombe's *Between Friends* (1982). The book, which was "never intended to be a novel," came out of a London women's discussion group set up after a 1980 conference on "The Problem of Men." Hanscombe explained in the introduction to the 1990 edition that:

> It took the form of letters between women for two obvious reasons: one was because only some of the material belonged to my own life, whereas the rest had been told by others round the table and therefore should be spoken in a voice different from my own. The other reason was that the material had been, and was, contentious and made us argue, rather than agree; and therefore it should appear in a form that allowed the arguing to be clear. Then there was a more hidden, third reason: having taken so long myself to find feminist ideas, I wanted to write something that would be easily and immediately accessible to all the women who would never be motivated to read straightforward polemic or theory; something that could be popular; something that could have a sense of relationships between women and that could have a smattering of "story."

(unpaginated)

The novel sets up a four-way correspondence among apolitical lesbian mother Meg, her old heterosexual friend Frances, radical separatist lesbian Jane, and her consciousness-raising partner, feminist heterosexual Amy. As they debate separatism, the mothering of male children, political lesbianism, nonpenetration, rape, and whether sexual identities are themselves patriarchal, Hanscombe is frank about feminists' differences and the limits of solidarity. Although Amy's letters bring Jane and Meg together, Frances chooses an abusive husband over feminism and cuts out of the epistolary circle. Yet the romantic ending, especially as mediated through a correspondence that will close in the embrace of its two central writers, retains an allegiance to the idea of a loving egalitarianism specific to women:

> I've had your snow letter and you're about to arrive and will have this waiting for you after our time together. No, and then—before, and after, I say yes to you Jane—yes—yes—yes. . . . Come soon . . . come quickly . . . stay with me, and go, and come again, and go, and come again. That's how it is, that's how it really is. That way there is always enough time, always enough space. . . . I love you. I feel embraced by you and I embrace you in turn. Keep

safe, my sister and friend and lover. Your woman's power is like my own—we need not fail.

(175)

Between Friends, like all these texts, registers the emotion of the early 1980s debates over "difference" but also highlights the persistence of letter writing as the expression of women's intimacy. As we can see in this closing letter, the paradox of this symbolic correspondence is a dream of women's reunion in which, in fact, there will be no need to write at all, in which separation is always matched by similarity: "go, and come again, and go, and come again." It is significant that Hanscombe describes the conference behind the novel as what transformed her from being lesbian to being lesbian-feminist. While debates over sexuality, race, and religion, to mention only the matters most prominent at that time, made many feminists move away from feminine identification rooted in the need for (lesbian) sexual liberation, Hanscombe has stuck with it, a fact that surely prompts her continued interest in letters as a form. I have already discussed in chapter 1 the epistolary poetry she published with her lover Suniti Namjoshi, and the love-letter-writing workshop for lesbians they ran together. Hanscombe and Namjoshi's poems and fictional letters have been included in two subsequent anthologies of women's letters (Dawson, *The Virago Book*, 26–28, 117–19; Kenyon, *Eight Hundred Years*, 28–30). Hanscombe has also drawn on lesbian and bisexual women's correspondences in her research into modernist women's writing (Hanscombe and Smyers, *Writing for Their Lives*).

The Three Marias' "passionately nourishing" letters, Wittig's "*écrivante féminine*," Walker's "dear sister," Hanscombe and Namjoshi's "fleshly paper," and, just as much, the silly, loving, angry, jokey, pretentious, and nervous letters actually sent and received by the kinds of women who read this literature in different ways personify the discovery of an erotic and spiritual identity among women. As a public art this epistolary form might be uneven, and these awakenings were specific to culture, race, and other identities as well. But as the record of a romance with the *idea* of political identity itself, these letters form an important element in the "corporeal soul" of feminism, as well as a literary culture based upon women's writing and reading for one another.

Christine McCauley, cover of the British women's liberation magazine *Spare Rib* (December 1980) showing a handwritten letter to an "agony aunt" for the Problem Page of a traditional 1950s-style women's magazine.

SR 102 is out December 18.

COPYDATE (the *last* day we can accept any items) for news, shortlist, classified ads —

NOVEMBER 18.

English – a language of oppression

* Dear *Spare Rib*,
I thought your article 'UN notices women' (*SR* 98) was great, and reflected the chaos that must inevitably arise when representatives of half the population of the world get together to sort out their problems within three weeks!

However, I was particularly disturbed at the language problem at the forum, and sympathized greatly with those women who felt so outraged at having no voice due to the lack of adequate translation facilities. Moreover, I frankly think it is supreme arrogance to expect English (American) to become universal in these circumstances — or French and Spanish. For many Third World women these are the languages of colonial oppression (at best), and the fact that they are used at such conferences must typify for many the patronising attitude of the west.

Feminists should consider adopting the use of an artificial international language — esperanto for example. Women would then be able to talk together on *equal terms* in a language which is neutral and has no disturbing historical or political overtones.

I would love to hear what other women who are interested in this problem think.
Yours,
Joy Bounds,
Ipswich

Give us disputes

* Dear *Spare Rib*,
I was so pleased to find your editorial and some letters in issue 98 about the lesbian/heterosexual women power struggles.

I like *Spare Rib* and like its appeal to women new to feminism as well as those familiar with the Women's Liberation Movement. My main criticism though is the lack of space given to discussing different political perspectives in the WLM and the emotional power struggles that accompany them. So when I saw issue 98 I thought at last! Some actual struggles brought into the open.

I was so disappointed that issue 99 had nothing further on that whole subject! As though it had even begun to be discussed fully! I am glad though to see the pieces by Irish women on their differences and political stand-points.

Please don't think I would like *Spare Rib* to be a forum for hatred, antagonism and disagreement. It *is* comforting that you have an editorial line on certain issues and that you write so supportively about more or less any aspect of the WLM.

But please give us the disputes too, otherwise it leaves an impression that is totally fake.

Such power struggles in the WLM today! White and black women, middle class and working class women, lesbian and heterosexual women, young and old women, religious and atheist women, and so many others. To discuss these power struggles in as supportive an environment as *Spare Rib* is would be invaluable to feminists everywhere.
Sandra Woods,
North London

College – tutors – sex

* Dear *Spare Rib*,
I'd like to share some of my thoughts on the 'Sex with Tutor' topic (*SR* 99). I'm a mature student currently engaging in such a relationship, recognising the costs and sometimes finding it hard to accept what I am doing, despite the benefits.

It's my first experience of College and, although I am 30, quite self-reliant, and comfortable in my relationships. I am as vulnerable as anybody in this new environment and anxious about the academic demands. During the first few days of the course my tutor seemed very attentive, and I felt puzzled, and then worried because I found him very attractive. I tried to keep control, and thought I ought to bring the whole thing out into the open. The alternative would have been to battle on self-consciously, not being able to be natural. I thought he would be able to suggest some way of controlling the situation, so I just said I was going to find it difficult being his tutee because of his attractiveness. He would have arranged for me to change to another tutor, but I decided against this because I thought I should be more sensible and over-

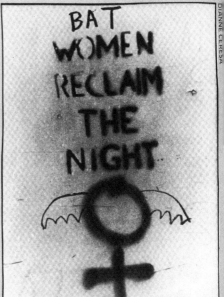

Graffiti on graffiti, spotted in Brighton.

come my inconvenient feelings towards him. This didn't work though and my desire grew along with interest on his part, so that lovemaking became inevitable.

At no time have I felt that having sex was part of my seeking approval from him as my tutor. In retrospect I feel I could have enjoyed an affair with him more freely if I had changed tutors, and this would have avoided the unequal power balance in that he is assessing my work and is the person to whom I should turn for advice on the work. This has caused me quite a lot of strain at times. Lover/learner is a real role conflict.

Another of the costs has been my concern about the attitudes of fellow-students, making me feel stigmatised. Fortunately I have made one or two good friends. I think that a liaison with a tutor may limit development of relationships with other students.

Deborah Cameron mentioned the convenience for tutors of knowing that the student will leave after three years. There are other ways of looking at this although many would not agree with me. It seems that this is a similarly neat situation the other way round — the student knows that there is a ready made end which might suit her, particularly if the tutor is showing signs of emotional dependency.

Of course I take responsibility for my own conduct in my relationship, and have still a lot of things to work out with him so he understands what has happened to me. I feel angry at what I see as his unprofessional behaviour, and at my own inability to overrule feelings.

There doesn't seem any easy way for women to stop seeking sexual approval — old habits die hard. But students who feel sexually harassed ought to request a change of tutor or if possible seek support from a more enlightened member of staff.
W
London

4 *Spare Rib*

The contrasting letters pages of *Spare Rib* (December 1980).

Twisted!

Dear Sisters,
In the Concise Oxford Dictionary (1972), I noticed a distinct case of overt sexism: — Nymphomania 'Morbid and uncontrollable sexual desire in women'.
Satyriasis "Excessive sexual desire in men."
   Would you agree?
In sisterhood,
S Lovett
Staines

Sexual repression

* Dear Spare Rib.
I have just finished reading Shere Hite's Report on Female Sexuality. If only I had read it earlier, I might not feel so bitter and used now. I write as one who was inhibited and ignorant and sexually repressed, did not know what or where a clitoris was until 17, did not climax until 20, or learn to masturbate until 21. Naturally sexual relationships were unhappy. Men were as ignorant of what would give me orgasm as I was myself, some even inferred that I was abnormal; being miserable and frustrated — it is easy to feel at fault.
   I think it's atrocious that 'sex education' should be limited to an explanation of how to make a baby and where periods come from. Girls and boys entering puberty should be taught something about the female genitals. Only the reproductive organs were mentioned when I was at school. Something should be said about orgasm and masturbation, especially to girls; society still does not condone sexual curiosity in women, also the female genitals are anatomically discreet.
A Spare Rib Reader
Staffs

Home delivery can kill

Dear Spare Rib,
I am a junior doctor in a big maternity hospital. Reva Klein's article (SR 98) on home versus hospital delivery omits a vital fact: home delivery can kill. In the last 24 hours I have been called to resuscitate a fairly typical six babies. Two had started breathing after all by the time I arrived. Two needed only the sort of help to get started which a midwife or GP could provide at home with simple equipment. The other two needed help which can only be given with more equipment that could possibly be taken to every home delivery, and before a flying squad could have got to them at home they would have been brain damaged or dead. Of these last two, one had good reason to be born in hospital (her mother had high

FRIDAY 19th DECEMBER
8 PM
BOP WITH US
THE MISTAKES + DISCO
ACTION SPACE
16 CHENIES ST
LONDON WC1
MIXED
WAGED £2.00
UNWAGED £1.50

blood pressure and went into labour seven weeks early), but the other would have been a perfectly good candidate for a home delivery as her only problem was the cord tightly round her neck, one of several completely unforeseeable reasons for not starting breathing.
   Have your home delivery if you really think the advantages outweigh the small risk of losing your baby because of it, but I don't think you can reasonably demand that a doctor or midwife who disagrees with you takes the responsibility of looking after you. I know only too well how many disadvantages hospital delivery can have, but most of them can be avoided by shopping around for your hospital, as Reva Klein suggests, and going into it as well informed as possible about the pros and cons of the procedure and drugs you may be offered, determined to have a real choice about each of them.
Yours sincerely,
Louisa Polak
Edinburgh

Beach litter

Dear Spare Rib.
Thank you for printing the readers letters and the addresses for the manufacturers of the Playtex tampons.
   I have never used this product but cannon fail to be aware of its manufacture. I live on a particularly beautiful, conservatively designated, piece of coast-line and every day its beaches are littered with bright pink, plastic, non-degradeable tampon applicators.
Yours faithfully,
Jane Burt
E. Devon

Message from a foreign prison

Dear Spare Rib,
I'm so tired of promising myself to sit down and write you some kind of poignant letter in which I express my thanks to you for offering me a free subscription to Spare Rib. I guess it's about time that I simply say THANK YOU!
   Prison is no fun anywhere . . . and I suppose it's no funner here in France than most anywhere's else . . . (though there's a lot of worse prisons spread over this world we live in . . .) Spare Rib provides me with many hours of reading pleasure and keeps me up to date as concerns what's happening . . . and what's not . . . and it really means an awful lot to me. I support you and respect the job you're doing to make people more aware. Keep it up.
With love and best wishes.
Jill Diamond
France

Men are irrelevant — women must change

* Dear Spare Rib Collective,
I have been reading Spare Rib on and off (mostly on) for about eight years now and enjoy it very much. Gnerally however I would like to see more debate and argument about issues and ideas in your pages, at the expense, I suppose, of straight reporting of news and events. The letters page is, for me, one of the consistently more interesting parts of the mag.
   The various bits and pieces on men, pro and anti over the past few months, have for example interested me greatly.
   It does seem to me that a lot of women (me included) apply a double standard in their personal relationships, being much more tolerant and forgiving towards men than towards other women, but I would dispute whether the logical conclusion is "all men are shits". Why not "all women are shits"? It takes two to tango and if by your attitudes, words and actions you show that you expect a particular form of behaviour from men, you really can't complain if you get it.
   In my humble opinion, the Women's Liberation Movement's worst enemy is not man but in fact woman. Men won't change until women do, and although countless women have made a start in many big and small ways, there are vast hordes out there who haven't. And why should they? No social structure retains the slightest degree of stability unless there is something in it for everyone. Women's traditional role is pretty cosy if you choose the right man — meal ticket for life, nice house, 2.4 children (or is it 1.8 now?). A ready made identity and reassuring roles to play; home-maker, wife, mother etc. Personal change on the other hand is threatening and painful.
   In all my years of reading Spare Rib, I cannot recall much if any discussion of either the fact that a great many women are still, at best neutral, or at worst actively hostile, to the aims of the movement, or what to do about it. Men are irrelevant, convert those women and everything will fall into place.
Yours sincerely,
Eileen Richardson
London

* indicates letter has been cut.

Letters continued on page 19.

Feminist Academics Like Letter Writing Too . . .

In 1982, Jan Clausen argued that "poets are some of feminism's most influential activists, theorists, and spokeswomen; at the same time, poetry has become a favorite means of self-expression, consciousness-raising, and communication among large numbers of women not publicly known as poets" (quoted in King, *Theory in Its Feminist Travels*, 102). In 1994, Katie King analyzed this as a part of a "cultural feminism" that for her was not "an equation with the anti-pornography movement" or "the political 'other' of 'radical feminism,'" but "the apparatus for the production of feminist culture. . . . This apparatus is the site for the feminist proliferations of new political identities in the seventies, eighties, and nineties through such 'writing technologies' as 'poem,' 'story,' and 'song'" (92). King accordingly looked at the complex layerings of "action, event, oratory, writing, political intervention and theory building" that lie behind many of the classics of feminist theory. Theoretical ideas did not simply germinate on their own but often remained in the form of art or oral communication. King shows how academic books are deeply influenced by conversations, are themselves indeed high-level conversations, but also how historically they crossed and merged with more popular, artistic, and often oral communications among feminists. Understanding this is crucial to fully acknowledging the contributions of theorists on the margins of publishing or academia, and generally to appreciating the politics of class and race that determine who uses which form, as the example of Bernice Johnson Reagon's influential "Coalition Politics: Turning the Century" makes plain, as it morphs from song to album cover to movement text and back again.

I see letters as cultural feminism in this sense: a literature of the movement that was also clearly a practice and could be—was—claimed as a theory, too, of political relationship. Letters were symptoms as well as causes, literary in the sense that they embodied (even as they ironically abstracted) a set of values about women's writing. Letter writing thus exemplifies King's argument that feminist "theory" is something that has come from conversation and daily argument across the borders of activism and academia, professional and homegrown. But I wish to do more than simply add letter writing to the landscape of "conversation and daily argument." Rather, we need to see how academics such as King want to validate this personal and informal kind of theory making, often explicitly adopting an epistolary form to pursue it. Although King herself does not do so, a striking number of feminist academics write about or through letters precisely as a way to demystify their work. Anne Herrmann, for example, opens her 1989 study of the "dialogic" writing of Virginia Woolf and Christa Wolf with the following—anonymous—address:

> Dear D., What a relief, finally, to speak to someone else. The inevitable theoretical introductions one produces to somehow legitimize one's position. The sense, too, often, that one is speaking to those who would rather not be listening, or listen because they assume they do it temporarily, waiting for us to let go of our resistance, and thus of our differences. But will it ever be the same?
>
> (Herrmann, *The Dialogic*, 32)

In "Dear ——; In Search of New (Old) Forms of Critical Address," Anne Bower similarly suggests that critics should consider "corresponding," that is, turn to "writing that enacts the idea of interacting *with* rather than acting *on* or reacting *to*," rather than "respond[ing]" to one another in the stylized competition of the usual academic essay:

> Taking letters seriously as a form of professional address could lead one to ask, with Susan Koppelman, why we scholars and critics do not spend more time exchanging true correspondence rather than creating articles. In a letter to a group of friends, Koppelman asks, "[W]hy do you write long essays that are speeches or position papers instead of writing letters to each other?"— asking further if it is "the patriarchy that teaches that discussion of literature has to take that kind of impersonal form, that non-dialogic form, that emotional-after-the-fact form."
>
> (156)

Notably, this essay appears in Amanda Gilroy and W. M. Verhoeven's *Epistolary Histories: Letters, Fiction, Culture* (2000), which the editors evidently hope will "return to the issue of women and letters, not in any essentialist way but as part of a materialist account of letters as a liminal form on the border between public and private spheres" (15). The design of the book reflects the same intention, by getting the contributors to "respond to each other's essays in a type of dialogic 'postscript,'" in order to "demonstrate the essential imbrication of the epistolary with both public and private discourses, for each is a personal and partial response that nevertheless enters, and is informed by, an ongoing cultural correspondence" (15).

The epistolary has been taken up as a feminist academic form in other disciplines besides literature, including philosophy, sociology, and law. For Ann Margaret Sharp, the epistolary shows the affinity between feminist and pragmatist philosophy in terms that once again stress its value as a record of individuals' experiences and emotions:

> There is a growing recognition among feminist critics that letter writing can be a valuable source of insight for critical inquiry. Letters reveal the cognitive and moral experiences of individuals, experiences that escape formalistic theories of moral and political principles, abstract standards of justice, equality and individual freedom. . . . By taking letter writing into account, feminist critics can better understand the importance of the everyday, the prosaic, as a source of individual creativity and social criticism. Letter writing reveals the complex dimensions of personhood and the tremendous gap that often exists between moral and political theory and practice.[1]

Carol Matthews and Marilyn Callahan also believe that "letter writing is a promising practice and research tool" from a feminist perspective, useful in "attempting to build egalitarian relationships" in academia ("Wilderness Stationery," 338).[2] Dramatically, they consider that women's alliances in epistolary fiction and domestic letters can guide the public realm of management policy and theory:

> Letters can provide an opportunity for women to move beyond mutual understanding and their own historical narratives to make their private worlds public, at least to one another. We believe that this opportunity is particularly useful in our study of women and leadership, a field in which it is often difficult for women to articulate their experience.
>
> The letters that women write to each other about their experience in the foreign land of academe and bureaucratic organizations deal with many of the same issues that travelers write to one another: Have you learned the language yet? How are they treating you? When are you going home? As we move into the new territory in the public realm, it is important that we acknowledge the strangeness of our experience and construct new realities where present bound-

aries or borders between the private and the public, the subjective and the objective, can be crossed or perhaps enlarged and inhabited.

(346–47)

Matthews and Callahan go on to propose that careful correspondence could break down barriers between academic sociologists, social workers, and clients.

More recently, Robert Chang and Adrienne Davis have examined the politics of positionality in law and literary criticism through a published correspondence, used "as a literary device to allow them to collaborate on this project while maintaining their own voices."[3] Debating critical race theory and feminist legal theory, they muse on "Critical Race Feminism" in a form that continually foregrounds their own border crossings: men's attempts to engage in feminist literary criticism, white attempts to engage in African American literary criticism, and general attempts to engage in black male, black feminist criticism.

These potential engagements with differences of power as well as perspective dramatize an important recognition. Epistolary discourse shows us just how far the conventions of academic as well as literary expression involve suppressing the evidence of particular relationship and the contracts that lie behind all writing. As King has argued, feminist theory has emerged piecemeal from conversations, privately circulated drafts, and articles in process, all of which have reflected important political conversations behind the scenes. But letters remind us that academics are part of an imagined political community, too, and have their own deeply emotional investments.

In all these examples, we see how the powerful association of epistolarity with feminist values endures in academic circles. Academics, however, may be as vulnerable as anyone else to the hope that the epistolary form will bring equal, reciprocal, even intimate relationships, despite knowing full well that their profession is both cutthroat and, in many ways, founded upon the discipline of abstraction. Anne Bower's essay, cited above, for example, is much more interesting in the light of a challenging "postscript" by Gerald MacLean defending the value of distance and impersonal exchange. But did she really envisage this kind of epistolary reply? MacLean notably also defends himself against his apparently "patronizing" appropriation of the epistolary form in earlier critical spats. The epistolary does force academics to drop some of their evasions. On the other hand, any idea that letter writing in itself will mitigate competition and disagreement may be naïve.

Perhaps the apotheosis of the academic feminist's romance with letters can be found in the American literary critic Elizabeth Meese's *(Sem)erotics: Theorising Lesbian Writing* (1992). In this book, Meese uses the full battery of deconstructive theory to pose all sexual identity as an effect of language and its social codes, and her own style is, for any general reader, highly abstract. Yet her constant conceit is that lesbian writing is a kind of coded love letter among women, moreover, one that slips through the structures of patriarchal language. Deliberately eliding textual and physical relationship, her epistolary address, as well as her punning, sensual style, attempts to draw the reader in as a lesbian lover:

> When I write my love letter to you, I want to bring myself to you, hand myself over. When I write about lesbian : writing, I take my life in my hands, as my text. Or is it that I take my text as my life in my search for a language capable of expressing what those words—lesbian : writing—mean when our fingers, soft and electric, just meet, pulled together by their own magnetically charged engagement as (though) they have a life, a movement, of their own. . . . Or as the pen makes it tracks across the body of the page, its friction and its struggle to mark the course faithfully, our passions inscribed energetically in the body of the language in the mind: a love letter.
>
> (3)

Meese's claims for the ontological power of lesbian (letter) writing are even stronger in the more personalized letters that intercut her academic text. The following suggests that lesbianism is itself a literary entity, even in its imagery of sexual role-play:

JULY 14, 1989

Dear L.
How should I address you in my love letters? L, my lesbian(ism), my Lover; my love, through the glistening pip, the shining tendril (of) your desire for me, the slender rod registering the relation of your frequency and mine. My task is to convert you and me to us. You are you. I want you to be separate so that I can feel the thrill of taking (you) over; composing you/me/mine/ours. For a

moment I construct you/me: inseparable, just as I write the word "us" or we—a rewriting of you/me. A momentary substitution. The "you" standing in for you is the machinery that makes these letters possible. Overdrive: overwrite. What is passion without the dream of a resistance, a difference even ever so slight, to be overcome as I push you down on the bed, a distance to be bridged as I cover your body with mine, I orchestrate and perform my desire on your smooth skin, I play the fuck master and take you (in). Perhaps there is not even a sound.

Love, L

(in Kay Turner, *Between Us*, 34)

Meese, writing in the late 1980s, states her wish to find a language as a lesbian distinct from that of a feminist. Her adoption of the love letter is as much about the rightfully exclusive language of lovers who share the same desires as it is a tool for deconstruction. Notably, the 1970s correspondence from Meese's friend Linda Farrer, which Meese donated to the Lesbian Herstory Archives, is flirtatious, witty, drunkenly maudlin, but not in the least politically concerned.[4] Meese's excessive, "unproductive" textual pleasure is clearly paralleled with an excessive, equally antireproductive sexual pleasure. But, like all these writers, she presents seduction as a literary and even moral affair. Her academic refiguring is equally a loving address to a wished-for lesbian community. Meese's textual lesbian thus carries shades of spiritual transubstantiation, just as her abstractly personal "open" love letter to "L" becomes an exemplary address to "lesbianism" as platonic idea. This is true, too, of the autobiographical note that accompanied the letter's reprinting—here presented as a real letter—in Turner's anthology:

L. and L. have many names. As I write this, they are me and Sandy, the woman I love and who makes me want to write love letters and to dream (sem)erotics. We met in Tuscaloosa, Alabama, in 1988, and have lived here together since 1989. In 1993, we celebrated our 90th birthday (my 50th and her 40th). Both of us teach at the University of Alabama.

(in Kay Turner, *Between Us*, 153)[5]

Meese poses the love letter as the visible edge of a "lesbian," even "feminine" language. Even though Meese aims to reclaim lesbianism from feminism's tendency to dematerialize it, she also represents it as a kind of ethical literature of women's invention, in which "the body of the language of the mind" for lesbians is more original than the discursive construction of heterosexual relationships. Lesbian feminism is a kind of subversive postmistress that will scramble the language of hetero-patriarchy with *écriture féminine*:

> "Difference"/"DifferAnce"—e/a/—what's the differ(e/a)nce? A letter here, a letter there. When a woman chooses not to measure up, she can be a lesbian and sometimes a feminist (if she thinks of it in particular socio-cultural terms). She posts a letter, "L," to those who care to read it. Every lesbian : woman might be one.
>
> (Meese, *(Sem)Erotics*, 87)

Through the seduction of language, Meese nurtures lesbianism as feminism's "magical sign" (King, *Theory in Its Feminist Travels*, 124–37).

Ironically, this might seem to romanticize away the sexuality that lesbians like Meese were fighting for so hard during this period. Writing, of course, can evade actual physical relationship, and we might speculate that many declarations of lesbian passion on paper were symptoms of doubt when it came to sex itself. Gina Mercer's epistolary autofiction *Parachute Silk*, for example, begins with a now heterosexual monogamous woman writing to her lesbian confidante to tell her that "I am 'in love' with a lot of women right at the moment. I just don't happen to be sleeping in their seductive beds" (1). Meese's note that a revolutionary woman might choose to be a feminist "if she thinks of it in particular socio-cultural terms" is a warning perhaps of the deceptions of her own romantic invitation. Or perhaps we should ask instead how the love letter as a metaphor for new political identity survived the vicissitudes of life in the women's movement? What, more concretely, happens to feminist epistolarity when love fails?

CHAPTER THREE

Velvet Boxing Gloves

MARCH 6, 1994,

Mi amor:
I haven't stopped loving you but the pain of our relationship has turned
me into a despicable, overly sensitive and insecure creature. . . . And two
pimples erupted on my left forearm; I know it's because of us. I HATE
MYSELF. I told you once that I didn't know if I could forgive you for
betraying me. I tried to let it go and believe that you were more confused than dishonest. Still, I DON'T TRUST YOU. That stained white
cap you wore when we first met turned me off, and so did that cheap
looking knotted gold earring. Your soft, low, polite voice and the way
you fold your hands made me tag you as insecure, conservative, and
unimaginative. I DIDN'T EVEN LIKE YOU AT FIRST. I agreed to
have sex with you because I had pre-menstrual horniness and I needed a
good fuck to get the blood flowing. I didn't think you'd be any good in
bed because you bored me with your talk of "caressing" women. But I
figured it was worth the risk because we'd never see each other again and
anyway, when you squeezed my thigh for an instant in that bus, I
immediately oozed. WE SHOULD HAVE JUST FUCKED AND
LEFT IT AT THAT. You told me that you didn't love her anymore and
that the magic had worn off. You portrayed her as an immature,
manipulative alcoholic who didn't even please you in bed. . . . You
wanted out, but you were never brave enough to leave. YOU LIED TO
ME. At first I thought that the close relationship you had with your
family was due to mutual love and business ties. Now I see that you let
them devalue your work, control your money, limit your life and our
love, and humiliate you for being a lesbian. I LOST MY RESPECT
FOR YOU. I believed in our dreams of sharing a life together. Feeling
tiny in my king-size bed, I made a space that waited for you. I wore your
ugly knotted gold earring like a trophy. I HATE YOU FOR MAKING
ME LOSE FAITH IN LOVE.

—tatiana de la tierra (quoted in Kay Turner, *Between Us*)

Why is it that reading other people's love letters is so often a disappointment—until they start arguing? It seems that in our leisure time we enjoy the spectacle of rejection, betrayal, and confusion but neither the bubble of encounter nor the deep peace of the post-commitment-ceremony bed. From a literary perspective, this is because happiness provides no story, for, paraphrasing Tolstoy, "happy feminists are all alike; every unhappy feminist is unhappy in her own way." It is for this reason that epistolary novels tend to be much gloomier than real correspondences. Feminists, as we have seen, sought to develop an aesthetics that might honor the egalitarian romance. But for universal entertainment, the letter that fails to arrive, that is burned or returned, remains the literary staple.

And yet, if this begins to open up the complexity of epistolary art, we are bound to notice that we would rather receive happy letters from our own correspondents. Family letters, love letters, letters to friends, and e-mails are the same in this respect: these everyday genres are invariably marked by their aim to reassure rather than to disturb. Letters from war zones, where it is traditional to chat about the scenery, the local food, and homesickness—anything but violence—make the principle obvious (Keshen and Mills, "'Ich bereite mich auf den Tag vor'"; Jolly, "Myths of Unity"). Though they may rightly deserve the contempt of literary veterans like Paul Fussell, who want the writing of war to be as bloody as its subject, in reality such letters exist precisely to conceal what might threaten or change the relationship in peacetime (Fussell, *Wartime*, 145).

The nature of epistolary pleasure is entirely different when reading your own rather than other people's correspondences. Yet in this chapter I am going to suggest that angry or disappointed letters are a substantial part of the feminist record. Of course, there were many brilliant campaign and lobbying letters that began from such stances, and these required an art in a different style. Full justice to these are part of another book, though I shall touch upon them in relation to the women's campaign against cruise missiles in chapters 6 and 7. Here I want instead to trace how letters were part of the movement's internal arguments. Women tried to negotiate sexual and emotional relationships with one another through them in deeply personal and often creative ways. Epistolary fiction most obviously explores the issue of women's differences. But the "open letter," a favored form of self-assertion, also importantly registered outrage at those women—typically young, white, educated, and able-bodied—who romanticized "sisterhood." Yet the epistolary conventions that decorated these very serious challenges velvet-glove them with a persisting rhetoric of shared community and the expectation of reply. Still more rhetorically ambiguous are the letters of lovers who attempt to end a relationship in the same politically informed way they began it.

I am aware of the ethical risks of raising old specters of hurt and betrayal. Yet letters connect us to some of what was so distinctive about the nature of the "personal-political" community. When we are fired by what Audre Lorde termed "the uses of the erotic" (Lorde, *Sister Outsider*), we see it is indeed hateful to be forced "to lose faith in love," as de la tierra so eloquently puts it in her letter to her "amor." Yet, I hope, we will also newly appreciate the literary and emotional interest of such writing.

Confidantes in Conflict

If the Three Marias' 1973 collective-love-letter novel to one another symbolized women's reclaiming their sexuality from men, their bitter falling out in May 1974, after the new Marxist government pardoned them, foreshadowed what was to happen under the sign of women's identity. Their divisions— Velho da Costa distanced herself from feminism in favor of communism and the Portuguese Revolution; the others allied with an independent Portuguese women's liberation movement—were ironically displayed in a published exchange of correspondence in the press using the style of their novel (Owen, *Portuguese Women's Writing*). This classic socialist-radical split of 1970s feminism, followed by many more political divisions of strategy and identity through the 1980s, gradually revised feminist uses of the epistolary motif. Although the Marias expressed central feminist ideals in asserting that the new woman's hand "sets down ideas in a letter that we write, not so much for another as for our own nourishment" (Barreno, Horta, and Costa, *The Three Marias*, 13–14), this turns out to be only a half truth. In fact, as women turn out to be as bad at "nourishing" as men, they write more sophisticated petitions to one another asking for support.

With the institutionalization and diversification of the women's movement through the 1980s, feminist epistles morphed from sweet nothings to all too many somethings. From a literary perspective, we can situate this in a long history of fictions that use lost, misdelivered, or misinterpreted letters as metaphors for the difficulty of communication. Margaret Atwood's novel *The Handmaid's Tale* (1986) and Mary Hocking's *Letters from Constance* (1992) are just two epistolary novels that track the differences and the distances between women despite a promised solidarity or affair. Atwood's legendary dystopian vision is not always thought of as epistolary, but the handmaid's cassette tapes are futurist messages in a bottle (Kauffman, *Special Delivery*). These "letters" reflect her extreme isolation, hoping only that in some other universe, the women who currently collude with men in oppressing the proletariat "handmaids" will come to their senses and join forces again. Mary Hocking's 1992 novel is far less political in articulation, but the quiet narrator's letters to her famous feminist writer friend about her life as a worn-down Catholic mother of six also figure her distance from other women's practical support. The friend's glamorous trials as a media intellectual and poet poignantly contrast with the narrator's attempt to avoid the public sphere, heightened by the death of her son in the Irish Republican Army, about which her correspondent has little to say. These novels fit what Janet Altman describes as the pattern of tragic epistolarity, culminating in the breaking off of the correspondence through death, misunderstanding, or betrayal ("Women's Letters").

But *Letters to Marina*, by the Italian feminist Dacia Maraini, written at the end of the 1970s and first published in 1981, pinpoints a more specific kind of tragedy within feminism itself. This stylized novel takes the form of a dreamlike series of missives sent by a novelist who has ostensibly retreated to an ugly seaside resort in southern Italy to get over writer's block and a miscarriage. But she is clearly also escaping her former lover, Marina, to whom she continues compulsively to write. Marina and her women's consciousness-raising group are portrayed as insatiable and devouring daughters, and Marina's habit of showing her sex frightens but entrances the writer. She is also resentful of Marina's contempt for her attraction to men. With each letter, she distances herself from Marina, beginning an affair with a young man who works in the Neptune Bar to which she goes daily to drink peppermint-flavored milk and try to write. She becomes friends with Basilia, a downtrodden, stringy neighbor who is beaten by her husband and equally devoured by her many kids, especially her son. Basilia is timid and deferential but becomes an emotional support, in strange contrast to her addressee, who inspires increasingly lurid accounts of maternal incest and the confusion of lovers with the writer's wished-for children. Throughout, men are presented as abusive, coarse, exploitative, as well as sexually irresistible; women, intelligent and mature, the only ones you can trust.

This novel is obviously resonant of specifically Italian movements—the good-for-nothing brother of the writer's friend belongs to a violent guerrilla group resonant of the Marxist Red Brigade, for example. But its struggle to make sense of new perceptions of women as desirable and as dangerous is general to the second wave of feminism. The letters, which are never replied to, speak of a fearful closeness, the ensuing need for distance, and the disappointment of both the maternal and the infantile feminist subject. Yet though the letters are the product of a fantasy life that must be escaped, it is these that pour out of the narrator, rather than her novel. The conversation with feminism, and between feminists as lovers, in other words, is nowhere near finished, even if the writer finds she has to do it at a distance.

The ambiguity of these epistolary fictions in which letters dramatize women's disappointment or distance from each other yet persist in constructing a relationship from one lover, sister, and dreamer to another is the paradox of the real letters that were sent during the 1970s and 1980s. Although they often intend to punch, these fists have soft palms inside softer gloves, their epistolary framing signaling a continued longing for feminist love. Nothing is more symptomatic of such ambivalence than the "open letter," a form that proliferated in the movement during the 1980s. Dena Attar's "Open Letter on Anti-Semitism and Racism," first published in the British radical feminist quarterly *Trouble and Strife* (winter 1983), for example, grew out of a letter to the editorial collective of Britain's then première feminist magazine, *Spare Rib*, in response to their collection of articles "Sisterhood . . . is plain sailing," published in July 1983. Addressed "Dear Sisters," and signed "In sisterhood," it is an extremely thorough explanation of the distinction between "Zionist" and "Jewish," and of why condemning Israel's 1982 invasion of Lebanon should not become an excuse for anti-Semitism. Much of the letter negotiates the editors' statement that the "women of colour" then on the collective had decided not to print any letters from Jewish feminists about the invasion, as they were "Zionist and/or racist." While filling in some of the racial as well as imperialist history of Sephardi Jews, Attar's letter also tries to claim the magazine back as a place for (anti-Zionist) Jewish feminist representation. Another powerful plea for representation within the community is Sara Atatimur's "In Defense of

Womyn: An Open Letter to Marj Schneider." Responding to Schneider's "cassette letter" of March 1987 on whether to change the name "Womyn's Braille Press to Women's Braille Press," Atatimur's manuscript takes the form of a twenty-seven-page, heartfelt autobiography about her own political consciousness as a deaf woman who came to support lesbian and gender separatism.

Audre Lorde's open letter to Mary Daly, accusing her of racial and cultural bias in Daly's *Gyn/Ecology* (1978), is probably the most famous of the genre, and it was a focal point in asserting political difference within the movement. At the same time, it is obvious that Lorde wrote out of a sense of betrayal by somebody whose vision was apparently so close to her own:

> Dear Mary,
>
> Thank you for having *Gyn/Ecology* sent to me. So much of it is full of import, useful, generative, and provoking. As in *Beyond God The Father*, many of your analyses are strengthening and helpful to me. Therefore, it is because of what you have given to me in the past work that I write this letter to you now, hoping to share with you the benefits of my insights as you have shared the benefits of yours with me.
>
> This letter has been delayed because of my grave reluctance to reach out to you, for what I want us to chew upon here is neither easy nor simple. The history of white women who are unable to hear black women's words, or to maintain dialogue with us, is long and discouraging. But for me to assume that you will not hear me represents not only history, but an old pattern of relating, sometimes protective and sometimes dysfunctional, which we, as women shaping our future, are in the process of shattering. I hope.
>
> (Lorde, "An Open Letter," in *This Bridge*, 94).

Lorde's tone seeks to educate within some, at least future, shared project; her declared hope is "to share the benefits of my insights as you have shared the benefits of yours with me" (94). But, as is the way with letters, the gentle opening address builds up to the "real business" within civility. Lorde's excitement at reading Daly's resurrection of the European Goddess turns into disappointment at the lack of any reference to African matriarchal myths, and finally to anger that indeed the only references to non-European women were horror stories of African genital mutilation, Chinese foot binding, and Indian suttee, or the burning of widows. Daly's point was that American gynecological practices were just as bad and proof that women's oppression was universal in scope and kind. But Daly had contextualized her critique of gynecology with many examples of Euro-American women's resistance, while underplaying that by black or African women. In this context, Lorde was further angered that Daly cited a poem of hers, "misused my words, utilized them only to testify against myself as a woman of color" (95).

Lorde's letter reclaims those misappropriated words under her signature in a clear statement of her authority. This ironically contrasts with Daly's apparent mere "finger[ing] through [the work of black women] for quotations which you thought might valuably support an already-conceived idea concerning some old and distorted connection between us" (95). At the same time, the epistolary form stages her wavering but still hoped-for trust in her addressee, part of an ongoing process disarmingly figured as "chewing upon." The ambiguity of the letter's status as dialogue increased when Lorde published it, in revised form, in *This Bridge Called My Back: Writings by Radical Women of Color* in 1981. Lorde annotated it with the explanation that she was doing so because Daly had not replied, after she'd originally sent it in May 1979, although they had discussed the letter in person in September of that year. In her words, Lorde thus "opened it to the community of women," a phrase that amplified the sense that the letter was a rhetorical challenge that now needed witnesses to take effect (Lorde, "An Open Letter," in *Sister Outsider*, 66). Short, powerful, and accessible, the letter duly became a manifesto of coalitional feminism. But it was surely also the shock of its personal address to a respected figure in the movement, of its uncompromising dare to whites, especially, perhaps, to lesbian whites like Daly, that was, and still is, so arresting:

> The oppression of women knows no ethnic nor racial boundaries, true, but that does not mean it is identical within those boundaries. Nor do the reservoirs of our ancient power know these boundaries, either. To deal with one without even alluding to the other is to distort our commonality as well as our difference.
>
> For then beyond sisterhood, is still racism.
>
> We first met at the [Modern Languages Association] panel, "The Transformation of Silence Into Language and Action." Shortly before that date, I had decided never again to speak to white women about racism. I felt it was wasted energy, because of their destructive guilt and defensiveness, and because

whatever I had to say might better be said by white women to one another, at far less emotional cost to the speaker, and probably with a better hearing. This letter attempts to break this silence.

I would like not to have to destroy you in my consciousness. So as a sister Hag, I ask you to speak to my perceptions.

Whether or not you do, I thank you for what I have learned from you.

This letter is in repayment.

In the hands of Afrekete,

Audre Lorde, May 6, 1979

("An Open Letter," in *This Bridge*, 97)

Lorde's argument—that women may be universally oppressed but are differently so, that the existence of gender-class does not mean that women cannot oppress one another—is now well accepted. But the significance of the letter form remains less obvious. One critic, Amber Katherine, recently suggested that radical white feminists still have not responded to Lorde's letter, have not yet "received" it in the political post. She points out that Lorde's demand was not for a change in theory, as postmodernists have treated it, but for interaction, fueled by a desire to make connections under complex systems of oppression (Katherine, "'A Too-Early Morning,'" 206). But I also believe that the letter is a velvet boxing glove, a gauntlet thrown down. Consider her warning, "I would not like to have to destroy you in my consciousness," and the double edge of her metaphor of a debt "repaid." Lorde's rhetoric of ongoing dialogue with Daly was surely at least a little disingenuous, as was obvious in her decision to go public with the letter without Daly's knowledge. Daly could not have been anything but shamed, perhaps rightly so. But the form of engagement also surely speaks of Lorde's own mixed emotions, the passionate hope that this opponent will care enough, even if only to fight.

It would be fascinating to know how effective such open letters really were in changing the views of their ostensible addressees, and also those of the implied addressee of the public with whom they were shared. Lorde's letter, especially alongside the other groundbreaking essays of *This Bridge Called My Back*, certainly played a part in a wider feminist discussion about difference when it became common classroom fare as a means to discuss racism and feminism. At the same time, Daly herself never "replied in kind," either by a personal or open letter. She did address the exchange in her book *Outercourse: The Be-Dazzling Voyage*, but this was published more than a decade later, and she continued within it to defend her universalist interpretation of women's oppression (232–33).

As a genre, these letters are symptomatic of an ambivalence about what women could share, and yet, equally, they rhetorically continue to invoke the feminists' obligations, debts, and even love of community, though it is a community that has become more painful as it has grown. This rhetoric also emerges in three other open letters that represent a less complex form of relationship. The first is a "letter to the women's movement" from "Republican Women Prisoner of Wars, Armagh Jail." Written on toilet paper and smuggled out, it was sent in 1980 and first published in *London Women's Liberation Newsletter* and reprinted in *Sweeping Statements*. This fervent description of the horrendous conditions of cell life, augmented by a "no wash" protest "for the retention of political status in this gaol," is vivid and violent, but it is couched as a straightforward "appeal" "to raise your voices in the demand for political status" (262), with no hint that they will be disappointed. Simple in a different way is the Women of the American Revolution's "Letter to our Sisters in Social Work," published in Robin Morgan's 1970 *Sisterhood is Powerful*. This open letter challenges middle-class social workers to stop shoring up patriarchal ideas of marriage and "legitimate" children and is clearly a call for them to *discover* feminism, but its tone is more berating than reproachful: "When will women social workers recognize our common bond with poor women, including unmarried mothers? We share with such women the common oppression of our sex. Every insult to a woman insults *you*" (525). A second open letter in *Sisterhood is Powerful*, presented as a "Statement on Birth Control" by the Black Women's Liberation Group, Mount Vernon, New York, is more comparable to Lorde's letter in its task of managing an internal division within a projected class. Addressed to "Dear Brothers," it opens, "Poor black sisters decide for themselves whether to have a baby or not to have a baby," continuing:

> So when Whitey put out the Pill, and poor black sisters spread the word, we saw how simple it was not to be a fool for men any more (politically we would say men could no longer exploit us sexually or for money and leave the babies for us to bring up). . . . Now a lot of black brothers are into the new bag. Black women are being asked by militant black brothers not to practice

birth control because it's a form of Whitey's committing genocide on black
people. Well, true enough, but it takes two to practice genocide and black
women are able to decide for themselves, like poor people all over the world,
whether they will submit to genocide. For us, birth control is the freedom to
fight genocide of black women and children. . . .

But we don't think you're going to understand us because you are a bunch
of little middle-class people and we are poor black women. The middle-class
people never understands the poor because they always need to use them as
you want to use poor black women's children to gain power for yourself.
You'll run the black community with your kind of Black Power—You on top!
The poor understand class struggle!
(Black Women's Liberation Group, "Statement on Birth Control," 360–61)

The letter ends, "Signed by: two welfare recipients two housewives a domestic a grandmother a psychotherapist and others who read, agreed, but
did not help to compose" (361). Like Attar, Lorde, and Atamuir, these writers are also working out competing interests within a community, here the
Black Power movement. The open letter has been an important form in
many political struggles besides feminism. It is interesting, however, to see
how this address omits the rhetoric of intimacy and desire so striking in
feminist battles. A limit-case example was Robin Morgan's poem "To a Sister Underground," published in the same 1970 *Sisterhood is Powerful* anthology. The woman in question was Jane Alpert, a former member of the leftist
revolutionary group Weathermen who had announced new loyalties to radical feminism as she went into hiding from the police. Morgan's public
championing of Alpert was highly controversial in movement circles because Alpert pronounced her feminist conversion in an open letter that simultaneously rejected any sympathy for sexist black men who had been
slaughtered in the Attica prison riots of 1971. Unsurprisingly, Morgan's petition provoked countering open letters (see Echols, *Daring to Be Bad*, 247–
62). Yet Morgan's poem remains typical of the romantic, epistolary, register
of so much sisterly address, even in the painfully opposed loyalties between
black and women's liberation:

Dear Jane:
It's funny, now, to write like this:/a letter I don't even dare shape like one/(not
that you'll probably ever read it, which may be the reason it can now be

written) . . . the reason (good as any other)/for this message cast adrift in a
bottle sent to/where you never would be anyway even if I did know/where you
are which couldn't matter less/is that it doesn't mean one damn disguise/which
woman I address it to, or how I sign it,/since all of us are underground./Each
sister wearing masks of Revlonclairolplaytex/does it to survive.

(Morgan, "To a Sister," xxxvi)

Uncertain as a sailor casting her message to the sea in a bottle, Morgan
writes her poem-letter as a substitute for more direct contact with Jane. But
despite the fragility of communication, Morgan believes that any woman
could crack the code to reveal a message of underground identity and, more
important, of love. The poem closes, "In sisterhood, in struggle,/and all
that,/but mostly because/I think I love you" (xl).

The distinctive tone of the epistolary narrative I am tracing is resonant of
women's intimacy, and I suggest that often even the most diplomatic or angry address contains a gesture toward this. Frances Ferguson, reflecting on
the nature of the epistolary self in generic terms, explains that the letter
writer is always by definition dependent upon her reader at some level. We
might say that this is the basic condition of all conversation. Yet Ferguson
goes further, suggesting that a letter writer attempts to create identity:

On the one hand, the letter has long functioned as a long arm of education
because of the letter-writer's genial desire to create or to expand a common
ground between himself and his [*sic*] correspondent. On the other, the letter,
precisely because it lays claim to a reply, registers an attempt both to generate
and to enforce resemblance between the correspondents.

("Interpreting the Self," III)

Evidently, the intensity of the aim of creating identity and the level of dependency will vary enormously, and writers like Lorde or Attar would probably
be surprised if their compositions about the importance of respecting difference were perceived in these terms. Yet their rhetorical mix of closeness
and distance, sisterhood and rejection, evokes this uncomfortable double-
ness. In this, they plumb the letter's essential duality as simultaneously both
demand and gift.

The proliferation of open letters of this kind is thus a collective example
of Lorde's political vision of the "erotic" as "a resource within each of us

that lies in a deeply female and spiritual plane" (Lorde, *Sister Outsider*, 53). And yet the open letter, over time, increasingly loses its illusions that women's unification will be magical or easy, becoming a genre about the bitter disappointment of failed or aborted love. Consider the palimpsest of academic essays about Jan Vermeer's famous seventeenth-century painting *Woman Writing a Letter*. In 1977, French philosopher Annie Leclerc saw in it an inspiring portrait of the private creativity of women writers and titled her own essay "La Lettre d'amour" as a kind of extension of what she presents as early *écriture féminine*. But American critic Jane Gallop in 1985 responded to this romantic "reclaiming" by asking about the silent maid standing behind the letter writer, and the conditions under which bourgeois women's writing was produced (Leclerc, "La Lettre d'amour"; Gallop, "Annie Leclerc"). In turn, British historian Carolyn Steedman argued in 1999 that Gallop romanticizes the maid, pointing out that many servants would have been literate in the seventeenth century and that letters may be just the place to uncover this buried history ("A Woman Writing"). On one level, this debate shows the refining of feminist scholarship. On another, the proliferation of internal differences directly undoes the erotic communion of women.

Nancy K. Miller and Peggy Kamuf's essay "Parisian Letters: Between Feminism and Deconstruction" perhaps most explicitly struggles with the letter as a form of women's intimacy. Published in Marilyn Hirsch and Evelyn Fox Keller's 1990 collection, *Conflicts in Feminism*, correspondence for these two North American critics is the space for polite dissension about the meaning of feminism rather than for female complicity. Miller, who was advocating coalitional feminism(s), hoped the anachronistic form of an open correspondence might avoid the necessity for restating entrenched positions—but she would not pretend the two scholars were writing as confidantes in the way of "the canonical female letter writer" (Kamuf and Miller, "Parisian Letters," 121). Kamuf, who saw even this form of feminism as an unworkable identity politics, riposted that "letters may dramatize . . . the effect of . . . unaccountable otherness on the discourse assumed by a subject presumed to know what she is doing. One is always addressing letters to an unknown address" (125). Miller and Kamuf's much more sober view of feminist letter writing resonates with a general move away from conversion models of writing, and consciousness-raising itself, as a representation of the coming to feminism. While personal address remained—and still remains—an element of feminist politics, since the early 1980s there has been an increasing doubt over whether its aim is the discovery of identity. Literary deconstruction of the idea of writing as presence has aided the disillusionment with epistolarity in that sense. For Miller and Kamuf, at least at this point, the ideal of letter writing itself seems dated.

Laurent Versini argues that education and desire are fundamental "vocations" of epistolary literature through the ages (Versini, *Le Roman épistolaire*). Feminist letter writers pursue both of them, but they are often torn between the two. Conflicts covertly express desires; a rhetoric of love decorates polemic. Political negotiation is a continual balancing act, endless in the way of correspondence itself. Wearingly demanding, it can drive the self into a defensive affirmation of identity, rather than the connection to which it ostensibly appeals. At the same time, it is that remaining appeal which is so distinctive and, sometimes, so heart-catching.

The End of an Affair

A short set of letters housed in the Lesbian Herstory Archives exemplifies the very real ways in which the politics of identity fired, eroticized, and also combusted relationships among women influenced by feminism, even (perhaps especially) when they were literally lovers. Although these raggedly incomplete letters were never intended to be published, they are even more eloquent than the open letter, and arguably more than the epistolary novel, on the painful end of an ethically conceived love. They speak of the personal investment in political relationship and of how writing itself was part of that ideal.

Sent in 1982 with an anonymous covering note from one of the writers because she had heard that "old love letters" were wanted by the archives, the letters are described as a correspondence between "a 21 year old white middle class jewish womon and a French Canadian irish catholic white working class womon, age 39."[1] The younger woman's letters, in a staggered sequence written between 1980 and 1981 (dated in the feminist calendar as 9980–81), are filled with passionate references to women's shared identities and lesbian feminist culture: poetry writing, moon worship, dreams, dancing, menstrual celebrations, and tarot and divinatory readings, including of the shapes of blood on the sheets. "Mmm, its sweet to know you as comrade/lover/sister/witch/and lunatic" (19 December 9980), she declares, assuring her that she loves "with her cunt," as well as her heart and wisdom. This language of bodily identification is matched by visual tokens of women's identity: a photo card of elderly women playing pool and another of a pistol-touting May Lillie in chignon, lace, and gauntlets. The collection also includes a ritual necklace "to celebrate your 39 years of survival and change." The necklace is clearly handmade and its thirty-nine beads, shells, crystals, feathers, are lovingly itemized in the letter for their protective, talismanic qualities.

This letter writer epitomizes a branch of political lesbianism allied with goddess culture; she refers to "devouring" current feminist literature such as *Sinister Wisdom*, *Off Our Backs*, "even *Ms*," including "2 timely articles in *sinister wisdom* on ♀♀ sexuality, one saying we are 'essentially' gentle lovers, the other arguing that we are simply repressed & that yes, wimmin do fuck." Her constant analysis of both herself and the relationship in these terms features typical concerns of lesbian feminism at that time: weighing whether the "raunchiness" that she clearly finds so delightful in her lover is something she should bring out in herself or whether that would be to be "male-identified"; feeling uneasy about having to see straight women as "a separate species." Excited over being able to talk to her lover about her new awareness of, for example, the politics of sweatshop labor, she is more troubled about her emotional reasoning over identity and difference, declaring that she is being "ANALYTICAL & CRITICAL" again but that she likes and learns from being this way. Shortly afterward she acknowledges that it has been only a year that she has felt herself able to be "spontaneous" and have "instincts," that when she is "calm, trusting, in touch with a spiritual way of living," she is not "all theoretical-intellectual." She remembers her lover talking of having to learn the jargon of the women's movement yet is glad she may be learning from her in this respect; she berates herself for remaining attached to the privileges of her class and her apparent earlier belief that she was like any other white Anglo-Saxon Protestant (inviting her lover to "call" her on whether she is being "classist") yet is angry that she has been made to feel alienated from her Jewish identity and guilty about claiming the name "lesbian." The letter ends, symptomatically, by expressing the problem of infinite regress in the identity politics she is embracing:

> I don't want to feel that lesbians are my enemies. I never completely made peace with my feeling that straight ♀ were another species. My tribe gets

smaller as I name myself in more ways. Oy, no wonder I'm confused now about what political work I want to do, as I make lists of groups to join & read notices, & avoid meetings. It was a different life last year, I was so plugged into a network of the health center—♀'s center—rape crisis center—G.C.N. . . . my groups & my roommates' groups.

The mediation of their relationship through a proliferating discussion of political "difference" is more bitterly expressed in the older woman's replies, written a year later. Angrily announcing that it was time for them to break up, that she had lost her sense of self, she reminds "J" that she is "not the last strawberry in the patch, though you were the juiciest." Three months later, she writes joyfully, having received a loving letter. Declaring she does not want to talk about her feelings on paper, she is full of newsy observations about the people in the café where she is writing, the children she works with, her pride at stopping some kids playing with water from a fire hydrant, and her attempts not to drink coffee. But by October, she refers to their pledge of honesty and truthfulness in an angry discussion where their differences of class, age, but principally race are signifiers of personal betrayal. Beginning with the acknowledgment that "maybe in some insidious way we are all racist, on a conscious or un-conscious level," she covers pages with accusations that it is she, not her Jewish lover, who has dedicated herself to learning about Judaism and anti-Semitism, proposing that her own "part-Indian" heritage has made of her a warrior who does not understand the resignation of some of the oppressed:

You have made our differences glaring & painful to me, when you rejected me because I was not a jew (one of the reasons) I almost went crazy with anger & pain & I couldn't understand how you seemed to know me so well in my spirituality & how hard I was trying to understand you as a jew & deal with my feelings of fear & hatred. It was all so complicated & it was tied up with my awe and my worship of your darkness yr hair, yr cunt, yr. spirituality yr powers, I know these feelings are real but it was so hard to relate to you as a sister as a warrior as another ♀ with a common bond of survival. You drew the lines, you created the boundaries, you refused to deal with hard stuff between us. You denied my experiences with jews in my own life & you glossed over my hatreds of what had brought me to these feelings. . . . I never got to hear or read yr poetry because you wouldn't let me & you excluded me from that experience. It seems to me that at times you just seem to learn what you have to for the occasion & that you don't go very deeply into matters. . . . You have separated us by tribes & I am not of yr tribe. . . . I said many things that I wanted you to deny to say were not true that you didn't leave me because I was too old & powerless & vain & insecure & I blamed you for all my insecurities. That is why I couldn't continue to hate you just to protect myself.

Realizing that she wants more from the relationship than her ex, the older writer presents their internal fight as a pitiful defeat of both of them by "MAN'S HISTORY." Yet this tips into a warning that oppression can become aggression if a sense of humanity is lost, choosing the clearly inflammatory example of the Israelis in relation to the Palestinians. The competition fuelling the letter finally emerges explicitly when she says she is tired of competing with her lover, how angry she is that the lover has been "willing to give up everything for some boring big cunt because she was a jew with a car & nice hands."

We see here the splitting of the erotic and the political and where the confidante founders in the face of her own idealism. The rejected lover rages not only about the inefficacy of the language of respect for racial difference she has learned but about the literary culture that had overdetermined the letters as a woman's intimate identity. The letters eventually become another marker of her exclusion, returning "cunt" to its association with degrading insult; she instructs her lover not to "write any more crummy poems about me." As in many literary epistolary seductions, from *Les Liaisons dangereuses* to today's e-mail hoaxes, writing has played its own part in the deception between these two lover-correspondents. It seems that the very expectation that the letter will "mirror" self to other, as part of an understanding of their difference, magnifies their isolation in their different "tribes." The legacy of this political isolation is resonant in the double-edged note that the younger woman sent with the correspondence to the Lesbian Herstory Archives (presumably having had her own letters returned to her by her ex): "I heard you wanted old love letters, so I send these to you instead of burning them. . . . thank you for providing a place to save our herstory when it gets to be too much to keep it at home."

The pleasure of reading breakup letters is rather embarrassing to explore. Perhaps the ones I have discussed here are pleasing and most painful to the same degree and will undoubtedly speak loudest to those, like me, who still identify with a feminist love story, especially a lesbian feminist one. Letters are valued not only for the relationships they bring to life but for how they are saved and edited; here the inadvertency and mystery of the snippet creates its own poetry. I do not know who these two writers are, having been unable to trace them without invoking paid Internet sleuths, which seemed worse than leaving it. Yet it is precious to me not only that they remain in the Lesbian Herstory Archives but that Deborah Edel, founding and still present archivist, encouraged me to use them as anonymous, hitherto unpublished herstory.

We cannot minimize the difference between public and personal letters, and I realize that much of the movement's inner heart is scrawled in letters not archived at all. At the same time, when these personal letters are seen as a form of literature, or even as autobiography, we can see parallels with the epistolary fictions, essays, and editions of the movement. They are ropes that twist together romance and realism, gift and demand, education and desire, rejection and dependence to form a literature that is not only rhetorical in the classic sense of an art of persuasion but eloquent about relationship itself. And yet it is also a story about letter writing, as part of that culture of relationship, an investment in writing that goes beyond the functions of informal networking or lobbying to pursue written identification and love between women. tatiana de la tierra, with whose letter to her former lover, Gloria, I opened this chapter, lists this "neurotic love letter: as part of her curriculum vita.[2] The weak yet all-powerful lost lover in her dirty white cap is still a muse, and de la tierra's attempt to hold together regret with fury does not preclude evident pleasure in both the writing and the publishing. Her poem "dreaming of lesbos," tells us that "the dream perfumes all of my days. I go to the post office and look for stamps with etchings of flowers and fruits so that I can send letters to the women who loved me in my sleep" (de la tierra, *For the Hard Ones*, 15).

PART TWO

Letter Writing and the Ethics of Care

CHAPTER FOUR

Theorizing Feminist Letters

I've been back in China for more than two months. I received several
elaborate cards and some messages from the members of the Chinese
Society for Women's Studies at New Year. They wished me good luck in
the coming year and they all wanted to know how it felt to be back home
and, most important, they wanted to get the 'latest news' from China,
especially about the preparatory work for the World Conference on
Women to be held in Beijing this autumn. Though I'd love to answer
all their letters, it seems I'm always too busy to do that. However the
more letters I owe them, the guiltier I feel.
—Yue Mei, "To My Friends in the Chinese Society for Women's Studies"

The first part of this book has argued that, over the last forty years, feminist letter writers have created a literature about women's political and
emotional alliances in both real and fictional address. I have charted how
some wrote passionately to each other, thrilled by their new sense of selfhood. Lesbians coming out alongside and even against feminism wrote love
letters to the idea of women's desire. Conversely, some, with histories in
black civil rights and struggles of other kinds, used letters to pose sober explorations of internal differences, which became a veritable modus operandi
in the early 1980s. I have concluded that, overall, letter writing initially ap-
pealed as a form of intimacy but became a genre for developing coalition
among very different parties. Does this trajectory show a loss of political
opportunity, the perennial disappointment of politics, or the maturing of
political alliance? These questions are still open among historians of the period, and no doubt each answer is true to a degree. My point thus far has
simply been to show that the letter between women is a trope of feminism,
particularly of the second wave, in which an idea of women's relationship is

intensely, often romantically pursued. Even in correspondences motivated by the wish to disassociate, I believe we can trace need and desire.

This chapter proposes to draw out the theoretical implications of what we might call feminist epistolarity. I have described these briefly in the introduction to the book, referring to debates about the aesthetic and social value of private writing and a model of the self as relational. However, as I suggested in chapter 2, we can now appreciate the extent to which feminist academics have themselves been pursuing their own love affairs with the idea of sisterhood, and with letter writing as part of that. In this chapter, then, I wish to offer a more comprehensive survey of existing epistolary criticism, which will put its own gendering in historical perspective, and compare it to the more established field of auto/biographical criticism. Moreover, I will press further the argument I have been making: that letters played out the question of women's identity and identification in a particularly ambivalent way, more loving, needier than in other genres. The second half of the chapter proposes that we can understand this more fully if we relate literary-political debates about letters to a range of feminist philosophies about ethical relationships that were widely publicized in the early 1980s. In the feminist ethics of care, specifically, we can find terms for much of feminist epistolarity and begin to understand some of the intense emotion involved in all of its elements.

Letters, Feminist Aesthetics, and the Relational Self

Letter writing as contemporary feminists *themselves* have practiced it has not yet been systematically analyzed—the reason, of course, for this book. But as the previous chapters have begun to show, feminists since the 1970s have been deeply attracted to the study of letters from women in past epochs and other societies, probably for the same reason that some years ago, I excitedly edited a collection of letters by women who worked as welders in the Second World War (*Dear Laughing Motorbyke*). Virginia Woolf, as usual, got there first, championing the forgotten art of the seventeenth century's Dorothy Osborne and the letters of working women in Margaret Davies's *Life as We Have Known It*. Like Woolf, the first impulse of second-wave literary scholars was to see women epistolarians largely as frustrated writers, making do within the confines of genre as they did in social role (Spacks, *Imag-*

ining a Self; Goldsmith, "Authority"). But this emphasis on "equality" of access was increasingly displaced by an attempt to understand and celebrate personal, domestic, or private letters in their own terms. Scholars like Caroll Smith-Rosenberg ("The Female World") and Tierl Thompson (*Dear Girl*) tapped neglected archives of women's letters as part of a reclamation of women's experience, notably inspired when it evidenced women's mutual support. Ruth Rosen and Sue Davidson's 1979 collection *The Maimie Papers*, for example, brilliantly revealed the surprising friendship of a Progressive Era Jewish "prostitute" turned social worker and Fanny Quincy Howe, her Boston-based gentile patron. Such private writings have been crucial in defining hidden female networks, friendships, affairs, and mentorings.

It is in this context that literary critics began to make more general claims about the relationship of gender to life writing. As Sidonie Smith and Julia Watson put it:

> Around 1980 the criticism of women's autobiography necessarily came of age. It was clear that new theories and generic definitions were required to describe the women's writing that had been recovered and was being produced. Why? Gradually it became clear to many feminist critics that academic scholars were complicit in broader cultural practices that valued women's writing only in terms of, and as the "other" of, men's writing. In publication, at conferences, in scholarly overviews, references to women's writing were often uninformed or condescending. Throughout the 1980s feminist critics intervened in what they saw as traditional reading practices that assumed the autobiographer to be male and reproduced cultural stereotypes of differences between men and women.
>
> (Smith and Watson, "Introduction", 8)

The belief that women wrote their lives differently than men was first proposed by Mary Mason in 1980, in "The Other Voice," an essay based on her 1979 excerpts from British and American women's autobiographies, *Journeys: Autobiographical Writings by Women*, edited with Carol Hurd Green. Mason argued that women have historically told their stories through writing about the lives of others or a significant other, in contrast to the canonical tradition of men's tales of public achievement as exceptional individuals. Although Mason was speculating about autobiography, the idea that women represented their lives in "relational" modes was enormously influential and reappeared in many analyses of letters, diaries, biographies, and even patch-work quilts. We have seen some of these in the previous chapters, but the sentiments are epitomized in Olga Kenyon's praise for "female letter-writing" in her 1992 anthology, *Eight Hundred Years of Women's Letters*, for women's refusal to be "authorities," for their plurality and their "relational, fluid styles of address" (xix). By 1988, Susan Stanford Friedman was summarizing a common critical state of play in "Women's Autobiographical Selves: Theory and Practice," an influential piece published in Shari Benstock's collection *The Private Self: Theory and Practice of Women's Autobiographical Writings*. Friedman challenged Georges Gusdorf's hitherto axiomatic argument that autobiography could only appear in societies with a concept of individuality, essentially the modern West. For Gusdorf, only individuals able to undertake philosophical introspection and then shape it into a literary unity could write autobiographies that were any good (Gusdorf, "Conditions et limites"). Friedman countered by arguing that women, people of color, and non-Westerners produce plentiful "life writings," and indeed precisely on the opposite condition of having enough *collective* consciousness, or what she terms cultural "mirroring," as well as material support, to do so.

This idea was to go much further than saying the letter has been designated a feminine genre largely because it, like women, it has been associated with the private and domestic sphere. Mason, Friedman, and their like seek to understand the deep conditions behind such cultural patterns and where, indeed, conditions of oppression can paradoxically produce creative responses. Moreover, where Gusdorf rooted his analysis of "the conditions of autobiography" in philosophy, Friedman's method was typical in drawing much more heavily on psychology; she described her approach as "psychopolitical." A key resource here was Nancy Chodorow's 1978 work, *The Reproduction of Mothering: Psychoanalysis and the Sociology of Gender*. Chodorow argued that because women are almost universally the primary caretakers of young children, girls' identity formation takes place in a context of ongoing relationship and attachment with their mothers, in contrast to boys, whose sense of self involves rejecting women's care. Part of what was so compelling about this was her celebration of such a psychology, which men, with their defensive shell of protected ego, might consider enviably unrepressed and capable of attachment.

But the excitement about women's "relational" selves soon ran into trouble. Smith and Watson again describe this in relation to the history of autobiography criticism:

If terms such as female relationality and fluidity promised theorists of women's autobiography a more enlightened model for exploring and revaluing women's experiential histories, some have since cautioned against privileging these characteristics as innate to women's experience rather than as culturally conditioned responses. Considering theories of maternal identification, Jessica Benjamin warns of the dangers of a "one-sided revaluing of women's position; freedom and desire might remain an unchallenged male domain, leaving us to be righteous and de-eroticised, intimate, caring, and self-sacrificing."

("Introduction," 18)

As with autobiography, epistolary critics have similarly reacted to what they feared were oversimple connections between "women's experience" and writing, with a battery of theories from poststructuralism to materialism, postcolonialism, and New Historicism. Linda Kauffman in *Discourses of Desire* (1986) argued that, through letters' diegetic, rhetorical structures, apparently lovelorn, weak women were ironically getting their own back. In her *Special Delivery* (1992), she moves even further towards looking at love-letter "modes" as deconstructive experiments with language, often pursued by theorists like Schlovsky, Derrida, and Barthes themselves. A later essay, "Not a Love Story: Retrospective and Prospective Epistolary Directions," champions postmodern epistolary satire and e-mail against what she casts as even the residue of her own earlier interest in romantic love. Michèle Longino Farrell in 1991 saw the prototypical female epistolarian, Madame de Sévigné as "performing motherhood" in her profuse, emotional, and gossipy letters to her daughter (*Performing Motherhood*).

A different challenge to the stereotype of the "relational" woman's life story has come from critics exploring how women epistolarians have *not* always adopted private modes. Elizabeth MacArthur, Dena Goodman, and Mary Favret find in the letters of French seventeenth-century salonnières and British romantic women writers a self-conscious political letter writing that comments on court and state affairs (MacArthur, *Extravagant Narratives*; Goodman, *The Republic of Letters*; Favret, *Romantic Correspondence*). The "extravagant multiplicity of relational models" Elizabeth MacArthur perceives in Madame du Deffand's letters to Horace Walpole show just how far such critics have helped to strip the romance away and historicize homogenous fantasies of "the relational self" (Gilroy and Verhoeven, *Epistolary Histories*, 9). Others have been engaged in puzzling out why it is that the most famous examples of sentimental, private letters, at least in novels, were written by men, variously suggesting that men's adoption of a "feminized" genre expressed the rise of bourgeois cultures of privacy but also the homosociality of many correspondences between men. Gilroy and Verhoeven introduce their edition of literary studies of letters, *Epistolary Histories*, by declaring, "the most historically powerful fiction of the letter has been that which figures it as the trope of authenticity and intimacy, which elides questions of linguistic, historical, and political mediation, and which construes the letter as feminine" (1).

There is no doubt that the last twenty years have seen sophisticated developments in understanding how letters are no more straightforward transcriptions of experience than are any other writings, even and particularly when designated as "private" or "personal." With these developments, it should be easier to historicize the celebration of "relational" life writing, along with feminist psychology, as part of a particular moment when women's "difference" from men became so appealing an idea that it overrode feminism's equal commitment to looking at how gender was socially shaped and its conjunction with many other constructs, such as class, race, culture, and the like. It is now more than a decade since Laura Marcus was able to perceive that feminist discourses of auto/biography frequently constitute "an ethics of (gender) difference, arguing for a new valuation of self in relationship, embodied and empathetic consciousness, identity as likeness to an other rather than as the self-same" (Marcus, *Auto/Biographical Discourses*, 220). As I have shown, we can see in the history of feminist epistolary criticism an even stronger version of this ethical investment. Whereas in autobiographical forms the move has been to question the terms on which the genre at least initially seemed to tie autonomy to masculinity, the feminized history of personal letter writing meant it could be immediately embraced as maternal inheritance. Moreover, its ephemeral, occasional nature perfectly fitted the search for "fluid" and relational self-representations. Feminists—myself included—have idealized letters as ethical forms in which we hope that some equally idealized relational self can finally be expressed.

And yet I am bound to observe that rather than returning to aesthetic or even primarily historical critical paradigms, critics have become ever more committed to ethical approaches. Further, in the context of what has been dubbed the "ethical turn" of criticism in the 1990s, it is striking that the concept of a "relational self" has only gained more value as it has diversified.

Indeed, some critics have gone back to the canon to show that men's autobiographies are also relational (Danahay, *A Community of One*; Broughton, *Men of Letters*; Miller, "Representing Others"). Paul John Eakin has used developmental psychology to suggest that autobiography itself originates in the early dialogues between children and their carers. He concludes that ethics may be the deep subject of autobiography (Eakin, *How Our Lives Become Stories*). Nicky Hallet is typical of today's epistolary critics in closing her essay on "the epistolary self" with the view that "for feminists, certain aspects of women's letter writing may dispel conceptions of overriding individuality lodged within generic assumptions of autobiography, replacing them with a sense of 'social self lodged within a network of others'" (Hallett, "'Anxiously Yours'" 115). At the 2006 International Auto/biography Association Conference, it was sarcastically mooted that even Hitler could claim to have had a "relational self," the term had become so loose.[1]

Perhaps ethics really are the deep subject of autobiography, and certainly of letters, despite the letter's flamboyantly rhetorical nature. It should be obvious that any promise to be "sincerely yours" can only represent a very local form of truth. But precisely to the same degree that we realize all letters are mediations of one interest or another, we only more quickly encounter the question of whether the writer is being *fair*. Is she dealing plainly with her correspondent? Or is she out to charm, to trick, to negotiate? It may be that feminist critics have allowed in the obvious questions, jettisoning arid debates about truth or art in the abstract. And yet, critics have found themselves unable to separate their analysis from the ethical questions upon which letters seem so evidently to insist, too often wanting the letter to be a "good form," just as the ephemeral, fragmented, patchwork "self" must outshine the logical, upright, defended, and consistent ego. Our task, then, is to take up the challenge of ethical analysis while simultaneously resisting its strange temptations to judge and condemn. In other words, we need to situate the ethical questions that letters and relational writings provoke historically, beginning with the philosophy of ethics itself.

The Ethics of Care: Writing the Contracts of Sisterhood

Ethics, as "the arena in which the claims of otherness—the moral law, the human other, cultural norms, the Good-in-itself, etc.—are articulated and negotiated" (Harpham, "Ethics," 394), is implicitly founded on an idea of relationship. Traditionally, at least since Kant, this has been defined as the adjudication of competing individual interests through a law of justice, whether religiously expressed as a church commandment, secularly in terms of enlightenment liberal democracy, or psychoanalytically as the superego. But in the same period that we have seen produce feminist epistolary and auto/biographical discourse, an influential group of feminist philosophers challenged this approach with their own version of the relational self.

The protagonists here were Carol Gilligan, Nel Noddings, Sara Ruddick, and Virginia Held. They argued that people were not the insatiable consumers and egoistic economic agents of Kantian liberal theory, nor even the free individuals of Marxism who no longer need to be defined by class. Rather, "though we often aspire to be free of the debilitating aspects of some group memberships and of various ties, we seldom aspire to be the unattached individuals of liberal theory" (Held, *Feminist Morality*, 812–13). Held and the other philosophers sought to understand and value people's ethical behavior in actual practices such as parenting, nursing, and friendship, rather than the traditional philosopher's case studies of an "ideal" subject with no personal ties, emotions, or physical context, working out legal or economic contracts. Along with this, they displaced justice as the key ethical term altogether in favor of one of "care." Although trained as a psychologist, the most well known advocate of this philosophy was Carol Gilligan whose 1982 work, *In a Different Voice*, outlined a "feminine" form of ethics in what had previously been dismissed as moral confusion:

> The reluctance to judge remains a reluctance to hurt, but one that stems not from a sense of personal vulnerability but rather from a recognition of the limitation of judgement itself. The deference of the conventional feminine perspective thus continues at the postconventional level, not as moral relativism but rather as a reconstructed moral understanding. Moral judgement is renounced in an awareness of the psychological and social determination of human behavior, at the same time that moral concern is reaffirmed in recognition of the reality of human pain and suffering.
>
> (102–3)

Comparing girls' and boys' responses to Lawrence Kohlberg's "puzzle" of whether to rob a chemist's to get otherwise unaffordable medicine for a

dying partner, she suggested that girls think through their felt responsibilities toward everyone's needs, while boys weigh up "rights" in the abstract.
In contrast to an ethic of justice, which hopes to treat everyone the same
through a principle of human equality, an ethic of care is premised on the
idea that "no one shall be hurt," in the face of the obvious differences between people and their needs. The psychology of attachment, which
Chodorow proposed as the basis for love rather than dependency, thus
found formalization in philosophical terms; Gilligan indeed explicitly
quotes Chodorow's argument that "girls emerge from [early socialization]
with a basis for 'empathy' built into their primary definition of self in a way
that boys do not" (*The Reproduction of Mothering*, 8). As Gilligan put it, "the
logic underlying an ethic of care is a psychological logic of relationships,
which contrasts with the formal logic of fairness that informs the justice approach" (*In a Different Voice*, 73).

Trying to rethink "the age-old split between thinking and feeling, justice
and mercy, that underlies many of the clichés and stereotypes concerning
the difference between the sexes" (69), Gilligan was typical of her time in
trying to value what she depicts as women's characteristic moral response in
its own terms, suggesting that men need to explore ways of being more
emotionally connected as part of their moral development. But she also said
that women needed to learn how to care for themselves as part of *their* moral
development, to disrupt the conventional feminine equation of "goodness
with self-sacrifice" (70). Deciding that justice and care were not only compatible but essential halves of a mature moral consciousness, Gilligan concluded that care was no excuse for martyrdom.

Yet this was the rub for feminists. Just as literary-critical claims for some
kind of universally "relational" femininity were soon being attacked, so care
ethics was quickly controversial for the same reasons. Despite the attempts
to argue for women's "self-care," other feminists were afraid this was a new
version of women's self-sacrifice, distracting from the urgency of the struggle for rights. Furthermore, care ethicists seemed to ignore women's lack of
actual caring behavior and to generalize wildly; many studies showed that
perceptions of morality are much more similar across class than gender (see,
for example, Xiao, "Class, Gender, and Parental Values").

And yet, my argument is that an ethic of care underlies the conception of
the feminist relationships dramatized in the letters by women during this
time. This is not to say that it always materialized—as we have seen, clearly

not. But even in failure, epistolary discourses and practices reached for the idea of liberation through a certain form of unquantifiable personal engagement. Constantly situating both self and other in local, often physical being, letter writers, and, indeed, letter critics, dreamed of and reasoned about equality or liberation through, rather than despite, relationship. We can see this formulated in care philosophers' repeated emphasis on the importance of conversation, such as Ruddick's analysis of mothers talking to their children:

> In aid of reflectiveness, they will likely develop conversational habits that are valuable when, despite their disappointment and incomprehension, they speak with, not at, their children. Reflective conversations allow for reinterpretation as well as revision of choices that may be disturbing to mothers. Despite temptations to mutual disavowal, mothers and children, in conversation, can experimentally and tentatively envision current options and future life prospects that are attractive to a child and acceptable to a mother, though she might never have imagined, let alone chosen, them.
>
> (*Maternal Thinking*, 117–18)

Similarly, Virginia Held describes the development of "mutually respectful and shared practices of conversation and behavior and mutually considerate and caring emotional relations" to be an essential aspect of a distinctively feminist philosophical worldview (*Feminist Morality*, 178–79). The idea reappears in Peta Bowden's 1997 argument that "the ability to listen to and to hear the voices of different others become ethical resources" because they allow "the possibility for activating relationships, for understanding differences among persons, for mediating and offering compensations, as well as claiming respect for one's separateness and expressing willingness to observe boundaries" (*Caring*, 173). Finally, Patricia Hill Collins argues that care ethics converges with Africanist traditions because of this emphasis on "value placed on individual expressiveness, the appropriateness of the emotions, and the capacity for empathy" (*Black Feminist Thought*, 216).

Feminists even hoped that just as personal expression could stimulate ethical behavior, writing itself would be stimulated by caring relationships, much as the letters of the Three Marias represented their erotic collaboration or as Elizabeth Meese framed an academic book as a letter to her lover. The choice of style itself could signify the attempt to write ethically as an alternative to the stripped, impersonal tones of conventional philosophy: Margaret Sharp argued for the compatibility of pragmatic philosophy with letter writing. Even in realist epistolary novels like *The Color Purple* (Walker), *Between Friends* (Hanscombe), or *English Correspondence* (Davey), we see the effects of a philosophical belief that individuals always make their choices in the context of relationships and in which reason encompasses emotion in such ethical modes as "maternal thinking" and "mindful feeling." In the preface to a later reprint, Gillian Hanscombe described her epistolary novel *Between Friends* in just such terms:

> As for me: I still think, when I read this or that passage, that all four of them—Frances, Meg, Amy and Jane—had a valid point to make and painful, problematic, fascinating, inconsistent lives to live. No woman's lot, under patriarchy, is simple, or logically systematic, or clearly laid out. And we still need—come the revolution—to extend imaginative sympathy, to find common ground, to develop compassion, to construct our vision, to define our ethics, to understand our own and each other's situation.
>
> (unpaginated)

Letters have repeatedly figured the community to be as close as a family. Virginia Woolf framed this in lamenting the loss of the "little public" that defined eighteenth-century letter writing; more recently, Dena Goodman has seen the same in the women-inclusive salons of early democratic letter writers; Nicky Hallett sees it in the intimate "interpersonal groupings" of Carmelite nuns' letters of the seventeenth century (Woolf "The Humane Art"; Goodman, *The Republic of Letters*; Hallett, "'Anxiously Yours'"). Although such literary ideas of community have historically been the privilege of tiny educated elites, recent feminism makes similar claims in dramatically more populist terms. Amy Erdman Farrell in 1998 analyzed letters to *Ms.* magazine as "the promise of popular feminism" (*Yours in Sisterhood*). Mary Thom in 1987 edited those letters to create not just a glimpse into a world of women's experience, that is, into women's difference, but a model of a certain kind of relationship:

> From the beginning, it was clear that the *Ms.* readers made up a very special community—mostly sympathetic to us and each other, sometimes querulous, always demanding. Perhaps because the editorial material of *Ms.* has so

profoundly to do with their own life choices, most letter writers are anything but detached observers. (As one subscriber wrote recently, "*Ms.* Is a good old friend. I like to read her before I go to sleep at night. We've been together since her birth.") And they show an astonishing concern about each other that has made the Letters to the Editors column each month probably the most popular feature in *Ms.*

(*Letters to Ms.*, xv–xvi)

Compare this to the claims that Noddings and others, such as Held, made for care as a principle of community making. In their point that a person is not divided into "a public or a working person and a private person," we recognize instantly the feminist truism that collective enterprises can also be understood as having "shared, relational" dimensions. Relationships of "trust and concern" developed in, for example, environmental and disarmament work or social policy, for these theorists, should be concrete and particular—family-ish—as well as abstractly communitarian (Held, *Feminist Morality*). The fact that an antinuclear campaign turns into the making of (feminist) community, for example, would follow as part of this ethics—something we will see embodied in the letter-writing circles of the women's peace movement. From the point of view of such ethics, ends cannot be divorced from means, and single-issue politics will always turn multiple, though notably in networks of still individualizable causes rather than party-style centralization. In a world perceived to extend through an elaborate network of relationships, the fact that someone might be hurt affects everyone who is involved, complicating the morality of any decision and removing the possibility of a clear and simple solution. Thus morality, rather than being opposed to integrity or tied to an ideal of agreement, is aligned with "the kind of integrity" that comes from "making decisions after working through everything you think is involved and important in the situation," and "taking responsibility for choice" (Gilligan, *In a Different Voice*, 147).

Yet, as is already evident in the previous chapter, the attempt to think about the personal in the context of the professional raises all kinds of problems, and feminist working relationships were the place to find them. Put another way, just as relationships of care can be intensified in letters, so they can amplify the special painfulness of care's failure. Here the proliferation of accusatory or aggrieved epistolary essays, the furious debates in women's letters pages, stylized personal letter debates, or even the ritualistic burning of letters finds its explanation. In Shula Marks's 1987 edition of *Not Either an Experimental Doll: The Separate Worlds of Three South African Women*, we are faced with a white patron's failure to interpret her correspondent's needs and eventual madness. But we are also confronted with white feminists' duties of care to black women today. Published jointly by the London-based Women's Press and the University of Natal Press in South Africa, the former of which had committed itself to prioritizing the publication of black and Asian writers, this triangle of tragic letters among a teenage Xhosa girl, her elderly white sponsor, and her black social worker in apartheid South Africa of 1949 resonates with its editorial context, in which the politics of race was center stage in the British women's movement. Marks explicitly interpreted the "differentiated meaning of the complex South African social order" as a means to rethink "sisterhood" in general:

> Unravelling these threads through the relationship of [Mabel Palmer, Lily Moya, and Violet Sibusisiwe Makhanya] inevitably undermines any simple-minded feminist assumption of the power of 'sisterhood' in which the fractures of class, age, and ethnicity are of no account. Equally, however, they share in a 'woman's world,' shaped, it is true, by different forms of male domination, but in which men rather than women recede into the middle distance.
>
> (*Not Either an Experimental Doll*, 40)

We can understand the intensity of disappointment when other feminists appear not to care, more specifically through an open letter on the politics of disability written by Maria Jastrzebska. She wrote to fellow myalgic encephalomyelitis (post-viral fatigue syndrome) sufferer Caiea March, who was editing an anthology on "women and ME," about her anger that feminist friends wouldn't look after her because "they'd had enough of self-sacrifice, of over-caring for others and not knowing how to put themselves at the centre of their own lives." Jastrzebska describes the failure of a personal correspondence with a former lover who was also training to be a healer, and the open letter seems a way for her to return to this exchange as an unsolved puzzle about "the issues of need and dependence—so complicated for women" (Jastrzebska, "Sto Lat Zdrowia," 111):

I seethed at the thought of her seeing clients on a professional basis while avoiding a close friend who had become so seriously ill. She said I didn't understand the pressures she had in her life. She couldn't keep on top of things for herself, she didn't even have time to get her washing done, let alone deal with my guilt-tripping her. We exchanged angry letters. In the end I suggested we meet to try and sort it out; she refused. Perhaps she thought it was too late for that. She said she wanted to leave behind situations like the one she'd been in with a previous boyfriend. Some time before she'd been lovers with a man who had also had a (different) chronic illness. This man had manipulated and guilt-tripped her and in the end become violent and tried to kill her. I was devastated by the comparison—I felt ashamed of not recovering—and I gave up.

(113)

The real exchange of "angry letters" mentioned in this displaced address clearly turned on what each felt the other owed and could expect, and feminist reasoning could be claimed on both sides. Jastrezebska's feminist friend's decision to stop looking after her because she had to "look after herself" checkmated Jastrezebska's need, her demand, indeed, her feminist *expectation* of care.

What happens when feminists disagree? The Three Marias' fallout after their trial and Audre Lorde's letter on racist white feminism raise the question of how an ethic of care works when conflict arises. In the context where "the law" has been particularized and "justice" embodied, community can appear to fragment into particularities, writing to regress into unmoderated clashes of need. This is another way of coming at the problem of identity as it played out politically in the women's movement. Although it was important to question the universalized identity of women as confidantes, the self-defeating spiral into ever more precise and ironically individualistic collectivities is all too well known. Politicizing the personal also meant personalizing the political in ways that sometimes collapsed the distinction between public and private altogether, with radical but sometimes unbearable implications.

Indeed, many letters may owe their origins ironically to the wish to avoid caring for somebody, as today's debate over whether Internet communities can ever substitute for face-to-face relationships reminds us. Care has classically been theorized as the response to someone's need as an individual standing before you; Emanuel Levinas's view is that we are called to moral responsibility when we can see and touch a specific other's need for help (*Totality and Infinity*). Much of feminist care ethics likewise begins from paradigms of physical care for a child or sick person, though, as we have seen, the care ethicists argued that it should include care for oneself as well. In contrast, letters, like the get-well card or even the phone call, can be more ambiguous as possible substitutions for such giving. Letters in this case dramatize the limit of care and hint that "one under the guidance of an ethic of caring is tempted to retreat to a manageable world" (Noddings, "Caring," 18). They can show how public life can ironically be scuppered by the insistence upon meeting the other as one who cares, for "when this reaching out destroys or drastically reduces her actual caring, she retreats and renews her contract with those who address her" (18). Again, we might think of the exchange between Maria Jastrezebska and her friend over how much care Maria could expect, and we wonder whether the friend broke off the correspondence just as she refused to meet Maria in person. Alternatively, a carer might return to the stiffer terms of justice precisely because care was felt to be too much to ask for. This is one way to understand the experience of falling out of love with "sisterhood" that activists so often describe.

Conclusion

Feminist literary critics have been astute in analyzing the life writer's "self" as something defined always in relationship and often in collective relationship to a projected "identity." To a degree, this is simply to acknowledge that you cannot fully appreciate life writing's meaning without historically contextualizing it, though occasionally a purely aesthetic approach will work. Letters, perhaps more than any other textual form, are often incomprehensible without reconstructing the context of the relationship that engineered them—for this reason they are really more of a "proto-genre" than a genre proper (see Jolly and Stanley, "Letters as/Not a Genre"). However, this "historical" turn prompts ethical questions that we have seen raised throughout life writing and feminist criticism since the late 1980s. Although letters rarely have the scope of autobiography or even biography for moral insight, their very embeddedness (if not embodiedness) in particular relationships raises instant dilemmas and questions of trust, duty, power, and fairness.

Feminist philosophers' attempts to develop the ethics of mercy, or in their terms, "care," remains compelling as a way to approach letters (and indeed all life writing), as it is premised on precisely this recognition of the particularity and dependency of selfhood. These ethics are worked out in the messy detail of real relationships, in which a sense of conflicting responsibility describes people's actual experience of moral dilemmas much better than an abstract weighing up of rights does. This also recognizes that each person's experience is unique and that pain in some respects cannot be quantified. The ideas that no one can speak for another and that political platforms must encompass individual as well as collective experience remain a touchstone for feminists.

I will draw upon both the notion of the relational self and the ethics of care in the following chapters. But the actual letters and letter-writing practices of second wavers show a much more precise and conflicted version of the relational self than either literary critics or feminist philosophers typically celebrate. This may be because the originators of the theories were themselves also mired in the assumptions of gender difference and women's internal sisterhood of the early 1980s. All of them were motivated by the movement's exploration of alternative values in terms framed as women's "difference" from men, by the hope of a new society freed from the uncaring world of patriarchy. But what is obvious is that the movement produced its own ethical dilemmas at the same time as a new level of ethical demand, expecting women not only to seek justice together but to care for one another in doing so. The trouble is that once you admit that people have needs as well as rights, you have opened the Pandora's box of the capacity to be hurt, to be vulnerable, in fact, for people to be endlessly needy. Letters from women in the 1970s and 1980s show just this confusing sense of a new space in which women could articulate new needs as well as new rights, although they were not necessarily clear about this. At their best, these letters also demonstrate the writers' commitment, and ability, to care for one another in both these capacities. But this was no easy task.

I will not at this point attempt to speculate on the bigger historical determinants of all of this, though the question will recur in the next section. Rather, I wish now to turn to two classic scenarios of "care ethics" through the prism of letters: mother-daughter relationships and the women's peace movement. Through them, I will further explore the idea of letter writing as the pursuit of ethical relationship as it was articulated in early 1980s feminism. Yet I will also suggest that letter writing was part of a world of love and ritual that went far beyond the conscious intentions, ethical or otherwise, of feminist letter writers or, indeed, literary critics or philosophers.

CHAPTER FIVE

Mothers and Daughters in Correspondence

Helen Claes to her daughter Christine, California, October 1974
Dad, of course is worried (so am I) but you are you and no matter where
you go I'll never lose you (dead or alive). I'll fear for your welfare at the
same time envying your strength of purpose to endeavor to do what you
must. Your letter reminded me of my own about Chicago written so
many years ago; when my life was new and exciting. I hope with all my
heart you have the guts I lacked to keep the fragile flame flickering. With
love and happy hope, Mom

Rita to her mother Mira, U.S.A., June 1981
I have never written a letter like this before in my short life. I feel good
about writing this and I would like to hear what you have to say. Ma,
perhaps, you and I still can be friends in this way that you and your
mother could not be. Let's try. I love you. Yours, Rita

—quoted in Payne, *Between Ourselves*

With Love and Happy Hope, Mom

W hen Karen Payne got the idea in 1978 to collect contemporary correspondences between mothers and daughters, she was looking for a
way to celebrate feminist values. For her, these private writings seemed to
describe, as she put it in her introduction to what became *Between Ourselves:
Letters Between Mothers and Daughters, 1750–1982*, "what women find moving, beautiful and worth *living for*" rather than the angry protests of wom-
en's liberation so easy a target for media criticism:

> I began work on this book with the idea that mother-daughter relation-
> ships in today's feminist climate would be under particular strains: that the

rapid changes in women's lives would create traumatic disagreements and differences in this relationship, which has been concerned primarily with teaching the traditional roles of wife and mother. I discovered that, when women challenge tradition, they do often feel that they must justify their actions, above all to their mothers. There is sometimes strong disapproval, even violent disagreement across the generations. But I also found mothers and daughters in the past and present who have encouraged each other to go far beyond the conventional definitions of good mothers and dutiful daughters, and have given each other crucial support in creating alternatives to values which tend to limit women's lives.

(xvi)

The book spoke of its time in celebrating women's intimacy as a method as much as a goal. A classic example of politicizing the personal, it also reflected the idea that liberation was nurtured in women's mutual encouragement "to go far beyond the conventional." Payne's files show that while planning the book, she was reading work on newly published passionate letters between women friends and relations from earlier eras, including Carroll Smith-Rosenberg's 1975 article "The Female World of Love and Ritual: Relations Between Women in Nineteenth-Century America," and Lillian Faderman's 1981 *Surpassing the Love of Men: Romantic Friendship and Love Between Women from the Renaissance to the Present.* Her project embodied a similar drive to discover a history of women's love in the archives. Although she presents some very difficult relationships, such as those of Florence Nightingale and Harriet Martineau with their mothers, maternal support for the extraordinary self-making of women such as Helen Keller, Hannah Senesh, or George Sand is more typical. The letters from Calamity Jane, Vera Brittain, and Jessie Bernard to their daughters showed mothers could be rebels, too.

Yet it is Payne's assemblage of personal letters from the era of the second wave itself that remains for me riveting as an example of the intersection of letter writing and gender socialization that I theorize in the previous chapter. These letters were not easy to collect, a fact that has comforted me in my own research! Payne's advertisement, sent to *The Guardian* Women's Page, *Mother Jones, Spare Rib,* "many newsletters in the women's liberation movement," and, interestingly, the commercial freebie *Ms London* (Payne, xi), invited submissions of "letters you have written to your mother or daughter to explain developments in your life that departed from her perception of "normality." These might include, Payne suggested, "explanations of what feminism means and offers to you, your adoption of non-conventional relationships, of lesbianism, of the decision to have an abortion, to join a political party."[1] I was not surprised to learn from Payne that in fact many of the more personal missives came through contacts, including Zoe Fairburns, Roz Baxandall, Ani Mander, Blanche Cook, Michael Kidron, Alison Weir, Annette Overby, Gillian Perry, and several women at the Women's Buildings in San Francisco and Los Angeles.

The result of this explicitly politicized call was a contemporary archive of writing from women who often had quite painful stories to tell. Yet it comprised, by and large, statements of "happy hope and love." Payne organized the book to augment this, beginning with the blessings of Helen Claes to her daughter Christine, explicitly against one editor's initial suggestion of opening with the more gruesome letters from suicidal Anne Sexton to her daughter Linda Gray. Payne's thesis emerges through her organization of the seventy writers into sections from "Killing the Angel in the House" and "The Men in Our Lives" to "Loving Women" and "The Infinitely Healing Conversation." Liberation must happen through, rather than despite, women's relationship. We are encouraged to believe that writing, especially writing letters, can cultivate the "relational self" and its ethics, even when this involves confrontation and confession.

Let me give some brief examples by way of introduction. Sixteen-year-old Indian American Rita states she has found a new "friendship" with her mother, Mira, compared to the much more fraught—and stiffly censored—exchange in Mira's letters from the United States to *her* mother in India in the early 1960s. Yet Rita's confession of her ambivalence about her mother's "over protectiveness" and wish for her to "become Indian" is couched in a letter because in person, "Words seem to fail on both sides."[2] Leslie, an American writer of Russian descent, signals the new relationship the letter to her mother will enact after her having read Adrienne Rich's *Of Woman Born*, in 1979: "Dear Mother (How different it feels to address you only [and not Father too]! How marvellous it feels to address you only!)" (303). The letter is written hot after scribbling pages of notes on Rich and explains to her mother the revolution in women's possibilities, the reasons that daughters are oppressed by their mothers, her own physical attraction to her mother as her first lover. While this has all the straight-faced fervor of the new convert, she tells us that her mother "loved my letter," and more letters of the same guise follow—though her coming out as a lesbian proves to be the limit to her mother's willingness to listen. Korean writer Chungmi Kim composes a poetic "Daughter/Mother Dialogue" of praise for a mother now too ill to speak (354–57). Judy Green Herbstreit, explaining her neglect of her children as a single, bread-winning mother, warns her daughter that "it is as disgusting to be a manipulative *child* as it is to be a manipulative *parent*" (289), closing with words of encouragement and a citation from the Bible. Isobel writes to her daughter Catherine from Australia that she was reading the feminist epistolary classic *The New Portuguese Letters*

> about the same time you were reading *Damned Whores and God's Police*, and it hit me as never before how cunningly the whole trap is set. You've been smart enough never to be snared because for most of us, once we have children, they (the men) know we are side-tracked for a long time.
>
> (44)

Here a feminist mother writes openly to her daughter about the "snare" for women of having children in a patriarchal society. Her reference to the Three Marias' own passionate correspondence about shared oppression suggests the model she is emulating.

Payne and the women who wrote to her were mesmerized by women's identity as a source of power and believed the mother-daughter relationship to be its crux. In this, they reflected, sometimes explicitly, contemporary feminist literature. Payne as well as her contributors, had been inspired by Adrienne Rich's *Of Woman Born: Motherhood as Experience and Institution* (1976), which was seismic in "recovering" motherhood for suspicious feminist daughters at this time. Payne had also read Nancy Chodorow's *The Reproduction of Mothering*, first published in 1978, and Dorothy Dinnerstein's 1977 *The Mermaid and the Minotaur: Sexual Arrangements and Human Malaise*. Both these books popularized the idea of relational identity, recommending that men would be liberated by learning to nurture, even as women would be freed from the coercive aspects of mothering and being mothered. Payne's notes do not show reference to the emerging philosophy of care ethics, as expressed in Carol Gilligan's *In A Different Voice: Psychological Theory and Women's Development* (1982) or Sara Ruddick's "Maternal Thinking" (1980). However, all of these proposed that mothers' relationship to their children was the test case for feminist notions of relationship in ways that resonate deeply with both Payne and her contributors' interpretations of their struggle.[3]

Letters have long expressed the idea that mothers have a particular legacy to give to their daughters, that daughters have a particular duty to their mothers, and that this exchange must be maintained even when the daughter leaves home. The unstoppable Madame de Sévigné is the most famous forbear, and her nearly 1,300 lovelorn and archly gossipy paeans to her married daughter on the other side of France have been canonized as the epitome not just of women's letter writing but of personal letter writing itself. The identification she projected made her letters textual mirrors for an imitating daughter, notwithstanding the fact that Sévigné's romantic tones reflected not so much the particularities of the relationship but a seventeenth-century courtly aesthetic (Michèle Farrell, *Performing Motherhood*).

Patterns of mother-daughter identification recur through the history of published women's correspondences. Lady Mary Wortley Montagu, famous for her publicly intended "Turkish Embassy Letters" about her travels as an ambassador's wife, also used letters to instruct her daughter in the limited lot of an aristocratic, educated, but still domesticated woman in eighteenth-century Britain (Spacks, *Imagining a Self*). For Fanny and Bessie Bussell, emigrants to Australia in the early nineteenth century, "letters became the very stuff of family life" in corresponding with their mother back in England (Clarke and Spender, *Life Lines*, xxvi). Caroll Smith-Rosenberg's analysis of the copious correspondences of mothers and daughters in nineteenth-century middle-class America showed how crucial they were in the education of girls for household management and marriage partly *through* maintaining "an intimate mother-daughter relationship . . . at the heart of [the] female world" of that society (Smith-Rosenberg, "The Female World," 378–80). Jenny Hartley writes of the "surrogate maternal comfort" that British mothers provided in letters to children in service in the Second World War ("'Letters Are Everything'"). Poet Bernadette Mayer is sarcastic about *The Desires of Mothers to Please Others in Letters*. Even where such intimacy was not the norm, as in the more recent cultures of adolescent rebellion, or where mothers have been the ones to leave, mother-daughter correspondences have centered on questions of identification and legacy, as we can see in Payne's own anthology.

Of course, education is an overriding theme in most letters between the generations for obvious reasons—the eighteenth-century Lord Chesterfield's letters to his son on the arts of diplomacy are just one of the more famous examples of men's use of the form. Using letters to persuade or teach is itself generic: classical and medieval theorists classified the epistle as a branch of rhetoric, and many genres of instruction such as handbooks, petitions, and essays have taken epistolary form. But the educational impulse in mother-daughter correspondence has often gone deeper, as it engages with the transmission of a gender identity founded on domestic relationships. For this reason, mothers' letters can be framed in the language of desire as much as of instruction, bringing together the "two epistolary vocations: the didactic and the sentimental" (Versini, *Le Roman épistolaire*). Equally, letters from daughters rhetorically negotiate needs and duties that are emotional as well as practical, expressing the way that love and nurture—and sometimes personal writing itself—have been the terrain and language of socialization as much as more obvious forms of instruction. Perhaps this is why mother-daughter letters seem to epitomize the letter's function as "a long arm of education," in their "attempt both to generate and to enforce resemblance between the correspondents" (Ferguson, "Interpreting the Self," 111).

The letter writers in *Between Ourselves*, like philosophers of care ethics, attempt to rework the primal tie of the mother-daughter relationship without breaking it. As newly politicized women, they protest against identities based upon domestic labor and sexual exchange. But their correspondences show how interdependency was embedded in ideas of women's identity and morality that Gilligan and Noddings were formulating at the time. Charlene Baldridge regrets "unwittingly pressur[izing]" in trying to coax her twenty-year-old evangelical Christian daughter to postpone marriage and kids altogether, while writing with laughing sympathy about her daughter's classic dilemma of charming charlatan versus suitable suitor who will "grow up to be a very boring middle-aged man." With a sense of the occasion she capitalizes her missive—"A Letter to a Daughter When She Did Not Know Which of Two Suitors To Marry"—but her argument is intimately framed, opening with the statement, "there can be no objectivity where we're concerned" (Payne, *Between Ourselves*, 41) and closing, "I see myself as a participant in a fertility rite as old as the world, and I can't help myself. The circle must be completed. You are my eternity, womanchild of mine. And I am sorry for this" (43). Baldridge herself had made what she described as "shatteringly naïve" choices about marrying young, giving up the chance of a career as an opera singer in the 1950s, and she had wanted her daughter to avoid her own mistake. Charlene chose to marry anyway. (She decided on the dull, sensible man.) Just as openly, Nan Hunt and her daughter compare their contrasting reservations about getting married to their current partners. While her daughter Diana fears her partner's lack of commitment, Nan as a woman who has "done" marriage and children already, fears for her daughter's loss of freedom. But her ultimate stance is:

> It was mainly when you wanted to settle for less, that I wanted to persuade you otherwise when you were growing up. Now, though I have no prerogative to do so, I'm still tempted at times to persuade you a certain way, but it is a friendly, loving and not demanding persuasion—just motherly inclination. I do more than tolerate, I *accept* your differences, and I love you very much.
>
> (47)

Diana, in turn, responded, "I can understand your fears about my men associations, I would feel the same if the tables were turned. . . . It is very hard for me to balance my dependent and independent feelings. . . . I love you" (47).

The turn taking in exchanges like these was surely the basis of Payne's argument that women so often encouraged each other to go beyond convention. It confirms "the continuation of an ethic of responsibility as the centre of women's moral concern, anchoring the self in a world of relationships and giving rise to activities of care" (Gilligan, *In a Different Voice*, 132). At their best, letters preserve this tradition of care even as it is "transformed by the recognition of the justice of the rights approach" (132). But often love did not square so easily with decisions to work or travel against expectations, to live with a boyfriend outside of marriage or marry someone considered unsuitable, to have sexual relationships with women, or to choose not to have children. On one hand, these letters open us up to how women's chances in life depend as much as ever upon changing their foundational relationship, how mothers and daughters need to find each other. But on the other, they show how hard it is to reconcile the desire for autonomy with support, justice with love, whether for the writers or for others. They remind us that in demanding both these things, feminism can become an obligation in itself. The consequent rhetorical mind games are evident in a 1980 letter from Jackie Page in Oregon to her mother Lynn Page back on the family farm in rural Colorado. A high school teacher, Jackie was thirty-five years old, with two children, and living with her boyfriend to her parents' great disapproval. As she explained to Payne in an introduction, Page had reproached her mother for never seeming interested in how she felt. Her mother had replied, "Sit down and tell me in a letter." Page consequently wrote:

> I feel like I'm approaching a time in my life that's more comfortable than anything I've felt right up to writing this letter to you. Now for sure I'm not talking economics when I say comfortable. I'm addressing my equivalent to your financial security/insecurity. The thing I'm talking about is self-confidence. I feel confident that I made the right decision in divorcing Ron; I am confident in the riches I possess for giving my children the confidence and desire to grow and live; I am confident in my own decisions, in my ability to meet responsibilities financial and otherwise; and last, but I assure you not least, I am confident in the love, affection and friendship I feel for Matt Blender from New Jersey. . . . Now I know you and Dad are feeling like I've acted horribly, like a bad child who really knows better. I've hurt your feelings, probably embarrassed you and disappointed you miserably and I feel sorry that it had to happen. I guess by your standards, all that is true about misbehaving, but not by mine. I feel badly for you both, though, that you don't have the confidence in me that I have. It would be so great for me if you could listen and understand when I say that I don't have all the answers, just like you don't. All we really do anyway is live through a series of accidents and mistakes, insights and successes. I'm not saying my way is better than yours, I'm only saying that it is my way and we can either part ways here or get to know each other somehow and see if we can practice some lessons in perceiving the world in our different ways.
>
> (Payne, *Between Ourselves*, 38–39)

Page's separation of her sexual relationship from her economic decisions and her definition of security as self-confidence are founded on notions of individual rights and her happiness as an independent individual. Closing her appeal for her mother's acceptance with the promise that she too accepts, she attempts to avoid a mode of writing as argument, explicitly saying that she is not offering a "defense," but rather an example, particularly in her description of the "riches" and "desires" she aims to nurture in her own children. Page wishes to be seen as caring—it seems to me she also really desires to care as much as to be cared for—and this conditions her challenge. This emerges more clearly in the letter she sent to Karen Payne to explain her submission to the book. It offers the defense she had tried to transcend: "One reason I felt I had to be so 'flip' and sarcastic in the letter was because she seemed to me to be so dreadfully closed-minded towards me as well as behind the times, or ahead—whichever."[4]

To talk of these letters as examples of ethical exchange, then, cannot be to say that they are easy or successful nor that they are the prerogative of women in any essential way. Changing the terms of family duty involves emotional as well as literary risks, visible in the arid polemic that sometimes swells the feminist address or the damply evasive reply it can engender. Jackie Page's mother, for example, did not keep the letter that Jackie had sent her because she considered it "unimportant": Jackie had kept a draft, which was what she sent to Payne. On the other hand, even the most heartfelt appeals do not guarantee a receptive addressee. Exchange possibly arrives only after years of delay in the emotional post, attempts to convince are stymied by desire or, conversely, drained of its affect. Many of the writers cannot face the genie their optimistic writing unleashes or find disappointment in the "uncorresponding" reply. "A letter, a letter, give me some paper," writes Morena in 1977, San Francisco, full of desire to "think of you simply as another human being rather than mommy." Yet, despite enclosing heartfelt journal entries about her black women's support group, she simply receives no reply (*Between Ourselves*, 387). Another writer sent in not only the polite letter she really wrote but the angry "what I wished I could have said," while another sent in a letter addressed to herself instead of to the mother she could not talk to. And Nan Hunt, after writing so lovingly to her daughter Diana about valuing their differences, annoys her own adopted mother, Bunny Flarsheim, so much with requests to film her in a documentary about growing older that she receives the admonishment: "I am *81* years old—look 181—feel 281—act 381. If I were to try to put the way I feel in a few words—I'd say I'm tired of loving" (195).

Teresa and Kate's Right to Choose

I want to consider the double edge of epistolary care more closely in a reading of the most extensive correspondence in Payne's collection, twenty letters between Teresa and her daughter Kate, dated from 1973 through 1979 and written between the north and south of England.[5] In this classic feminist scenario—a daughter wishing to raise her mother's consciousness, a mother responding with loving admonishment—letter writing is both a neutralizing space for argument and the expression of intense mutual need. But fundamental questions about both women's identities are also at stake, not only in terms of gender but class and ethnicity, which becomes fully apparent from Kate's editorial notes. Kate's grandmother had died while giving birth to Teresa in 1930 in the Great Depression in Ireland, and Teresa had gone into domestic service at fourteen years old, the Army at eighteen, and marriage to a railway worker at twenty, moving to England in the process. In her disastrous marriage, despite health risks, Teresa had four daughters, of whom Kate was the second. The excerpted correspondence begins when Kate is at university in 1973, eighteen years old, recovering from two suicide attempts and being berated by her mother who has found her contraceptive pills.

Teresa's letters, particularly in the earlier part of their correspondence, support the traditional model of women's letter writing as familial in content but also in form: a mix of confession and advice that articulates identity as emphatically relational:

4 OCTOBER 1974

Re: your state of mind, I feel really helpless, it's a horrible feeling being unable to help or even understand, for instance I cannot see how you feel that you have destructive powers . . . Kate, we all have our share of sickness even death, we all reach the depths of misery when we feel that life is not worth living, we all reach the heights of Joy when our World is perfect and life is Wonderful . . . When all is said and done all we can do is say what course of action is the best to take for *me* and if you are married and have kids you want what is best for them because you love them more than yourself. I sometimes wonder if being married and having a couple of kids would help you to a peaceful mind, never being able to jump in to any decision without first saying how will it affect my wee helpless loveable dependent children and believe me it may change your nature to a certain extent but having to go against the grain does strengthen the *character*. As I see life, it is full of injustices and all we can do is fight to the death for those you love, fight injustice as far as possible, don't envy anyone anything. Envy really is a disease, the World is full of Goodies and Baddies,

and all you have to do is decide which you are going to be and then get on with
life, they say that Right always prevails but like a lot of people I often wonder
about that.

(Payne, Between Ourselves, 225)

What is best for "*me*" is "what is best for [the kids] because you love them
more than yourself." Although the letter offers advice, its authority is based
in a feminized mode of dependent desire, in which letter writing itself is
part of a submission to a perplexing yet ever-demanding relationship. Teresa
asserts that having children aids a peaceful mind, but a few words later, it
becomes apparent that this is only by "going against the grain," by changing
one's "nature." Her professed worldview is therefore one of resignation to
suffering, renouncing "envy," and counseling acceptance—however unjust
the world is. The language of the church naturalizes her suffering as a moral
rather than political state. When pushed by Kate, however, she explains her
situation economically: divorce is "not practical, where would the money
come from to keep two homes going?" (223).

Kate's letters to her mother, by contrast, ostentatiously refuse the stance
of "wee, helpless, loveable child" that her mother constructs for her. Political reflections fill long and emotional letters as she finds feminism and also,
though less explicitly, a new class consciousness, at university. Against her
mother's view that motherhood is a woman's fate, she joins the newly established National Abortion Campaign in 1975. But the early declarations of independence that accompany this later soften as she embraces the feminist
interest in mothering of the later 1970s. Writing in 1977 after having seen a
play about mother-daughter relationships, she rejects "the forces that have
divided us," quoting the play's optimistic uniting of their two parts—"Even
some revolutionaries are lovers, even some poets have babies." She goes on
with a lyrical tribute to their differently corresponding correspondence:
"Mum I love, you, Mum I'm glad I got away from you, Mum I *love* you and
I wish you would come too" (231; her italics). Clearly the hope is that desire
will be educated through desire—that mother and daughter can be confidantes as well as comrades in struggle.

The letters record a crucial stage in the history of feminist activism, in
which we see the kinds of personal experiences that fuelled it. They also represent a writing process between a mother and daughter in which the status
and meaning of mothering is explored for both parties. Without suggesting

that letter writing was the only, or the most important, factor in the dramatic change in their relationship, it is undoubtedly a force for private conversion. Correspondence goes beyond the traditional feminine specularity, constituting as well as reflecting, digging deep into the political terrain of their relationship. But the real difficulty of the exchange is indicated by what they do not say, revealed instead in Kate's editorial notes—her father's rape of her mother, her mother's drinking and fury at her younger sister's pregnancy and suicide attempt, Kate's abortion and breakdown. Kate's most explicitly political letter, indeed, was never sent. Written on 5 May 1975, it describes with religious fervor her attendance at a meeting about defending women's right to abortion against a Private Member's Bill introduced by a right-wing Labour MP, James White, which was aimed at decimating the British 1967 Abortion Act. She suggests her mother would neither have supported nor understood her:

> An anti-abortionist tried to wreck the meeting, but got shut up by a very good woman doctor who told him what it's like trying to save the life of a woman who's been driven to the backstreets. . . . I am full of anger and pain, dreading that this Bill should become law, dreading that there should be more tragedies like the one she tells us of. But I cannot show that pain, I have to be strong. I have to be organizational.
>
> (226)

In this paradoxical admission of the pain she says she cannot show, she constructs her mother as a hurtful kind of confidante. In contrast to "an old lady of 80 [who cared] enough to drag herself out into the night" to come, having endured five illegal abortions and nine children, Kate accuses her mother, "I expect you're thinking I'm completely cracked to tell you all this, to which I can only reply that I guess most of the things that really interest me seem cracked to you, cracked, irrelevant or wrong" (226–27). In the gap between the narrative of her life in the campaign and the address to her mother lies the gap between her mother as fantasized witness and as fantasized adversary. This ambiguity is also evident in her cry that "God knows I hope that I should never need an abortion, but I cannot separate my fate from those of the women around me," for the letter's very account is part of an attempt precisely to "separate her fate" from that of her mother. She uses the tragic necessity for abortion ironically to challenge her mother's view that children, who tie her to an oppressive husband, must deny a mother (at least one without independent income) her own life and happiness. Yet this polemic ends by revealing the writer's abject dependency upon her absent reader-mother. This certainly supports her argument that women should have more choice over the terms of mothering, but it takes her into a realm where choice is no longer possible for her, that of her own birth. The letter's political account thus doubles as an inquiry into her mother's love for her and the terms upon which she herself was given life. Kate retrospectively comments on the letter that she is "very embarrassed by the boasting/defensive tone," which "started off jolly and gradually got more defensive and angry" (225–26).

It is true that as an expression of physical distance, letter writing evades many of the troubling issues of power, irrationality, and physical dependence that motherhood involves. But although on one level Kate and Teresa's exchange evades the messiness of physical relationship, it is infused with physical memory, as resonant of their correspondents' bodies as love letters. Kate's unsent letter in particular exemplifies the strain of attempting a purely enlightened conversation, and it is no coincidence that it is about abortion rights, for the topic, like the letter, paradoxically separates and joins the daughter to mother as Kate tries to question her mother's most profound teaching. On the one hand, Kate tests her powers of language to ward off her mother's pessimism. But like women poets who have written about abortion through apostrophe (the technique of addressing an inanimate or absent object or person), Kate is also compulsively summoning her mother's presence (Barbara Johnson, "Apostrophe"). Under her political debate about reproductive choice she is attempting a much more difficult animation through writing—her own. The fact that she was unable to send the letter makes this a poignant case of self-birth, as divided as mother-poets speaking to progeny they did not give birth to. Yet it remains symptomatic of the desire to continue a relationship, to give birth to the self that exists within that conversation. Kate's apostrophe is much like the unexpected discovery that Susan Neulander Faulkner made in a letter she had written to her dead mother to tell her that "at last I am free" (Payne, *Between Ourselves*, 358). Strikingly, however, Faulkner describes her new aloneness as a hollowness, "just as—I imagine—a woman must feel after giving birth. For in a strange way, you were like a physical entity within me, a part of me that belonged to my body that filled a void within me" (359). Faulkner's image discovers that she is her own mother's mother, as well as that she can now create herself as she wishes. Yet both Faulkner and Kate find that writing also uncovers a dependence upon and identification with their mothers that they had not bargained for.

Reading through old letters from her mother in 1977, Kate was convinced that "both our ideas have changed" (229). That year, she mentions her mother's coming with her on "the abortion demo" and "taking those antifascist leaflets to work." Two years later Teresa filed for divorce and went to stay with her sister in the United States. Her letters to Kate from this period show a startling new sympathy towards "Women's Lib" (253), even reading the feminist magazine *Spare Rib*. A telling sign of their reconciliation is Teresa's teasing response to Kate's account of a friend's labor:

> had to laugh at you having sympathy pains—how she of the compassionate Heart suffers eh. Pleased to hear that the birth went well, that Sally had kind and considerate people with her, that must have made all the difference. It made me think back to all my births. Liz a breach birth and me in Birmingham alone. . . . Your dad was in the Army still and it was many years later that the thought occurred to me that the Army got compassionate leave for births—but not him—he didn't ask for it—he came home six weeks later—I wonder why? I know the answer to that.
>
> (250)

Teresa's view of Kate as a maternal force of her own, though on better terms than Teresa herself endured, seems compatible with Kate's rhetoric of sisterhood: "I feel we are friends as well as mother and daughter" (229). The last letter in the sequence, written by Teresa in 1980, informs her daughter that she has written to Margaret Thatcher to protest against the "Corrie" Amendment, an eventually defeated bill that would have drastically reduced women's rights to abortion. Perhaps most encouraging of all is a letter not included in the book. In 1983, Kate wrote to Karen Payne herself, who had become a friend, to tell her about life as the mother of a new baby of her own. Her portrait of economic struggle and domestic craziness living abroad with an irresponsible artist-partner, on one level, shows her frustrated discovery of the powerlessness she always feared, alongside a passion for her child. But determination not to repeat her mother's martyrdom feeds into not just the beginnings of negotiations with her partner but a joyous closeness with her mother.[6]

The subject of reproduction that is such a leitmotif in this correspondence obviously reflects the continuing terrain over which mothers and daughters negotiate a deep education in gender and sexual roles. As the classic ground for women's sense of their responsibilities to others, it is also the place where the ethical element in Kate and Teresa's exchanges becomes clearest. Kate's defense of abortion rights is initially deeply offensive to her mother, not just because it is presented as a political argument against her mother's Catholicism but because it apparently rejects the ethic of care that has sustained Teresa through her own suffering. But Kate spends very little time defending "rights" in the abstract. Rather, in using letters to try to appeal to her mother emotionally, she presents a revised "relationality" that rejects her mother's presentation of motherhood as self-sacrifice for a view that "responsibility for care . . . includes both self and other" (Gilligan, *In a Different Voice*, 95). Moreover, Kate's work in the abortion rights movement turns out to be not only about the right to choose but the need to *be chosen*, rather than simply the fate of a mother too beaten down to have resisted her husband. Kate's letters are little births, little acts of choice within relationship. At times, indeed, Kate demonstrates more "maternal thinking" than Teresa, in the sense that Sara Ruddick defines it as "a discipline in attentive love" (*Maternal Thinking*, 123). In comparison, Teresa's letters can seem manipulative. Yet she can be the more human of the two, softening her daughter's relentless sense of mission by gently joshing "she of the compassionate Heart."

Conclusion

Payne hoped that publicizing mother-daughter letters like these would fulfill Mira Hammermesh's call for a "cult of birthmanship which would complement, rather than replace the art of destruction," offering "creative models of wholeheartedness, and birth—not ideal fantasies."[7] We could, indeed, think of these letters as forms of "art" or "creative models." They can be moving and compulsive to read, though, as always with letters, they require extensive editorial contextualization and can still seem fragmented. But an ideal of relationship, especially between mothers and daughters, as an engine for mutual change goes beyond questions of aesthetic satisfaction. That change prompts the discovery and telling of new needs, whose ideal response is care. And this in turn redefines the *practice* of letter writing for these women.

We might justifiably name this practice therapeutic. That is, letter writing becomes a form of self-healing, one that quite literally works through conversation. In this way, arguably, it brings its own support to the feminist revision of care's object from children or men to other women and oneself. As for lovers, the letter between such physically involved parties mediates, rather than simply abstracting, the body and its less tractable language. Geographic distance might seem to make it harder to be close to someone, and certainly, classically, philosophies of care are based on the effects of physical nurture and response (Levinas, *Totality and Infinity*). But, in Kate and Teresa's correspondence, literary manipulation does not efface so much as repeat an intimacy that is both troubling and liberating. Writing manages at once to preserve and displace the rhetoric of fateful blood bond for a chosen family of emotional, sexual, or political allegiance, much as did the idea of "sisterhood" itself (Hirsch, *The Mother/Daughter Plot*, 165). Letters, then, can be a scene of a bloodless reproduction, an emotional labor that can be painful but often gentler than embodied conversation.

The therapeutic reformulation of the interdependence of mother and daughter proposes that care for the self—and saying it in a letter rather than in person—will solve the conundrum of their mutual oppression and transform old forms of specularity. But it may set up new orthodoxies and expectations that prove even harder to maintain. At the same time that someone like Kate follows the dictum of preventing harm alongside lobbying for justice, she is challenged to the limit in the face of people's self-harming behavior, or what Freud termed our "commitment to unhappiness." Conversely, someone like Jackie Page could perpetuate the very problem of self-sacrifice, duty, and covert power struggle that feminism was trying to solve.

The letters Payne both discovered and provoked trace some of the kinds of personal changes most prized by second-wave feminism in getting to the psychological centre of structures of gender oppression. They also trace the risk to individual relationship such exploration could involve. Yet the idea that particular, interested love, of the kind that mothers may especially transmit to their daughters, could be the platform for how to love ethically, how to be ethical lovingly, mesmerized many feminists at the time (Noddings, *Caring*). Indeed, some considered that if daughters and mothers could learn to really "correspond," women's unconscious anger or fear of both dependence and difference *within* the movement would also disappear (Jacobus, "Reading Correspondences"). Hence, many writers and artists wrote publicly in the guise of personal letters or literally drew on them in more public writings. The Belgian filmmaker Chantal Ackerman in *News from Home* (1976), for example, used her mother's reproachfully longing letters to her as the soundtrack to footage of New York city streets in one of her series of psychoanalytically inspired films of "unalienated feminine language" (Cerne, "Writing in Tongues"). Sylvia Plath's *Letters Home*, edited by Plath's mother Aurelia (1975), and *Anne Sexton: A Self-Portrait in Letters* (1977), edited by her daughter Linda Gray, were rites of passage for many women because they pitted mother love against the deathly expectations of 1950s femininity. Terry Wolverton read a letter to her mother about being sexually abused by her stepfather as the closing act to a one-woman performance, *In Silence Secrets Turn to Lies/Secrets Shared Become Sacred Truth*, in 1979, explaining that "ending this silence is a gift that I give to my life and to other women's lives, and that ultimately this is the most sacred gift that I can ever give you, Mama, my own truth" (quoted in Payne, *Between Ourselves*, 59). Merle Woo's "Letter to Ma," in Cherríe Moraga and Gloria Anzaldúa's *This Bridge Called My Back: Writing by Radical Women of Color*, pleaded for her mother to understand her lesbianism and the racism they both faced. Brenda Prince's "Letter to My Mother," about being gay, was accompanied by a double portrait of the two of them in Jo Spence and Joan Solomon's *What Can a Woman Do with a Camera?*. SDiane Bogus writes touchingly to her dead mother about her own children as a lesbian mother, an open letter originally published in *Lesbian Tide* in 1977. Alice Walker influenced a generation of African American women in valuing a maternal tradition of creativity as the handing on of "a sealed letter they could not plainly read" (Walker, *In Search*, 240). Bogus's letter was subsequently anthologized in *Double Stitch: Black Women Write About Mothers and Daughters*, a literary quilt and one long love letter between the generations.

Moving out from the questions any child has of her parent, or parent of her child, these visions hope that in solving the puzzle of the intimate difference between a daughter and her mother, love will permit wider political change. But how do such personal and public politics intersect in practice? In the next chapter, I want to look at how these ideals worked when they were adopted as a principle of community in the early 1980s peace movement.

CHAPTER SIX

Writing the Web

Letters from the Women's Peace Movement

Dear women,

The US air base at Greenham Common in Berkshire is the first place in
Europe where 96 Cruise missiles are to be sited in December 1983. Since
September 1981 women have been camping outside the main gate of the
air base, protesting against this decision which has been taken without
consulting the people of this country. . . .

    As women we have been actively encouraged to stay at home and look
up to men as our protectors. But we reject this role. We cannot stand by
while others are organizing to destroy life on our earth. It is not enough
to go on demonstrations. We must find other ways of expressing the
strength of our opposition to this madness. We have one year left in
which to reverse the Government's decision about Cruise missiles. There
is still time to stop them.

        With peace and love, from the women at Greenham Common

          —The Women at Greenham Common, 1984

It is not accidental that the philosopher Sara Ruddick saw the women's
peace movements of the early 1980s as a prime example of mothers taking
their principles into public, where traditional feminine values could be transformed through feminism into radical politics. As with the Madres protesting
the "disappearance" of loved ones under the Argentinean and Chilean military regimes of the 1970s, the drama of women's protests at this time seemed
to be a symbolic manifestation of a "women's language" of loyalty, love, and
outrage, though soon sanitary towels and lesbian ankhs joined pillowcases
and children's toys on the barbed-wire fences of the military bases. "In their

protests, these women fulfil traditional expectations of femininity and at the same time violate them," Ruddick wrote in *Maternal Thinking*:

> Preservative love, singularity in connection, the promise of birth and the re-
> silience of hope, the irreplaceable treasure of vulnerable bodily being—these
> clichés of maternal work are enacted in public, by women insisting that their
> governors name and take responsibility for their crimes.

(229)

Anyone who has been part of a protest for more than a week or two knows intuitively that campaigning is intimately related to community making. Sociologists and anthropologists who have analyzed the social life of protests have, however, been especially struck by feminism's emphasis on personal and public relationship as a method of organizing as well as a political goal. Writers such as Alberto Melucci and Kate Nash have considered feminism a "new social movement," defined through lifestyle and values as much as the demands for economic or political representation more typical of traditional class struggles (Melucci, Keane, and Mier, *Nomads of the Present*; Nash, "A Movement Moves"). The emphasis on mutual care was indeed flamboyant. It seemed that feminists hoped to facilitate "preservative love" among themselves: "singularity in connection, the promise of birth and the resilience of hope, the irreplaceable treasure of vulnerable bodily being."

Letter writing emerges as an important, though unappreciated aspect of both the making of this community and the attempt to extend its values. In part because of its innovative use of direct action, where hundreds of women literally left home to live on the verges of an American military base at Greenham Common, Berkshire, community making became crucial to the early-1980s campaign to prevent the stationing of nuclear cruise missiles in Britain. But I will focus on how this notion of community was extended, at least in principle, to those who were only visitors or never even got to the camp, through letters. In this sense, we can understand campaign letters, like the more personal letters from the same period discussed in previous chapters, as forms of life writing with often intensely personal investment.

Letter writing is, of course, a staple of all political campaigns—any campaigning handbook will contain a section on lobbying and petitioning (see G. Scott, *How to Get Rid of the Bomb*). It is also one whose art and function as an organizational tool are invariably underestimated (Stotsky, "Writing in a Political Context"). Although the demographics of letter lobbying is too little researched, it seems that women, perhaps those who would be unwilling or unable to participate in more public demonstrations, are reliable petitioners.[1] Lynne Jones, one of the most indefatigable campaigners at Greenham, considered that letter writing "appears to be something [women] are good at. It provided the starting point for German Women for Peace, and the basis for the Women's Day for Disarmament. Personal letters can also cross political divides in a way that written propaganda cannot" (L. Jones, *Keeping the Peace*, 147). But in the women's peace movement, letters' role as an internal binder and mediator was especially interesting. We can understand it in much the same terms as the campaign's primary symbol, the web. Like the wool that both bound women together and obstructed police and military agents, letters were a means of political lobbying and of identification and resistance. As such, they also tried to enable the campaign's ideology of decentered action, in which local and dispersed actions, or even simply personal identification, were supposed to be as valued as those taking place in the more public eye at the military base.

Letter-Webs: Greenham as Virtual Community

The thirty-six women, four men, and assorted children who initially marched to the Greenham Common Air Base in August 1981 to protest the siting of American nuclear cruise missiles there intended neither to create a community nor to write about it. They were going simply to protest an intolerable situation where Europe seemed likely to become a theater of "limited nuclear war" between superpowers dramatically scaling up the Cold War. Yet, when the men left and the ensuing women-only camp became a lifestyle, the campaign precipitated an extraordinary flowering of feminist direct action at military bases across the world, in which women's lives were turned upside down and permanent friendships created. Equally, while letters were initially written to drum up support and attention from the press and Parliament, as well as to explain actions to the base commandants, the needs of the thousands of women who heard of and wanted to be part of the party generated a new set of letters intended to create and sustain a community network. Letters poured in to the makeshift camp from day one, one organizer recording "well over a hundred" in a letter of September 1981 and the delivery of "variously-addressed mail and telegrams of support from all over the country."[2] And, reciprocally, letters came from the camp: open letters and chain letters; hand-written, signed newsletters that often reproduced individuals' letters within them; letters to and from protestors in prison for their creative peace-mongering. Letters are an integral detail of Barbara Harford and Sarah Hopkins's portrait of the camp during the first year:

> An enormous structure of polythene, tarpaulin and branches was built as a communal area. Just inside the doorway was a cauldron hanging from a wooden tripod over the ever-smoking fire surrounded by orange boxes and camping chairs. At the back of the structure there was an opening to the kitchen caravan; along the wall was a large table with leaflets, badges, photos and donated flowers. A noticeboard *displayed letters*, messages and posters advertising events. In one corner was a stack of material, old sheets and paint for making banners . . . and wool for weaving webs. Local people offered the use of their baths and telephones. Daily chores such as fetching water, *answering mail* and washing dishes took longer as the weather grew colder. There was also lots to do in the new 'office'. Typewriters, donated stationery and a duplicator made it possible to keep the media informed, organise actions and *make links* with the people in the groups who were offering help.
>
> (*Greenham Common*, 23; my emphasis)

The letters that arrived at the camp were often simple offers of help. A touching example comes from a woman writing "To the women at Greenham Common" regretting she had not had the courage to stay overnight after attending the huge "embrace the base" demonstration on 12 December 1982:

> At the moment I work as a secretary (which is a pretty useless thing to do), I am 25, I don't have any dependents to worry about (so I could go anywhere) but then I don't have any particular skills or talents either so, you see, I'm not sure if I would be any use to a peace camp. I really do want to join a peace camp but what I want is secondary to what is best for the peace campaign.[3]

As the campaign evolved, correspondence naturally expressed the friendships as well as planning among those already involved in the campaign. For example, Juley Howard jokingly wrote to Ginette Leach from prison in 1986 about her new vegan clogs after describing her tour of Dutch peace

Ed Barber, Greenham women reading letters. Originally titled "Greenham Common, October 1981." From Barber, *Peace Moves: Nuclear Protest in the 1980s* (London: Chatto & Windus, Hogarth Press, 1984), 32–33. Photograph by Ed Barber, text by Zoe Fairburns and James Cameron.

camps;[4] Zohl de Ishtar from Women for a Nuclear Free and Independent Pacific became the focus for many Australia-Europe correspondences; and Carole Harwood maintained letter links with women in War Resisters, New York, after participating in taking the U.S. government to court for planned genocide in November 1983.[5] Having just got back from Greenham, Julie at the sister Seneca Women's Encampment for Peace and Justice, wrote to say that "we should all put out more energy to create a tighter connection with our entire family!" and to invite women at peace camps all over to "keep in touch and let us know what you are doing and how you are feeling."[6] Indeed, the post was so important that the campers organized with the local post office for a postcode to be created for their settlement.

Naturally there were overwhelmingly practical reasons for the importance of the post—ensuring correct delivery of money and parcels and making the case that the camp was a real domicile, necessary for the right to claim unemployment benefits and avoid deportation.[7] In my interviews with a range of Greenham campaigners, though, few actually *remembered* writing letters. But a closer look at the scattered papers that remain from the camp shows that letter writing was inextricable from the development of the campaign and indeed was what distinguished it from the conventional peace movement. For letters were part of its much-lauded decentralizing networking strategy, a strategy that produced support groups, sister camps, and individual "Greenham women" and men sympathizers all over the country as well as in the United States, Italy, Australia, New Zealand, Ireland, Denmark, the Netherlands, West and East Germany, and elsewhere (Eglin, "Women and Peace," 252).[8] If we are to understand the ways in which Greenham fostered a sense of community, we need therefore to consider its virtual as well as its material aspects and where writing went alongside direct action in ways hitherto overlooked.

The immediate references for the Greenham women's protest style were the Spinsters, a women's affinity group from Vermont who had woven shut the gates of a nuclear power plant with wool, string, and rags, and the Women's Pentagon Action, who also used weaving, puppetry, drumming, and keening as part of their civil disobedience against U.S. policies toward Latin American in 1979 and 1980. These brought with them what became *the* prime symbol of the camp, the web. Drawing on traditional associations of domestic weaving and matriarchal religions, the Greenham women made their characteristic action the weaving of wool across military areas, gates, and fences and as ties around and among protesters, as a feminist mode of protest. The web soon appeared as a motif on publicity, banners, postcards, shawls, scarves, and t-shirts (Y. King, "All Is Connectedness").

But an equally distinctive aspect of the web as it was taken up through the peace camps was its expression of a relationship among women, and as such, it was a virtual structure, more purely symbolic than wool or human chains. Indeed, much was made of its "invisibility." Sasha Roseneil, a sociologist who lived at Greenham as a young woman, analyzes the web as an image of classic anarcho-libertarian "new social movement" organization, operating through networks that are fluid, horizontal (reticulate), autonomous, and informal (Roseneil, *Disarming Patriarchy*, 72). To a far greater degree than the symbols used by traditional movements such as political parties or trade unions, which are concerned more narrowly with economic self-advancement, or even by the more institutional peace movement, the web figured the role of identity in the Greenham campaign, an inner as well as outer focus distinctive of postindustrial movements (Melucci, Keane, and Mier, *Nomads of the Present*). The web, in other words, emblematized an aspiration to unify ends and means. It was a declaration of values that even women who had never met, or who could never come to Greenham, could share. Roseneil eulogizes:

> An intricate pattern of individuals and groups, joined together by almost in-visible threads, the Greenham web might have appeared fragile, but its strength rested in this supple translucence. The threads which linked the women could not be seen by those who looked for the traditional markers of political organization, but they were clear to those they bound together. They were the ties of friendship, emotional and affective bonds, shared val-ues and an identity forged in common, the identity of "Greenham woman." The invisibility of these connections to outsiders was protective; it made the Greenham network hard to locate and almost impossible for its enemies to infiltrate. And like a spider's web, the building of the network was never fin-ished; it was continuously in creation, never static.
>
> (*Common Women*, 69)

As both a literal method of organization and an ideal, the web of people was an imagined community not only because of its "passion to transcend the physical location" (68) (which therefore made it dependent upon tech-nologies of communication) but, as Benedict Anderson puts it, because it was conceived of as "a deep, horizontal comradeship" (*Imagined Communi-ties*, 7). The tenets of the women's peace movement were profoundly egalitarian—nonviolence, decision by consensus, and a holistic, emotional as well as intellectual approach to change (Roseneil, *Common Women*, 113–39). As we shall see, such comradeship was not always achieved, though the contradictions between ideal and reality were nowhere near the size of those of the national communities that Anderson describes. Indeed, the campaign was from the beginning informed by contemporaneous feminist debates about women's differences from one another and the importance of each in-dividual's experience. Many women worked hard to prevent the internal dif-ficulties that the women's movement had been experiencing through the 1970s.

In philosophical terms, we can understand the web as a concrete mani-festation of the ethics of care. Obviously, justice was a key aim of the move-ment: the right of citizens not to be used as pawns of the superpowers. But the aim of preventing the stationing of cruise missiles in Britain was always articulated as the minimum in an argument about nonviolence as a principle. Individuals were to live the message. In refusing to divide either military planners or protestors into "public" and "private" selves, the seemingly highly abstract political issue of nuclear disarmament was personalized as the need to develop trusting and concerned relationships simultaneously on the global and individual levels. Significantly, this approach spanned campaigners of diverse political backgrounds. In the early years, the camp was dominated by mothers who explained their motives as love and concern for children. Their terms were similar to Ruddick's argument that "preservative love," rooted in an understanding of physical need and vulnerability, may be the best chance of "preserving the life of humanity" (*Maternal Thinking*, 65, 81).

As increasingly radical feminists and lesbians were attracted to the campaign, the emphasis became much more on women's need to look after one another and assert a different kind of value system than patriarchal militarism, with its hollow rhetoric of "democracy," "choice," and "freedom." But the model of nonviolent community remained key to the way resistance was conceived. Indeed, it was precisely this shared ethics that underlay the camp's ability to span "feminine" and "feminist" concerns, liberal and radical feminisms, and thus its phenomenal popularity in the first three years. It is significant that the "faint-hearted feminist," Martha, the protagonist of Jill Tweedie's popular column in the British newspaper the *Guardian* at that time, supported the Greenham protests. In her weekly "letter from Martha," Tweedie as editor of the *Guardian's* women's page, begged sympathy for educated and opinionated women who nevertheless accepted a bored and restless lot as unpaid wives and mothers, through the conceit of having Martha plead the moderates' cause to her radical separatist friend, "Mary." But when Martha and her sexist civil servant husband Josh spy Mary in the television coverage of the 12 December 1982 "Embrace the Base" action, hanging baby clothes on the military fence, Martha feels Mary has got things "into proportion," while she is merely minding the kids back home. Josh, spluttering at his exclusion from women-only action, accuses Mary of stealing the clothes from an Oxfam shop: she "wouldn't know a human infant from a Sainsbury's Christmas cracker until [she] pulled it and no funny hats fell out" (Tweedie, *More from Martha*, 86, 104). Tweedie's point was that "many housewives were overlooked in the explosive beginnings of the Women's Movement," that "no one fights for what *is*, only for what might be" (4). Against the odds, Greenham seemed to move between both. As one flyer had it, "We use this imagery

Merrily Harpur, cover of Tweedie, *Letters from a Fainthearted Feminist*.

[of the web] because we are trying to create new conceptions of how people live and work together. The web is a symbol of how everything is connected and all things depend on each other to survive."[9]

It is in this light, as much as the practicalities of a campaign run on a shoestring, that we should understand not just individuals' letters but the epistolary character of the campaign's literature. Its fortnightly newsletters were personalized with handwritten, signed articles and drawings.[10] Sometimes newsletters were literally presented as letters. "Welcome Women," opened one of June 1983, doubling as a handbook for the proposed "Rainbow Dragon" action. Its sign off was "LOTS OF LOVE TO ALL YOU OLD DRAGONS FROM ALL THE OLD DRAGONS AT THE CAMP XXX."[11] A report on the "Reflect the Base" action of December 1983, in which crowds of women held up mirrors towards the fence, ended: "Dear 30,000♀ . . . It would be nice if some of you or all of you came to stay at the New Year, We've got lots of room."[12] Personal letters to the camp from prison or abroad were recirculated in the newsletter, and friends kept in touch through their pages. "Farewell my friend," began a note to "Dina" in one, "I am sure I speak for all the Wimmin at camp when I write this. . . . I am sure that even though you are not at camp in body you are here in soul to help us along as you have in the past. LOVE YOU NOW & FOREVER WILL MISS YOU XXXXXXX KIRSTY."[13] And one long and heartfelt letter from Agata Ruscica, an Italian feminist at "La Ragnatella" or "Spider's Web" camp in Sicily, explicitly referred to the web as both her political motivation and her connection to other women:

> The drop which makes the vase overflow (!) came with the arrival of 2 women from Greenham Common camp. One is a photographer and brings slides with her of the camp. At the same time I receive a message from Greenham Common; it's *a living message, speaking a language of women in which I find myself completely*. At this moment I must and want to take up the issue of peace again and understand why I had put it aside. . . . *What pushes me is that this imaginary thread*, which some Sicilian women are building with the women at Greenham by going to Comiso on the 12th, continues to exist and other women strengthen it; that we will be there on the 12th at Comiso and we will be there 'separate' because we mustn't 'liquify' as always happens in a world that doesn't represent us.[14]

(my italics)

One of the inducements to an epistolary style was the much-discussed principle of the need to "speak only for oneself." Writing in the form of personal address avoided the difficulty of (mis)interpreting another's interests. This principle was put forward in the opening piece of the first newsletter, photocopied in February 1983 and hand signed "Barbara,"[15] and was again reiterated in the "editorial" of *Womyn's peace camp green & common february news and Bristol newsletter* (1983):

> this newsletter has been produced roughly once a fortnight since september of last year. Mostly it has been written by a few ♀. . . . we agreed that we would like to widen out the scope of the newsletter, both by more ♀ writing and by ♀ writing about different things, especially about issues currently being discussed at the camp—♀'s struggle in other places, how we spend money, our differences from greenham Women Against Cruise, nonviolence, and so on . . . What we write about and how we write are affected by our individual viewpoints, and, as you know, there are many different ♀ at the camp. we have decided each to sign what we write, to make clear whose accounts/ideas you are reading, and to make it easier for you to know who to find to make comments/criticisms . . . please write and tell us what's been happening in your area . . . Judy & Annie (indigo ♀ camp) [punctuation as in original][16]

The exception to this individualized approach were the pieces written by the "unruly bunch of Bluegate ♀♀" who started their gate in the July blockades of 1982 and were known for both their working-class base and partying. But these too took letter form, as a "gossip column" of tales of invasions of the base and confrontations with bailiffs addressed and signed off as a collective letter: "yours in peace & sisterhood, Blue Gate ♀♀♀♀♀♀";[17] or "See you s♀♀n, lots & lots of love."[18]

Carol Stibbs, who received the newsletter as a member of Cleveland Greenham support group, viewed the newsletters as "crucial in conveying" the camp's vision of "non-violence, consciousness-raising or the making of connections, and spirituality" to women supporters outside the camp."[19] Notably, she comments on the personalized style in this regard:

> They are immediate and inspiring as they are written by individual women who, if you have been to Greenham, you will probably have met; they come

direct from the camp informing you of their trials and tribulations which are usually not reported elsewhere; they have a wideness of vision and an internationality which is strengthening and empowering; and they are fun—they are full of hilarious, audacious incidents told with joy and humour.[20]

On one level, this showed that the community was a small one. On another, the motif of the personal address emphasized intimacy and respect as an aspiration no matter how far-flung its readership. Julia Emberley and Donna Landry, two American women who visited the camp in 1985 having read about it in the States, were disappointed by the worn down and unfriendly campers they met. Nevertheless, they praised the communications authorized by the camp for what they saw as a successful principle of dispersing power through virtual community:

> The strategy of Greenham-ness works at reversing and displacing the hierarchical relations between such concepts as "centre" and "margin." . . . In the coverage of Greenham that the women themselves have authorised, this attempt at a practical deconstruction of militarism and its relation to hierarchies of gender and power becomes explicit. The women legitimate the circulation of images of themselves in particular forms: postcards—that cheapest of forms, combining verbal *and* visual communication—books, film. The postcards reproduce richly textured, black-and-white photographs memorializing moments of protest at Greenham, especially the encircling and closing the base on 12 and 13 December 1982.
>
> (Emberley and Landry, "Coverage of Greenham," 491–92)

Perhaps the most characteristic epistolary expression of the web as virtual community was the chain letter. A low-cost way of publicizing events, it was repeatedly cited as another example of a women-centered method (Carter, *Peace Movements*, 109). The most famous and successful example was the chain letter advertising the Embrace the Base action of 12 December 1982. The following anonymous, handwritten letter leaflet was first sent to 1,000 women, who were each asked to copy and send it to ten friends:

> How we Spin and thread ourselves together as Women for this day—To make it strong + effective. . . . .

How we Spin and thread ourselves together as Women for this day — To make
it strong + effective············

You are a spring and if you copy both sides
of this letter and send them to 10 other women,
who then do the same, who then do the same, etc.
we will become rivers that will flow together on Dec. 12th
and become an ocean of women's energy. Believe it
will work and it will work.

Greenham chain letter. Reproduced from Cook and Kirk, *Greenham Women Everywhere*.

You are a spring and if you copy both sides of this letter and send them to 10 other women, who then do the same, who then do the same, etc. we will become rivers that will flow together on Dec. 12th and become an ocean of women's energy. Believe it will work and it will work.

(Cook and Kirk, *Greenham Women Everywhere*, 107)

Alice Cook and Gwyn Kirk, who reproduced the letter in *Greenham Women Everywhere* declare that the chain letter "was an inspiration for many women, giving them a chance to participate on their own terms' precisely because it was so unconventional a political appeal (105). Stephanie Lelland comments that "true to the Greenham style it was artistic, imaginative, but barely legible. . . . We sent out copies of a revised and legible chain letter to thousands of women both in the British Isles and overseas. . . . The chain letter as an idea was beautifully simple, and it worked" (Lelland, "Greenham Women," 119–20). Privately disseminated through women's friendship networks, framed personally, and encouraging personal additions, the chain letter reflected Greenham's principled anarchy, in which "gatherings at Greenham were initiated rather than organized" (Roseneil, *Disarming Patriarchy*, 101). Such initiation, by implication, was open to refusal, but if accepted, would promise a greater form of inclusion. Alice Cook describes receiving the letter thus:

I had been to the camp several times but had not taken an active part for a few months. The letter came out of the blue. . . . I didn't read so-called "impartial" information in a newspaper. This was a personal communication addressed to me, requesting things of me, making it plain that *every* woman was included, was important. Not only did I copy the letter, but I spent a long time considering who to send it to. I didn't send it to women who I thought would hear about the action anyway, nor to women who would never go to such a demonstration. I sent letters to women I thought would be interested but had not become directly involved. I felt that the spur of a personal letter might spark off enthusiasm. As it turned out, several of these women were at Greenham on 12 December.

(Cook and Kirk, *Greenham Women Everywhere*, 106)

As we saw in Agata Ruscica's letter, the 12 October chain letter refers to and represents "the web" by rewriting feminized imagery of delicate water and weak thread as strong forces that "work" by adaptation and fluidity. And like Ruscica's animated description of the thread "pushing" a "living message" in the communication from Greenham, here, too, both images unite passive and active. Women spin and flow but they are also *themselves* supposed to be thread, springs, rivers, who simply by physically uniting will be able to challenge the military. This works at the level of letter writing—or even letter xeroxing—as copying and sending the letter is syntactically represented as itself a kind of spinning and flowing in the repetition of "who then do the same," the unfinished series of elliptical points and the use of the present tense. In these ways, the conception of the letter was of a piece with that of the action itself, in which women held hands around the base and decorated the wire with mementoes, indeed sometimes letters themselves.[21] As one version of the text had it, "This is a chain letter with a difference. We'll meet as a living chain. See you at the chain-link fence!"[22]

The 12 October chain letter's imagery and syntax exemplify the web's coalescing of women's special relationship not only to the cause of peace but to one another. Sometimes this idea of this special relationship ironically stretched the notion of the letter in going beyond the need to write at all. An appeal to "beam energy to the camp" at a set time, to fill balloons with breathed wishes and float them over the base, or to "join us in our laughter, & the ripple will become a tidal wave," proposes an almost telepathic relationship between women.[23] Admittedly, this was no different from many popular uses of letters, which assume a continuity between speech and writing and disregard the medium entirely. Epistolarity has long been positioned on the border of oral and written cultures. Yet in the telepathic, we see the end point of the web's conception of a virtual, indeed, an ideal identification, even as it is paradoxically figured in writing. This was very different from the usual campaign or open letter and its specialized and abstracted literacy relationship. It was part of the concept of "Greenham Women everywhere," similar to other radical feminist calls that we have seen reflected in the personal correspondences of sisters, family and lovers: "Any woman can be a lesbian"; "All women are sisters under the skin." In this romantic idea of identity, literary and physical aspects of protest were brought together.

Part of what made Greenham's web so radical as a social movement was its internal critique of campaigning itself, protesting patriarchal valuing of public over private action. It was understood that many women would be unable to leave children, jobs, partners, that, equally, there were many other entrances to the military-industrial complex that needed vigilant webbing up, even if they were hidden at home. In principle, you didn't even have to have come to the camp to be a Greenham woman. Communications, across the spectrum of public and private letters, therefore, held together the idea of women's identity with a policy of decentering, the seeding of actions elsewhere, and the equal worth of the visible and the invisible action. As a flyer for the June 1983 Rainbow Dragon Festival advised on "Linking with women in other places": "If you don't live in Britain and cannot come (or prefer to spell it out at home)—choose a place where you are and join us in the Dragon Feast for the Future." The same leaflet advised on "WHAT MEN CAN DO TO SUPPORT" thus:

> Please show your support by respecting . . . the concept of women only space where ♀ can re-discover our long forgotton selves [*sic*]. Men + older boys can help by organising children's Fire Dragon Feasts & Creches *in local areas*— leaving mothers free to come on their own if they want to. Your financial help is also welcome. Best wishes to you all from the women at the camp . . . [24]

In one newsletter under the heading "the web is growing wider," women were urged to send "telegrams, messages of support to these amazing people," the Alderson Family, the last from a group of aboriginal landowners in Koongarra, Australia, and to the Australian government protesting Denison Mining's attempt to force them off their land to start uranium mining. The same newsletter carried a piece from Feminists Against Nuclear Energy, who were thinking of setting up a camp at Smithfield U.S. army installation in south Australia; suggestions to "refocus the campaign to your own local military installations"; and advice to "send a chain letter to women suggesting they write a sympathy letter to companies supplying military bases" and to "write to NFZ councils urging them to black these companies." And one letter from "The Women of the Orange Gate" announced that they would contribute at least half of donations they received "towards the struggles of less privileged women through-out the world."[25]

Feminist community has often been conceived of as explicitly, even ideally, physical in its more utopian forms of lesbian feminist "land" or in urban friendship networks, as much as in direct action campaigns like the women's peace movement. But technologies of communication and literary cultures have also been crucial to the functioning of protests that aim explicitly to nurture "imaginary" as well as literal community. The feminist peace protests that coalesced at the base found an important resource for making virtual community in articulating a collective identity of "Greenham woman" through personalized address and epistolary networking. As the "web" conveyed it, this identity aimed to encompass recognition of differences and the political equivalence of actions across public and private, perhaps even across physical and literary spheres. And, just as much as in physical community, it wished to take the care and responsiveness of intimate relationship into that virtual political space. The high idealism this represented is exemplary of what has been seen as postindustrial social movements' unique altruism. But if the web became powerful for the women it held together, how powerful was its weaving for the military, patriarchal, and imperialist complex it wished to disarm—and who got left out? I will turn to these difficult questions in the next chapter.

CHAPTER SEVEN

Do Webs Work?

Letters and the Clash of Communities

Dear friends,

I am deeply committed to the cause of peace and reconciliation in
 our world. I applaud every person who is willing to seek peace and
pursue it with conviction and perseverance, especially those willing to
take personal risks to live their convictions. . . . While there is a bright
and peaceful spirit that draws us together in this great cause, there exists
a dark spirit that separates us. I am grieved and hurt by the presence of
that darkness.

Perhaps there is a bit of perversity shared by all of us. Perhaps it is even
inherent in the human spirit, that we persist in our approach to gates and
boarders [*sic*] that are closed to us. Just as some of you feel drawn to the
locked gates of the Depot to make your statements for peace, so too, I feel
drawn to the perimeters of the Encampment to make my statement for
peace and reconciliation. . . .

I come, but I find my way into the peace encampment barred because
of a God given difference over which I had no choice. I am male, and I
can no more change that than the Black or Chicano can change skin
color. . . . When I approached the encampment last week I experienced
what it means to wear the label 'other.' I was excluded because I belong to
the 'other' group. No one took time to discover the person who exists
inside my 'other' body. And so I am in pain today. I see more clearly how
humanity's peaceful coexistance [*sic*] is jeopardized whenever our
perception of 'otherness' obscures our perception of the common
humanity and shared convictions which make us one.

—"Epistle to the Peace Encampment," John Wenger Berquist DeHority,
Seneca Falls

Sheer weight of local public opinion is vital and necessary to bring more and more pressure on the district councils to have these atrocious law-breaking trespassers removed. They have for far too long caused endless hardship to residents in and around the Greenham area. . . . I hope that the silent majority will support RAGE.

—Betty Warr, Ratepayers Against Greenham Encampments,
Letter to Newbury *Weekly News*

W e may accept the role of community in protest as inevitable, perhaps even essential to many feminist goals. But, more directly than other kinds of life writing, campaign letter writing asks us to judge a community's efficacy in the wider political context. In this chapter, I ask how Greenham's decentered, holistic approach appeared to the general public and to the peace movement at large: were its "letters" decipherable by them? From this perspective, we begin to see that letter writing becomes part of defensive cultural definition and boundary making as it creates virtual community, despite the very hope that there would be no end and no edge to where "Greenham" stopped and started. Louise Krasniewicz has traced a similar "clash of communities" at Greenham's sister camp at Seneca, New York, and in this chapter I spotlight her accounts of how letters were a part of this.

In the immediate term, the Greenham camp was vilified by the tabloid press because of what it viewed as the "squalid nuisance" and "filthy" lifestyles of the women, particularly as the camp grew less maternalist and more lesbian-feminist in orientation (Young, *Femininity in Dissent*, 56, 60). Led by such media smears, the mainstream peace movement became increasingly confused about how to react to Greenham, many considering that the "gender" issue had "distracted" from the peace one. The British Campaign for Nuclear Disarmament (CND) even commissioned a report in 1983 on public perceptions of the camp. It concluded "the Greenham women are burying a potentially popular cause in a tide of criticism levelled against them on personal grounds" (quoted in Young, *Femininity in Dissent*, 140), although the rank and file of CND was on the whole always more sympathetic to Greenham than the party-oriented leadership (Byrne, "Nuclear Weapons and

CND," 120). Feminist antimilitarism was even less popular among mixed movements outside the Western European–American context. Vaclav Havel, then a leading member of the Czechoslovakian Charter 77 human rights group, described in 1985 how "two appealing young Italian women" petitioning in Prague met with almost uniform disinterest from local women dissidents. He explained this in a general "open letter" to the Western peace movement, describing Central Europeans' "intense fear of exaggerating our own dignity to an unintentionally comic degree, a fear of pathos and sentimentality, of overstatement, and of what Kundera calls the lyric relation to the world." If Western peace-movement rhetoric trailed shades of hubristic utopianism for oppressed Czech dissidents, feminism was positively "dada . . . overstated, enthusiastic, lyrical, histrionic" (Havel, "The Anatomy of Reticence," 307–8).

Even feminists closer to home were divided and also used letters to say so. In 1983 Ann Pettitt, Annie Tunnicliffe, and others on the original "Walk for Life on Earth" to Greenham certainly thought that the camp had lost its political direction. Ten of them produced a revisionary chain letter as an (in the event unsuccessful) attempt to get men as well as women to attend a demonstration at Greenham, arguing that "we *must* rise above the female/male conflict" and offering advice in "dealing with confrontation with hostile women."[1] If Pettitt's arguments were couched in liberal humanist terms, other feminists had different concerns. Onlywomen Press critiqued Greenham and the women's peace movement from a radical lesbian perspective as glorifying women's traditional self-sacrifice. Their concerns were fed by petitions such as the East German "Women's Letter," sent in October 1982 to the chairman of the GDR, Erich Honecker, which protested against the conscription of women on the grounds that these "totally new obligations on women" were "a contradiction of . . . womanhood," as "we women feel we have a special duty to protect life, to support the old, the sick, and the weak" (Sandford, *The Sword and the Ploughshare*, 97–99). The fear that women were losing sight of their interests in joining the peace movement also produced at least one open letter, Sophie Laws's address to the "Dear Sisters" of Women Against the Nuclear Threat and the Women's Peace Alliance (Lesley West from the Leeds WONT group provided an open letter in reply).[2] Socialist feminists such as Lynne Segal worried about the Greenham group's essentialism, and black and working-class feminists argued that unless peace activists recognized the underlying economic and racist-imperialist issues that drove the arms race, disarmament would remain solely a white middle-class issue (Segal, *Is the Future Female?*; Brown, *Black Women*; kris, "Ain't We Wimmin Too?").

The infrastructure of the postal-delivery service also registered the evolution of rival groups at the Common. In 1987, the Wages for Housework/Kings Cross Women's Campaign assumed control over Yellow/Main Gate, where post and funds were delivered, in response to which the rest of the gates asked the post office to deliver correspondence instead to Violet and later Blue Gate.[3] Chain letters and newsletters disseminated such internal conflicts. One newsletter produced in 1986 begins, "Well, after almost a year we have finally got a newsletter together," adding, "a lot of women have been receiving a 'Greenham' chainletter which has been going around for quite some time now. We'd like to dispel the information carried by it and as far as we're concerned the facts are far from the truth."[4] After cruise missiles had arrived in November 1983 and the camp became more hardcore, response to calls for demonstrations dwindled. The call for "10 million women" to come in 1984, also advertised through a chain letter and chain "cajoling," largely fell flat: as one diarist at the camp joked, "we may not have ten million women, but we do have ten million fleas and they are breeding rapidly."[5]

It would be wrong to suggest that the dwindling of the women's peace movement's political credibility was principally the fault of the camp. The enormous turnout in 1982 and 1983 was attributable to a particular convergence of forces that captured the popular imagination—government talk of "limited nuclear war" and "civil defense"; the election of hardliners in the West and an intractable Soviet government; the Falklands war; and the nationalist element of "no cruise." And the peace movement as a whole lost its platform once the superpowers began to negotiate in the mid-1980s. However, the women's peace movement's special emphasis on personal identity and cultural change does raise particular issues about the movement's turn "inward," even as this was idealized in terms of a web that encompassed women everywhere. Was the emphasis on women's identity in protest a diversion from the nuclear campaign? Was it even a muddling of feminist aspirations to organize through a decentered and multiple "web" of issues and contacts?

Rituals of Community at the
Seneca Women's Encampment for Peace and Justice

I have suggested that the making of community in the campaign was not a by-product or diversion but a key element to its ethics. However, this could work in ways not necessarily understood by the public or, importantly, by the women themselves, and for that reason could backfire. Louise Krasniewicz's anthropological study of Greenham's sister camp, the Seneca Women's Encampment for Peace and Justice in New York, which was set up the summer of 1982, is instructive in this regard. The highly principled group at Seneca intended their demonstration to make connections between the nuclear issue and many others, prominently feminism and racism. Perhaps even more than at Greenham, this brought a cultural dimension to the protests, intended to perform long-term political change. But Krasniewicz argues that the women's use of circles, chanting, or even their choices in food, clothes, and role-playing and the dislocation of mostly urban women to a rural and isolated environment functioned as a kind of rite of passage or ritual. This involved a "separation from everyday life that leads to an evaluation of that life," taking them into a liminal state in which the rules of society were overturned, and then, usually when they went home, reintegrating them "into a new or renewed social order" (Krasniewicz, *Nuclear Summer*, 127).[6] Some of the most cherished ideals of political living at both Seneca and Greenham—of equality, spontaneity, sacredness, foolishness, simplicity, and unselfishness—were in fact classic features of liminal states: available because they are marked off from the everyday self. Moreover, they worked as rituals in part precisely because they were only semiconsciously performed.

These same aspects of liminality were incorporated into the protest actions: keening, die-ins, weavings, dressing up, the use of "women-centered" images of the circle, web, labrys, and peace signs. The effect was a powerful, even ecstatic experience of bonding for many women, visibly acted out in the physical circles used for meetings, singing, or chanting. But as the circle manifested metonymically, this involved a closing off from and even expulsion of those elements that did not agree to its terms. Krasniewicz cites a couple of letters to the camp from local women who suffered from this feeling, one from two who had gone to the camp as Christian pacifists complaining that their tastes in food and clothing had been mocked and one from a local woman very distressed to receive a form letter from the camp "office" with a blank space in which her name had been written, asking for more of her helpful coffee mornings (232). Another woman wrote with a long list of the ways she felt "betrayed" by some women's damage to the camper van she had lent the encampment.[7] John Wenger Berquist DeHority, who objected to the encampment's women-only policy, described himself as feeling as rejected as he imagined Mexican Americans must feel when prevented from taking part in the "American dream."[8]

It was not insignificant that local women found the integration of the "liminal" world of the camp and the everyday the most difficult, with so little transition between the spaces of the encampment and their own identities. As Krasniewicz points out, compared to the circle, the symbol of the web was not so obviously premised on a ritualized closure in its enshrinement of decentered action and even identity. Letters as a material aspect of the web's "imagined community" of women who did not meet or who only visited the camp occasionally were thus less likely to register such conflicts. There were, indeed, an extraordinary number who addressed diary-like accounts of their daily lives and feelings to the camp as a collective: "Oh rebel wimmin," "Mary" wrote, back in Wisconsin, "How my heart yearns for you!"[9] Betsy Aswad thanked "Kim, Pam, Aja, Margit, Coyote, Nell, et al," for the best letter she'd ever received: "I laughed out with delight. You brought it all back for me— . . . the camaraderie, the silliness, the clutter of cats, wildflowers, hammers, and vegetables."[10] Linda Field (later Wurther) wrote to "Benjamin," the camp cat, for over two years about her slow separation from her husband as she fell in love with women's community, and she was still writing to "Sisters and Cats" in 1989.[11] Schoolgirl Shell-Lee Miller also maintained a long-term pen-friendship, stoutly recounting her many skirmishes with antifeminist, racist, or homophobic classmates as well as dramas with homework, babysitting, and boyfriends.[12]

But there was one way in which letter writing very definitely did reveal the more problematic nature of the community, and, indeed, in which letters' own ritualistic dimension is revealed. This was in the letters between the camp and locals, including the military, and between locals and the regional media. As at Greenham, the women were conscientious about explaining their actions and used letters as part of a much-discussed program of outreach: "The Community Outreach Web" filed replies under "Constructive

Criticism & Concerns (Especially 'Why a Women's Encampment?')" and "Dislike Mail and Odd Letters."[13] One example was a letter was presented "*To* the Commander, Seneca Army Depot; the Secretary and Department of Defense; to the President," accompanied by a loaf of bread offered "as a symbol of solidarity" and roses (Krasniewicz, *Nuclear Summer*, 119). The letter explained the gift as "a symbol of the alternative world we are working towards where both the body and spirit are nourished rather than threatened with extermination" (131). An open letter to the townspeople was also leafleted, and letters were written to the sheriff informing him of planned protests, their rationale, and nonviolence (159). One particularly dedicated mediator, Pam Flanigan, detailed the 9,000 newsletters, talks, and videos at local universities, conferences, and other peace groups, as well as daily protest and monitoring of military activity, in a letter to one local newspaper precisely as evidence of the camp's political coherence:

> If you are only interested in "off-beat religious rites" and women's sexuality, read no further. This is a boring letter about peace work at the Women's Encampment for a Future of Peace and Justice. It is not sensationalist, titillating, or guaranteed to outrage some segments of the population. In short, it won't sell many newspapers. The Post-Standard's recent articles by Janet Gramza and resulting Editorial, claim that we at the Encampment have lost our focus. I suggest that you at the paper check your camera, or perhaps the cutting room floor. These are the pictures that didn't make it into the paper.[14]

However, Krasniewicz shows that the dialogue emblematized in this kind of outreach was not straightforwardly effective, if effective at all. For the local community and the military were *equally* bound by ritualistic and unconscious practices and ideas, which became defensively mobilized when faced with the threat of "difference within" that the women posed. Krasniewicz here suggests that the "imaginary" dimension of communities speaks not only of what holds them together internally but what defines their boundaries:

> The way to distinguish communities, Benedict Anderson asserts, is by the style in which they imagine themselves. The encampment, for example, imagined itself as a united group of women with spiritual, political, emotional, and

physical bonds built on a foundation of common womanhood. The local residents in and around Seneca County saw themselves as one cohesive, uniform group of simple, conservative, peace-and-quiet loving people living in the typical rural small town in America where dramatic occurrences are rare, people are friendly and helpful, and outsiders are rightly viewed with suspicion. The local residents confirmed this image for one another in a variety of ways, *most effectively through comments to newspaper reporters and letters to the editor.* Statements by local officials usually helped reinforce the image. One judge, presiding at a hearing for some arrested encampment women, began his session by saying, 'This whole thing has disrupted the peace and quiet of the community, and threatened the safety and welfare of the community.' . . . Even a letter that supported the Encampment confirmed that 'in our small, quiet community, unaccustomed to political protests, the demonstrators may seem like troublemakers bent on disrupting the peace of our towns.'

(83; my italics)

Letter writing, as implied here, was central to the parole between the two groups and, notwithstanding the women's attempts at "open letters," drawn into the less controlled aspects of defining community identity. Part of a narration of events taking place through many "texts," including clothes, food, flag, and gossip, letters had a particularly visible role in the local press as a classic mechanism of imagined community. Indeed, most Seneca County residents got their information about the camp solely from newspaper stories and gossip. Ironically, the development of the web's own "imagined community" of feminists was mirrored in the parallel coalescing of a reactionary idea of a patriotic, neighborly Seneca in the letters columns. Letters to the editor of the *Seneca County News* included "Don't Let Feminist Cause Overshadow Nuclear Weapons Fight" (Krasniewicz, *Nuclear Summer*, 200) and judgments of protestors as dirty, not properly dressed, pushy, or drifters trying to find a cause (204). The dramatic blockade of a protest walk by locals on Waterloo Bridge prompted a wealth of letters and calls to local and regional newspapers, in which fractures in both camps were visible: "Some letters supported the bridge blockade; others condemned the citizens of Waterloo for acting in an unacceptable and unAmerican way; all contributed to a lively discussion that continued for the rest of the summer and revealed the divisions and factions in the local communities" (220).

Letters that drew the lines between their conflicting ideas of community were also exchanged directly between locals and protestors. The most telling correspondence was that with a local businessman (who marketed evangelical Christian icons) and self-styled patriot Emerson Moran. Moran had initially "gestured" to the campers by inviting them to attend local churches and then by offering them an American flag to celebrate July Fourth. He followed his offer with a note addressed "Dear Ladies," which reminded the women that he had arranged for a press photographer to photograph the display of his flag on their porch, if accepted, and if declined, that he would likewise tell the media (Krasniewicz, *Nuclear Summer*, 120). A consensus decision by the women not to accept the flag, against some women's wishes, meant, in one woman's words, "we were stuck with having to write him a letter," which was signed by six of the encampment organizers "on behalf of everyone involved in the Seneca Women's Peace Encampment" (104). The letter began by thanking Moran for his "gracious offer" and followed with three paragraphs of reasons why the flag was an inappropriate symbol for the camp compared to "international symbols of peace and justice," even though "like many symbols, the flag means different things to different people" and that many women from the camp felt positively toward it. It ended by hoping that Moran would "accept our refusal of your donation in the spirit of American political dialogue."

The letter, addressed individually to Moran, did not appear in the press, but Moran wrote an open letter back to them that he made sure did, in which he declared the letter from the women "stares back at me from my desk" and "takes more than one reading to understand" (106). Quoting from Abraham Lincoln and the Pledge of Allegiance, he set the women's letter as evidence of their treachery to their country and hypocrisy in claiming the right to protest. A week later he followed this up with a letter to the editor of the *Finger Lakes Times*, copied to President Reagan, Governor Mario Cuomo of New York, state and federal legislators, the Seneca Army Depot, and the American Legion and VFW posts of the area. This letter asked his neighbors to display the flag everywhere as a challenge to the anticipated "carloads of demonstrators" (111). A bevy of letters to the editor followed from residents, mostly ironically thanking women for reminding them to be patriotic and agreeing with Moran that the "test" offer of the flag had revealed the women's true character. By the end of the summer, six women from the camp did write back in an "open letter to Emerson Moran" in which they put it clearly that the flag had not been "a well-intentioned gift." They concluded the letter with the question, "Next time, why don't you just send a pizza?" (116).

The convention that letters signify polite dialogue can obscure their function as part of a wider symbolic language of gift giving that involves covert tests on the loyalty of the recipient. As we saw in the open letters among feminists, the strongly educative impulse in the genre "registers an attempt both to generate and to enforce resemblance between the correspondents" (Ferguson, "Interpreting the Self," 111) that may be more powerful to the degree that it is unconscious. A broader moral of the Seneca story is that local hostility cannot be reduced to conventional political or underlying economic interests, such as the inconvenience caused by large-scale arrival of protestors or the threat of losing income derived from the military base. For it involves a level of unconscious relationship that theorists of new social movements are only beginning to acknowledge (Mueller, "Recognition Struggles"). As well as having political arguments with each other, locals and campaigners were also engaged in controlling community boundaries against internal as well as external dissent. This, of course, proves that the camp was successful in destabilizing rigid ideas about gender, sexuality, and national identity, as Krasniewicz concludes, albeit at the price of deeply disturbing most locals and making the nuclear issue secondary for the public at large. While many locals had bad memories of the summer even ten years after the event, and some men had ironically enhanced their sense of conventional masculinity in "standing up" to the women, the camp had certainly proved that there was an intimate relationship among patriarchal, nationalistic, and militaristic rituals that structure everyday American small-town life.

The powerful intensification of the normal processes of identity making that took place at Seneca was not so obvious in relation to Greenham, where the camp was distinctly more anarchist and provisional and whose membership was always more fluctuating. The American pagan priestess Starhawk's letter home about some Greenham women parodying her with a "scandalous toilet paper ritual" wonderfully contrasts the two protest cultures (Starhawk, *Truth or Dare*, 248–52). But in many ways Greenham was also a "liminal space," magic for those touched by the web but frightening and alien for those not. Women suffered verbal harassment and increasing attacks by locals and soldiers, including the daubing of feces and pigs' blood on camps, hot pokers being thrust through tents, and the arrangement of three male stripteasers to perform near Blue Gate (Roseneil, *Common Women*, 240; Belfrage, "Down Among the 'Wimmin,'" 795). The local papers were also full of angry letters from local residents, notably those belonging to "RAGE: Ratepayers Against the Greenham Encampment," who had announced themselves in the paper with a cartoon of a fat woman with boils, protruding breasts, and a crucifix earring, sitting astride a missile. The caption read "Send a Greenham Camper on a Cruise this summer" (Blackwood, *On the Perimeter*, 49, 55).[15] Open letters presented to commandants or soldiers gained frostier receptions as time passed: the presentation of one letter, along with a Japanese symbol for peace, a paper crane, on Nagasaki Day a year after the camp's establishment, provoked the removal of the women to a distant part of the base (Hopkins and Harford, *Greenham Common*, 61). Most disturbing of all were letter-bomb threats from locals (138). It is notable that mixed peace camps, such as at Faslane and the Clydeside base for Polaris submarines, prompted much less local antagonism (Carter, *Peace Movements*, 130).

The ideology of "Greenham Women Everywhere," as we have seen, also contained its tensions. Despite its principle of a centripetal web of difference, it could invert to a centrifugal concept in which identity had to be managed in a manner that could be painful for those who were judged to threaten it. One woman remembered the trauma of watching a woman being expelled from a ritual circle.[16] Another woman who had been late for the "Embrace the Base" demonstration wrote to her lover of the "raw" feeling she felt having missed being one of the 30,000 strong chain: "The majik was strong, even tho my personal pain about not being part of the circle was screaming inside me."[17] Another problematic example of the idea that women were in instinctive communication with one another is clear in a circular letter sent in October 1982 among friends inviting women to join them on Friday evenings "to 'beam their power and energy' to the women at the peace camp at Greenham."[18] The anonymous letter explained that they should be "thinking perhaps of one woman who they might have met or know there; also, at women (people) who are on the inside of the camp, trying to help them open themselves to the 'other' (i.e. our) side of the meaning of the base and peace camp." This instruction breaks off to remark that "whilst I was there recently, a huge American car drove out of the gates driven by a very smart black woman." This observation receives no comment but this itself speaks of the potential breakdown of the assumptions of women's identity that underlie the letter, combined with a fascination of both the rare sight of a black woman at Greenham and the clear evidence of her being on the other side, signified in the archetypal image of power, the American car. Whether or not it is the intention that this woman should receive the "beaming," the letter's subsequent suggestion that the "destructive energy" inside the base might burst out of its own accord confounds the sense of uncertainty about the relationship between those "inside" and "outside" the women's movement as much as the base.

One of the most moving epistolary productions to come out of the protest was Lynne Jones's "Open Letter to an Unknown Woman at the Falklands Victory March Day 1982." The letter dramatizes the failure of dialogue between mothers of soldiers and peace protestors at a parade of soldiers returning from the Falklands war. The "unknown woman" Jones addresses was a mother who had been chatting to the protestors, who were at that point incognito, sharing her profound relief that her son had survived the war, but who was "incomprehending, distressed" when the protestors hoisted a banner and turned their backs on the parade. "We share the same values, you and I," writes Jones, but the terrible gap in any understanding of this truth is obvious in the event of an open letter that will never be read by its addressee, only by other feminists and pacifists.[19]

Should We Be Writing to the Government Instead of One Another?

If anthropologists such as Krasniewicz and historians such as Anderson are right, much of what defines a community is unconscious and, in that sense, difficult to access politically. Naturally, this poses a special conundrum for communities formed in protest. Here we find a bigger context for the problems of personal relationships in the movement. Not only do individuals come into campaigns bringing needs and demands difficult to accommodate (even as they may be the reason for their politicization), but campaigns *create* new needs in the intensity of their own demands and their construction of insiders and outsiders. As I suggested in chapter 4, the movement in turn produced its own ethical dilemmas, at the same time as a new level of ethical demand in expecting women not only to seek justice together but to care for one another in doing so

I want to conclude, however, by contrasting the kinds of letters written as part of "the web" with more traditional forms of political petitioning. Any campaign will tell you that it is crucial to do this, although today e-mail and fax lobbies are usually the way in for lazier activists. We are often reassured that all incoming letters are read and filed and that "when an issue arises for legislative action, the weight and size of the folder often makes a difference" (Schneider and Lester, *Social Work Advocacy*, 252). Kate Douglas, recently celebrating the compatibility of traditional "letters to the editor" with Web site lobbying, summarizes:

> The "Amnesty International Letter Writing Guide" attests that, letter writing has greatly assisted in the freeing of political prisoners, in strengthening individuals, in stopping torture, in bearing witness, in improving prison conditions, and in demonstrating that there is a global community interested in defending human rights. The website contains testimonies in the form of direct quotes to suggest the direct political impact that letter writing has had on particular human rights campaigns.[20]
>
> (Douglas, "Witnessing on the Web," 46)

But the citizen's letter is stereotypically a comic genre. One thinks of pages of shaky handwriting in capital letters, metonymic of the unreasonable expectation that "Disgusted, of Tunbridge Wells" could actually have anything politically useful or realistic to contribute.[21] In my view, writing to uninterested representatives requires undoubted creativity as well as stamina, in the face of depressingly uncertain response. Deirdre Rhys-Thomas in 1987 published her 114 letters to largely male authorities—everyone from Dr. Spock to the local County Emergency Planning Officer in charge of providing bunkers to the pope, as *Letters for my Children: One Mother's Quest for Answers About the Nuclear Threat* (Rhys-Thomas and Owens). But however artfully she played on her disenfranchisement as an "ordinary" middle-class mum outraged at the threat to her children, we might not be surprised at disillusionment after four years of being fobbed off with contradictory and evasive replies. Rhys-Thomas found relief at Greenham—even as she wrote to her mother to reassure her that not all the women there were lesbians.

Another extremely persistent and imaginative letter lobby was that of the Hackney Greenham Women's support group, who worked with the Oxford Research Group to correspond personally with chief military personnel in Britain and abroad. Each woman "adopted" one man with the sole proviso that they had to maintain the exchange as long as possible. Karen Payne, editor of *Between Ourselves: Letters Between Mothers and Daughters*, was one of the group. She recalls that several of them were enticed into serious ethical debate, but only one or two who were already retired became supportive of the peace movement.[22]

Letter writing to public authorities, like lobbying, petitioning, electoral campaigning, and litigating, is an assimilative strategy that reflects a movement's belief that the political system is receptive (Rochon, "The West European Peace Movement," III). The imminent threat of war radically undermined this belief for many in the early 1980s. And, as a whole, the feminist movement has always been extremely ambivalent about these methods of fulfilling its more revolutionary goals, especially in Britain, where there have been comparatively few formal pressure groups (Rochon; Gelb and Palley, *Women and Public Policies*, 50).[23] Sometimes petition seems to be pointless. My own member of parliament has taken to writing wearily back to me in the form of "Dear Margaretta, I know what you think about nuclear defence . . ." Dutiful protest-letter writers like myself can only enjoy Kathy Acker's backhand letter to "President Nixon" in her 1986 novel *Don Quixote*: "Please accept my apology that my left hand isn't forming these letters correctly. I wasn't sent to Oxford or anywhere, so what I do to write is cut crosses into the insides of my wrists. I write in fever" (106–7).

The feminist stress on the inseparability of political ends and means and of the public and private touches on a general disenchantment with conventional political representation and economic goals that has found expression in many new social movements as well as the celebrated apathy of the contemporary voter. We should not then underestimate the significance of such alternative communities and the proposition that an ethics of care is relevant to the public as well as private sphere. Letter writing has played its part in expressing political shifts that extend well beyond the women's movement, constructing the imagined unity of groups when letters are published or circulated, asserting identities as well as relationships in dialogue with fantasized others. Although the times that defined the campaigns at Greenham and Seneca have gone, these aspects of the epistle are more important than ever in the age of electronic communication and globalization.

PART THREE

The Right to Be Cared For:
Letters and the Life Cycle of a Social
Movement

CHAPTER EIGHT

Care Versus Autonomy

The Problem of (Loving) Men

Dear Man,
I am writing to let you know
that I'm a woman, now
to remind you of the scars you gave
me, left me
to remind you of the nights I cried
to remind you that I was not your bride
to remind you that I was a total stranger
to remind you that my mother was your wife
to tell you that I'm taking you to court
to tell you that the charge is
RAPE . . .

— "An Open Letter," Patricia Hilaire

The story of the women's peace protests demonstrates the feminist commitment to fulfilling individual needs along the way to political solutions. It also reveals the less obvious fact that communities of protest create their own needs. Being in the movement awakened primitive desires to belong and fear of being excluded from the tribe. From that point of view, we can see how the care extended by the community depended more than its theorists would have wished upon markers of membership, of feminist kin. Letter writing helped to maintain this kinship virtually, even as its physical signs comprised diet, clothing, and language, as well as the rituals of circles and labryses, webs and benders. Letters, however, also registered its borders when addressed to the newspaper, government, local townspeople, other social protest groups, and even dissidents within. In the case of Greenham and Seneca, "kin" was most fundamentally defined by gender, the group "women" (womyn, wombin, wimmin), although it was a peace protest that had initially included men and whose honoring of difference within was literally expressed in Blue Gate's working-class lesbians, Orange Gate's middle-class internationalists, Yellow Gate's multiracial Trotskyists, Green Gate's ecofeminists, and the like. Other "letter-webs" from this period, which have yet to be traced in depth, trace the solidarity of black lesbians or disabled women, the diasporic ties of Eastern European dissidents, and the supporters of the Sandinista struggle in Nicaragua.

At times these virtual communities amplify ethical relationships of care, offering personal responses to others' needs and rights over and above a general assumption of equality. At other times, we see that letters in fact evade the real demands of such ethics, abstracted from physical confrontations or needs and often prompted by the wish to conceal or soften conflict. The missives to and from "Greenham women everywhere" or the changing staff in the wooden-porched "office" in the Seneca Women's Encampment for Peace and Justice, which I read avidly in feminist archives large and small, were undoubtedly passionate because the community was so strongly "imagined," and thus, in part, imaginary. In Krasniewicz's terms, it was liminal: magical because it felt like a holiday from ordinary life.[1]

More problematically still, letters can express enhancing demands, perhaps taking advantage of distance to do so, without necessarily enhancing response. The aerogramme from Samoa to "all ♀♀♀ at the Δ," disputing the claim she was asking too much reimbursement for her fundraising tour, for example, probably did receive a reply from the harassed "office workers" at Seneca.[2] The workers also replied to Phyllis Sawyer, who wrote to say how wrong it was that her peacenik adolescent son was not allowed to visit her at the encampment.[3] But what about the women who expected that their mental-health conditions be supported by the community? What about, indeed, the needs of the townspeople and the military employees? As in the letters between mothers and daughters, we begin to see specters of unconscious as well as conscious demands that pose wide-ranging questions about a culture that acknowledges, even encourages, their expression.

In this chapter I want to build upon the insights that Krasniewicz has offered about the unconscious dynamics of community making both in the Seneca Women's Encampment for Peace and Justice and in the local town of Romulus, which marshaled itself against the protestors. I will attempt to confront the ironic ways in which this seemed to prize care on condition that it was restricted to those in the "web." In doing so, I will also turn to the question of men in relation to the feminist relationship, as the most obvious boundary of feminist community. How are men represented—or not—in the kinds of correspondences I have been arguing were central to feminism at this time? Four letter-stories, the first one my own, will trace the difficult relationship between care and autonomy that underlies the question of feminist community.

Trying Not to Care

I remember quite clearly my decision in 1986 not to have any further serious interactions with men. I did not include my father or two brothers, and, to be fair, I had never had any male friends to speak of. My only boyfriend to date had been an ethereal Marxist two years earlier, who left me after six weeks for an anarchist feminist. I was twenty, finishing university. It was a sunny day, and I was wheeling my bicycle across the site of the English faculty, and I saw a friend of the Marxist whom I had half-heartedly been trying to gather courage to flirt with. My mind was full of images from Marleen Gorris's film about a serial killer, *Broken Mirrors*, recently screened by a visiting speaker from the English Collective of Prostitutes: women's bruises, women chained in cellars, women's sexual annihilation. No, I would not talk to Martin.

The charismatic, slightly bored, and angry ECP speaker, however, had shown the film as an example of all that was wrong with the moralistic "victim" politics of some radical feminism at the time; her point was that sex work was work and should be treated as such. My feeling was that neither stand was right. Or, as I put it in my diary then, "Though I fervently agreed with their analysis and perspective (as far as I can emotionally accept Wages for Housework principles), I have also been influenced to commit myself to separatism. It's very odd and ironic how these two decisions have happened inside me at the same time." The bleak dystopia of men existing for the delight of torturing women could not be right as a paradigm. Yet the hardline, bullying materialism of Wages for Housework did not seem to allow for the joy and conviction of women's alliance. I had been in a young feminists group at school; I had decided I was bisexual (or rather, "romantically open to the universe") when I was about sixteen and I fell in love with a girl

Dearest M,
                25·xi·87

          Many thanks for the letter. The photo's class (have
you any idea how rare photos of me smiling are? It'll
be a collector's item some day.)
          Where do you meet these people? They
just suddenly appear in your letters: A___, C___,
M___ (I didn't know Isanna had a lover at the
moment). And how had M___ heard of F_____? Is
she Irish? Or is she a damned-and-may-they-rot-in-hell
cretinous Troops Outer? (no offence) Or is she actually
interested in Ireland? (Difficult to believe. 98% of
the population of England think Ireland IS NOT a Political
issue. Most of my English friends among them.) I'd like
to be back in C'bridge for a few days — maybe in
February or so — to catch up on people, see you +
A + J___ + maybe get a look at these various
odd new people who have appeared.
          Separation: I'm afraid I'm turning
into a reformist in my old age. Seeing politics and politics
in action leaves me with a strong, if rather depressed,
belief, in changing the world by the slow, eroding
process of committees + reports + the changing of
people's attitudes + the keeping open of the channels
of information + cooperation + the enabling
of people. Of fragments becoming a whole, of
participating in as many things as possible.
I cannot see a deprived area of Belfast
simply as an area where women are exploited.

Letter from a friend of the author, 1987.

at summer school, and then my sister's best friend age seventeen. At that
time I had also gone to Greenham with my local CND chapter, a mixed
bunch of older beards and worthy types from my white, middle-class town
in the southeast of England. On alighting from the coach, I was in a different world: seeing women living outdoors, so roughly, so independently, so
butch. Tingling sexual feelings told me I had a potential. For me, feminism
was about what was right with women, not what was wrong.

   So began for me ten years in which I withdrew from men and loved
women, including two five-year relationships. But I could never resolve the

10:00 am

Dearest S____,   May 4th '88

I got your letter yesterday and it was just what I needed; apart from your intriguing social encounters, I was very interested in what you said about being Irish, and Irish in England. I could say that the gist of what you said isn't unfamiliar to me, but I was thinking about how still it shocks me to read how England's cultural imperialism is such a ~~real about~~ real experience for you - because of course I don't feel it at all, it is like the air (warm air) that surrounds me. Ireland still seems a very faraway place to me, the questions you have to negotiate everyday, like for finding a nice Irish speaker who he could imagine settling down with, (maybe not a good example?) ~~they~~ seem to belong to another world. Very often I remember what you said in your letter about separatism, that separation is a luxury that precious few can afford.

When I read your letter yesterday my heart stony and my head smarting still, with the crazy thoughts that I have been having about A____ these past few days, it seemed like an embrace back into ~~the~~ our difficult whole. A____ ~~matter~~ fills my mind and heart and lead me more ~~and those~~ into the ~~way~~ life of women, which, without wanting to sound trite, is a mysterious world surviving somehow intact in the larger official one _ Every nuance of emotion and soft subdued curve of cheek, it is like walking through a storm of feathers. Men seem less and less interesting everyday

Letter from the author to her friend, 1988.

conflict within myself about how inhumane and uncaring I felt I was toward men. I believed it to be ethically necessary to act so in order to care sufficiently for women, which meant being truly autonomous myself. Although I have reams of diary pages on my growing excitements and conflicts about being "a lesbian," "femme," about the Cambridge Women's

Resources Centre politics and my M.A. in women's studies, about my motorbike-riding girlfriend and her fiercely judgmental working-class politics, the letters from my own life that express this culture are diffuse. First, there are my exchanges with "I," the anarchist feminist whom my Marxist boyfriend adored and who subsequently encouraged me to come out. I have effusive letters to my sister's friend and Wages for Housework convert. I have, above all, five years of correspondence in broken French with my Belgian welder girlfriend, whom I saw every few weeks when one of us would come over on the Eurostar. That was a romantic passion to end them all. Our letters remained loving veils as our conversations in person silted up, and eventually I came face to face with the need to let men back into my life in the only way I really could, romantically. Needs that could not be denied; needs that the letters do not express.

Caring for and fiercely about women, as I understood and felt it in the movement at the time, was a crucial step to gaining autonomy *as* a woman. Yet it concealed two paradoxes. Confusingly, it produced new dependencies as I increasingly sought the approval of the lesbian and feminist communities in which I moved. Secondly, as care for some increased, care for others diminished. In my case, and the case of a protest like Greenham's, this was precisely along gendered lines, although, as at Seneca, race, sexuality, class, age, disability, and nation tested and produced other lines where care began and ended.

Two more "letter-stories" from the British women's peace movement of the early 1980s demonstrate these twists more eloquently than my own. The first is fictional, and yet, as a centerpiece of the one novel that came out of Greenham, it encapsulates some of its ideologies. *Mud*, by Nicky Edwards, who herself lived there through 1983, concerns a somewhat jaded former peace camper named Jo, who is writing a play about First World War soldiers in order to understand "men's motives" for going to war. Befriending a First World War widow, Ada, Jo gets to read Ada's letters from her husband John from the front in 1916. But far from discovering his struggle or pain as a soldier, she learns instead of his misguided complicity in being a good husband:

> I saw what Ada meant about him not telling her anything. The longer he was out, the less informative his letters were. After a year, they were almost

straight formula notes, with very little of himself coming through, as if he was in another world from which he could not make the mental effort to drag himself back and would not drag her into. He thought he was trying to protect her from distress, but it seemed all of a piece with him not being able to bear hearing a bird singing in the one blasted tree left standing in their hundred square yards of nothingness. No part of him could be spared for another life. So he talked about the weather and grumbled about the food and kept the woman he used to talk to 'not like most blokes would' at arms' length, for fear that she would make him realise that not all the world was a muddy ditch in the middle of a war. . . . I felt angry for her sake, as I put the last of the say-nothing, don't-risk-a-feeling letters down. What a real man. How bloody British. 'There, there, dear, don't you worry about me. I'm fine.' Of course he wasn't. Making endurance possible, by putting whatever unmanly feelings made him able to talk to her aside for the duration. Making killing possible.

(Edwards, *Mud*, 54–55)

Here military censorship is overdetermined by the everyday self-censorship of British masculinity in the misguided name of "protecting" women. The duplicity of letter writing, especially in war, convinces Jo that the only serious way to stop the appalling scene of war is not to get men to talk but to listen to the women who ambivalently supported them.

But Edwards's novel is equally symptomatic of the new kind of communicative difficulties that arose from feminist antimilitarist protest. For while *Mud* protests the separation of men from women in war, there is an ironic parallel between life in the trenches and life at the peace camp, where the intense, dangerous, and primitive conditions as well as the women-only community counter the desire to communicate to those "outside." Although Edwards's protagonist criticizes the First World War soldier John's inane letters home to his wife, she, too, finds that she is unable to write a word about her experiences when she is at Greenham—even to her woman lover, with whom she eventually breaks up. Life at the all-women camp is so dramatic, immediate, all-encompassing that there is an almost traumatic adjustment period on return to what feels like a "civilian" life of heteronormativity. Indeed, Edwards conveys no confidence in communication between men and women for the immediate future. While she champions the need for men to stop censoring their feelings and for heterosexual couples to break down their barriers, the narrator herself prefers to be separatist. She tries to explain to herself as much as to the baffled and critical outsiders that her going to Greenham was about "finding a real women's space for the first time, after years of polite feminism, always prey to co-option in the let's-not-be-too-threatening-here world of giving them credit, they are trying, the poor lambs, mixed politics. Not having to compromise. . . . Women treat each other as important. No time to lose" (112–13).

Sasha Roseneil's sociological study of Greenham shows that the decision for the camp to be women-only and the ensuing flowering of lesbian relationships there were crucial to its magic for the protestors and arguably for the camp's political efficacy, too, at least in terms of its feminist aims. As she put it:

> Greenham was an arena in which [the hegemonic construction of] 'woman' was deconstructed and rejected, and alternative notions of 'woman' were formed. The woman of Greenham was different in many respects from the woman of patriarchal creation. She was a woman who transgressed boundaries between the private and public spheres, she made her home in public, in the full glare of the world's media, under the surveillance of the state. She put herself and other women first, acting according to her conscience, taking responsibility for her own actions. She dressed according to a different aesthetic, in warm, comfortable clothing, removing many of the markers of femininity, but often adorning her body in ways which celebrated her independence of fashion. She was confident and assertive in the face of authority, rejecting its power to control her behaviour, testing it and taunting it. She developed close friendships and often sexual relationships with other women. This woman was stepping outside many of the restrictions of patriarchy.
>
> (*Disarming Patriarchy*, 156)

The gauge for such a transformation was precisely that it was women who came as mothers protesting on behalf of children rather than for explicitly feminist reasons who underwent the greatest politicization toward feminism and personal change (157). In her interviews with thirty-five protestors, Roseneil showed that more than half who had identified as heterosexual when they first went to Greenham became sexually involved with women (158).

My second story belongs to one of these women, Carole Harwood. Harwood first went to the women's peace camp at Greenham in 1982, and she was imprisoned for dancing on the nuclear missile silos at Greenham Common Airforce Base in 1983. By that time, she and her husband had been together for six years, having met as mature students doing a history degree in Wales.[4] Carole's letters to her husband during the two weeks she was in Holloway prison and his much longer missives back to her reverse the traditions of domestic letter writing as the extension of a waiting wife's role as well as the gender paradigms of men leaving home for war. His are filled with comical stories of cooking, looking after the kids, and commitment to both feminism and the peace protest, often touchingly illustrated with cartoons of the two of them and of Carole and "her sisters." Carole's alternate between jokes and earnest philosophizing, written to him but also to her three children, whom he was looking after, and to her other male lover, with whom her husband was good friends.

Carole and her husband were children of the 1970s, liberal, nonmonogamous, and together involved in other political causes, like the antiapartheid movement. Yet it did not wholly surprise me to find, in the archive of her papers and Greenham memorabilia, another cache of letters from her new lover, a woman she had met at the protest. They were the pattern of the romantic letters I have described in the first part of this book: at once frothily seductive and utterly excited about the idea of the writing itself as an existential leap into a new women's reality. Once again, lesbianism seems less a symptom or a cause than a historical and necessary passion. In interview with Roseneil, Carole celebrated Greenham's importance in these terms:

> One of the things that I feel personally is that it brought the possibility of a lesbian lifestyle to the surface for women . . . from all backgrounds. It's put 'lesbian' back into the vocabulary. They might have been burly, and they might have been muddy, and they might have been grubby, but . . . people didn't say they're a gang of well-meaning housewives. They said that they're a gang of dykes, and on balance they were right. I think that's been very important. And the idea that women can take control of their own lives, and take control of other people's lives, and can say to politicians, we're not going to have this sort of shit.
>
> (Roseneil, *Common Women*, 316–17)

For many women at Greenham such changes were threatening to male husbands and partners (Roseneil, *Disarming Patriarchy*, 150–51). Carole's decision to incorporate a lesbian relationship into an already nonmonogamous household and to balance mothering with the needs of two lovers was perhaps unusual. But her letters to her husband and children from Holloway prison were cheerily conventional, worrying about whether he was surviving domestically, about their exam results, and what the news coverage of the protest was. When Carole again leaves the family in November 1983 as one of five British women who took the United States government to court as a last-ditch strategy to prevent the deployment of cruise missiles, her journal is filled with passionate identification with Greenham's politics and her worry about leaving her children, leaving little clue as to the complex sexual relationships that sustained her.[5] And while her husband continued to write morale-boosting letters to his "superwoman," they said nothing of his own transgressions and difficulties at home. In these circumstances, the letters of peace campaigners are ironically like those of military couples, conditioned by their need to preserve relationships and for that same reason both reassuring and deceptive. It seemed, and, to an extent, *was* genuinely physically dangerous to protest at Greenham. But, as in Ada and John's different war experiences, correspondence had to contain another worry, in Carole's new relationship and its political implications.

I want now to tell a still more precise tale of how letters expressed the separatist logic of the era, in which feminist goals seemed to require an uncompromising wall between the women's "community" and those who might undermine it. We will also see in it the same loggerhead confrontation between feminist values of autonomy and of care. This story the writer told me herself, sitting in her kitchen a few years ago, in response to my question, "What was the most memorable letter she had ever written or received?"

The Last Letter to a Man

S had been pen-friends with Graham while working as an au pair on leaving school. When they first met in person, they looked at each other and felt like soul mates. She was studying languages; he taking an art degree. It was the early 1970s. She was a wild Quaker and loudmouth; he a quiet, more inward-looking person. Without telephones, and being young, they wrote to each other a lot. S told me that at that time, "A lot of [our correspondence was] just philosophising about art and books and god knows what. . . . *None* of it romantic. Although it's there between the lines. . . . It's a bit like writing a bloody sonnet. Just get it on the one page."[6]

Then S wrote to tell Graham she had become lovers with a woman. He "was fine about it," perhaps since he himself was getting involved with men. However, the new girlfriend was not a simple discovery of sexual preference, but part of S's growing feminist politics. She explained in a letter to her new lover:

> After leaving [university] I still was very involved with Graham, but felt that had to go because being with you made me see that a whole new reality lay ahead for me, if I wanted to take it—& so I knew that ♀♀ were where it was at and that *you* were the ♀ I knew and wanted to know, and to know more of.

She explained her politics clearly too, in a "coming-out letter" to her parents: "Don't ask yourselves where you went wrong bringing me up. That's not what makes women love other women instead of men. Women are just more accessibly loveable right now because they're learning to believe in themselves. To hide this from you would be to deny myself." S got more involved in the women's scene. "An Open Letter To The × Women's Centre," which she wrote under that title in 1977, shows her position evolving:

> My former 'political education' was of a basically anarchist nature, and I had lived out ideas of collective childcare, had helped run a bookshop collective and a collective press. There was very little theory involved, but these precepts had undoubtedly made a profound impression on me, because they were lived out in practice. Here I was in a lesbian feminist group—and I suddenly wonder if I am a feminist after all? What is a feminist? I found, on reflection, that I think feminism is a cross between anarchist politics and sexual politics (that was the bit we women amongst the anarchists were always harping on . . .), with the emphasis on women's self-definition, on women working towards autonomy, I suppose. The conclusion I came to was that I had spent the last four years pretending I was bisexual, never quite able to come to terms with

my feelings for women (because at the time I couldn't bring myself to trust them?) and deluding myself that I was getting the best of both worlds. Having opened my eyes at last to this aspect of myself, I began to take a look around me, at the people I was spending my time with and especially at the Centre, as the focal point of the WLM in ×. And what did I see? . . . There were undercurrents of resentment towards the lesbian women, which were nevertheless not openly expressed. I suddenly saw the complete inappropriateness of men being allowed into the Centre.

It was in this context that S moved to a remote farm to be in a women-only community. She wrote to her sister to tell her where she was but requested that her parents, particularly her father, whom she had felt abused by as a child, was not to know her address. There remained one "awful task," to write to Graham, with whom she was still good friends. This she described as one of the hardest letters she had ever written in her life, and it was so painful for her at the time that she did not feel able to show me the text itself. The gist of the letter was she had to be "in a total man-free zone." She said she knew he really loved her, that he would "just respect this," and that "I shall *know* that by you not responding to this letter." He did not reply.

Marilyn Frye as early as 1970 distinguished separatism from assimilation by saying they bear the same difference in degree as that between revolution and reform. "The theme of separation . . . is there in everything from divorce to exclusive lesbian separatist communities, from shelter for battered women to witch covens, from women's studies programs to women's bars, from expansions of day-care to abortion on demand" ("Some Reflections," 62). But she also asked "what is it about separation, in any or all of its many forms and degrees, that makes it so basic and so sinister, so exciting and so repellent?" (63). It is surely precisely its plain announcement that one neither needs nor cares for the other against whom one has so long been defined. In the case of nationalist separatists, fighting usually ensues; small but passionately driven troops take on the vastly superior forces of the dominant state. In the women's movement, independence was declared through a parallel, if physically peaceful, guerrilla action.

The cultural revolution involved in "the primacy of women relating to women"—as the Redstockings Manifesto had laid it out (Redstockings 21)—was a gambit premised on the same logic that characterizes ethnic or nationalist separatists seeking indigenous distinctions or workers who cultivate class-consciousness in order to overturn class hierarchies. The revolution will eventually "end the imposition of all coercive identifications" (21). But in the meantime, as many have observed of separatist cultures in the 1980s, the preservation of cultural purity within an imagined community overtook the goals of wider social transformation (Martindale and Saunders, "Realising Love"). The lesbian ethics elaborated by Sarah Lucia Hoagland, its best known exponent, is about identity rather than goodness, pursuing the interests of (already self-defined) lesbians rather than exploring a lesbian perspective on moral dilemmas that are the most acute when they cross community boundaries (Hoagland, *Lesbian Ethics*; Martindale and Saunders, "Realising Love"). Note, however, that the pursuit of autonomy so enshrined in lesbian ethics and feminism itself is always accompanied by the quieter assumption that *among women*, or lesbians, or whoever is in the community, care will equally prevail. Though lesbian ethicists have distinguished themselves from the heterosexualized scenarios of "care" ethics (Card, *Lesbian Choices*, 77), all these communities share a vision of personalized community and "to each according to her need" against an idea of abstracted "masculinist" individualism. Indeed, the very heart of lesbian ethics proposes that erotic love between women will nurture goodness between them, and vice versa.

Autonomy for women, then, as I have argued throughout, is often implicitly accompanied by the assumption that women should put their care for one another before any heterosexual desire for men. The common formulation of "prioritizing" women could thus involve its inverse, ceasing to care not just what men thought, but about them at all. Yet S, like myself, later seemed unsure about this formula. Was this because withholding care, even when you are oppressed, fundamentally contradicts the ethics that I argue lay at the heart of much of the movement's process? How did separatism square with the ideal of prioritizing the *individual*, respecting her own autonomy, let alone responding to her needs? S's "last letter" to Graham, she told me,

> led to us being out of contact for 8 long eventful years, . . . & it took many more years to right the wrong that I did to him through sending this letter. It is one of only 2 things in my life I truly regret—not the writing/sending of it, but the hurt it caused; the other thing I regret is burning all the letters from the 5-year relationship we had together.

We might almost say that there are two letters in this envelope: the ideal one, which expressed autonomy, and the real one, which rejected and hurt Graham; one that expressed her need for separation, the other that recognized that this need could not answer his, nor indeed to her own wish to care for him.

It is perhaps no accident that Graham was brought back into S's life in 1985 with an urgent appeal for care, ironically again arriving by post. S remembers picking a letter up "out of the letter box at the end of the lane" outside the farm, in which she discovered that Graham's brother had died:

> And I just went straight back to the house, sat down, wrote a letter to him, put it in an envelope, and walked all the way back up to the postbox and that was it. Just by return. It wasn't from him. A friend, another mutual friend, the one [through whom] I first met him, that I've known since I was a child—he wrote to me and said that Paul had . . . killed himself. Paul had already had an accident. An accident! Had jumped out of a third floor window on a trip some years previous. And was paraplegic. . . . *I'm* impulsive and wild, but Paul was worse. . . . And so, I got in touch with Graham immediately but I also wrote immediately to his mother. . . . So I'd kept up this correspondence with his mother. Well, when I met Graham again, he was very cool, very civil, very proper, and everything was fine.

And so she began corresponding with Graham again:

> [Graham] wrote me a letter . . . and he said, 'it was very nice to see you but the only way forward is forward. I don't want to rake over all this stuff. I don't want to talk about it.' So I thought, 'well, this isn't really for me to call the shots here, is it?' . . . Because he said, well I still feel like we've got a lot to offer each other, if that's what you want. So I thought, well, yeah, he's very wise. He's right. This is amazing that he's been this generous. So we would see each other and postcards flew backwards and forwards.

Regrets, confessions, and letters followed, yet S's commitment to women remained:

> I said, 'look I *really* want you to know how bad I felt about burning the letters and I want you to know how bad I felt about writing you that [goodbye

letter]—well, not so much writing it as sending it. I *know* that I caused you untold grief. And that I *value* beyond anything I can ever put into words the fact that you respected my request.' And I said, 'I don't know how I'm *ever* going to make any of this up to you.' Because, if he'd decided that he never wants to speak to me again for the rest of his life, that would have been my bloody karma coming home to roost and I would have had to accept it! . . . But he said, 'well one of things that's really pissed me off about this is not so much that you weren't there when Paul died, I could have got in touch with you but I didn't.' He said, 'what *really* pissed me off when Paul died was that *you* got all *matey* with my mum and started writing letters to each other.' So I said, 'well, that's what my woman-identified sexual politics is about. I'd written a letter to him saying I'm really sorry about Paul and I'm sorry I wasn't there for you'—[and he] didn't respond to that letter. That was his choice. I wrote to his mother: she *immediately* responded. And I responded in kind.

Sixteen years after she and Graham resumed corresponding, S cherishes what she has of their letters:

I created this document that's got photos of us in it and all these quotes [from letters] and it's like a chronology of how the relationship was between us, up until 1985 when we started seeing each other again and became friends again. And I made two copies of it and I sent one to him, 'cause I thought, 'this is how it was and I want you to know'. But it *was* a bit of an audacious document, really, because it was like me saying 'look, I want to *celebrate* the fact that we'd *survived* 28 years of *every* vicissitude that you could chuck at two people'. Including you know, totally divergent sexual identities, death, loss, babies and—everything! You could put up a bloody monument to that. Privately.

Conclusion

The ideology of men and women's complementarity has been enshrined in published correspondences, epistolary novels, and dramas. War correspondence is its archetype; letters, e-mails, and text messages home from military personnel to wives and families in recent wars in Bosnia or

Iraq, for example, still celebrate patriarchal as well as patriotic ideas of a gendered division of labor between home and front, notwithstanding the increasing presence of women in combat.[7] Men, it goes without saying, have made their bargains with patriarchal systems, and there are certainly enough epistolary literatures of their own that say so, from Saul Bellow's 1964 jilted writer *Herzog*, to J. Robert Lennon's 2003 paranoid, sexually repressed *Mailman*, poet Robert Duncan's tirades to Denise Levertov, and David Grossman's neurotically amorous bookseller in *Be My Knife*. There are few self-declared letters by men interested in feminist ideas, though we might count among them Joan Nestle and John Preston's *Sister and Brother: Lesbians and Gay Men Write About Their Lives Together*, Chris Hassett and Tom Owen-Toole's irritating *Friendship Chronicles: Letters Between a Gay and a Straight Man*, and, more recently, the letters on the feminist.com Web site posted by "men supporting the women's movement."[8]

I do suspect that in the attics of activist men, as well as women, we might find epistolary records of men's engagement with feminism, supporting women's opportunities and rethinking their own masculinity. However, my interest in this chapter, as in this book, has been to follow the story of women's love affair with one another through to the separatism that, for a significant minority, logically concluded it at that time. The "letter-stories" I have narrated here, like my own, equate women's sense of autonomy with cutting off feelings for those designated "men," in addition to campaigns to give women economic independence or political rights. Of course, many never identified with this step, or refused to take it, perhaps those more avowedly or comfortably heterosexual. Gender separatism also became an axis of disagreements among women who wished and needed to retain solidarity with men, particularly those who shared other oppressions. As Michele Wallace puts it "the difficulty of black feminist movement [is] that we black women had neither the will nor the means to risk standing together against black men on any issue" ("To Hell and Back," 438). Those who felt unable to privilege one identity were the first to find any essentialism problematic. Yet many "bisexuals" like myself did their best to commit to care for women "first," for what seemed to be, and sometimes was, a political necessity. For me, my very uneasiness about the divisions this established made me even more polemical, since I knew it required sacrifice to maintain. In this I was a child of my time, as well as my class, my race, my Protestant heritage, and my education. In the early 1980s, separatisms were being repeated in all of the expressions of difference, producing the ubiquitous "open letter" to sisters who were felt to have disappointed, discussed in chapter 3.

Although I have focused this chapter upon the question of men, it is just one example of the underlying trade-off between autonomy and care. If autonomy required separation, feminists tended to present this as quite different from the individualism of masculine culture. Instead, the maternal, the emotional, the romantic, the erotic were prized in relation to those designated "kin" but suppressed, repressed for those not. We might say that for gender separatists, women got the higher ethical treatment of care, men the barer law of justice. Yet, as I discovered, this could bring an unhappy conscience and, ironically, the repression of caring and loving instincts. This always felt at least as wrong, to me, as the sacrifice of potential political allies in men who supported feminism or who shared other political struggles. When the "community" then apparently failed to provide, the confusion was often deeply painful.

CHAPTER NINE

The Paradox of Care as a Right

This is not a need to confess, rather a desire for recognition.

—Susan Abbott, letter to her mother, Miriam, 1979

Letters uncover much of the spirit of feminist relationship in its early phases—its ecstatic, transformative qualities, as well as its determination and principle. Letter writing was part of an imagined women's culture, "the feminist counter-public sphere," as Rita Felski has named it, as well as a practical element in the construction of a network (*Beyond Feminist Aesthetics*, 166–67). I have suggested that this culture included the identification with *letter writing as a practice*. Being a "letter writer" did not usually go so far as to become an identity in itself: only "S" really presented herself to me in that way, and I consider that this is what distinguishes her in literary terms. However, many suggested that writing love letters to other women was one of the rituals involved in being in "the scene" in the way one woman told me "when I realised that I was a lesbian through my contact with wonderful women in the movement, I started some letter writing with lovers and ex-lovers which [was] more passionate than any previous letters to and from men."[1] This went along with reading literatures that metaphorically, and sometimes literally, constructed a world of women writing personally, seductively, exclusively to other women. The publication and consumption of edited letters was another aspect of the ritual, though a more elite one perhaps. Letters were "women's forms," like diaries, though not necessarily feminine in the way of literary stereotype, nor symbolic of women's unity. Alice Walker's image of the forgotten creativity of earlier African American women as "a sealed letter they could not plainly read" (*In Search*, 240) is resonant of the very real histories of the poor, working, and racially oppressed that the everyday letter could record, and the distinction between white and black feminisms. Mary Helen Washington remarked in 1987 that "educated daughters" in the black women's movement needed to open this letter, "to have their mothers' signatures made clear in their work, to preserve their language, their memories, their myths." Yet this invitation to come out is also a going in, a deciphering that loving readers are simultaneously recoding. Washington warned: "Before these signatures can be read clearly, we will have to free the mother from the domination of the daughter, representing her more honestly as a separate, individuated being whose daughters cannot even begin to imagine the mysteries of her life" (quoted in Ruddick, *Maternal Thinking*, 39). This command to respect the mystery of the other might also be read as the creation of a new mystery in the rituals of black feminism.

Yet rituals forcibly exclude as well as include, as women of color themselves so clearly observed of white women's groups (Omolade, "Sisterhood"; Geok-Lin Lim, "'Ain't I a Feminist?'"). Letters preserve communities and their myths as much as they create dialogue with those outside. At the same time, they record internal struggles and the repression of dissent, although often covertly. Within the feminist epistolary culture of care, in particular, we are constantly confronted by demands and the difficulty of meeting them, by romance and burnout. The letters tell us of the pressures to conform in a movement so committed to making the means match the ends. And, toward those designated outside of its culture, the political aim of autonomy becomes the justification for ceasing to care at all.

The pattern I am summarizing here bears some relation to the well-documented "tyranny of structurelessness" in activist groups, in which anti-authoritarian ideals became the cover for internal power struggles. Jo Freeman famously formulated this as early as 1970 after her experience of being "trashed" for displaying leadership qualities in the Chicago women's liberation movement (Freeman, "The Tyranny of Structurelessness"). Freeman's other bitter reminiscence of her downfall is sadly characteristic of the thirty-two passionate but often pungent accounts by movement pioneers recorded in *The Feminist Memoir Project* of 1998 (Freeman, "On the Origins of the Women's Liberation Movement from a Strictly Personal Perspective").[2] Letters add to the emotional record of the more-celebrated life-writing forms of movement testimony, autobiography, coming-out stories, and diaries. They take us once again to the puzzle of utopian communities and especially the new social movements that are committed to their creation as an engine of social change. They also point to the history of what happened next. As the grassroots turned professional, the ideologies of queer, postcolonial, hybridity, and transnationalism inevitably displaced the culture of pure identity with promises of more tolerance, inclusiveness, political subtlety, and hope, just as lesbian feminism and cultural feminism had previously revealed the superficiality of 1960s sexual libertarianism and equal rights. The relationship history of feminism told through letters reflects the archetypal dialectic of identity making and its dissolution in political campaigns.

But I do not want to talk about this evolution in the familiar terms of moving beyond "identity politics." For it seems to me that letters are special for what they show us of relationships, whether individual or communal. What are we to conclude about the "relational self" of feminist ideals? Did the internal maintenance of a world of "love and ritual" undermine the political aims of the movement? Such are the inevitable thoughts that arise in a cultural study of political texts. In this chapter I will return, then, to what feminist philosophers have said of care when conflicts arise. I next consider some feminist theories of citizenship in this light. I conclude with a brief foray into some third-wave letter writings, to see how feminist community is evolving.

Me or You First? Care, Autonomy, and Feminist Citizenship

An ethics of care asks us to accept that some people get more because they need more, because of an unequal context, or even simply because it avoids violence. This is morally more ambitious than simply giving everyone equal dues. Andrea Maihofer formulates it this way: an ethics of care insists on "the possibility of different normative 'truths' and the corresponding recognition of different moralities, while the traditional conception of justice allows only for one truth or rightness" (Maihofer, "Care," 388). Virginia Held similarly argues that the discourse of "rights" as the yardstick for ethical judgment is rigidly inflexible because "rights necessarily lead to dichotomous determinations that there is or is not a given right and that it has or has not been violated" (Held, Rights," 506). By contrast, feminists have posited personal response to need as more suitable for dealing with many moral dilemmas than the traditional "blind" justice of legal arbitration. Yet what do we do when people's needs compete? When they overwhelm?

The actual challenge of living with difference, with inequality of need, has been obvious from the literature of the movement itself. But this literature has also provided a solution, which lies in the proviso that one must also care for oneself. This is the nub of the matter for feminists wishing to reclaim "female" or "feminine" values without merely re-entrenching self-sacrifice or pretending that women are either all equal, all the same, or all good. Carol Gilligan's founding text, *In A Different Voice*, claimed that care for the self was a moral duty, giving the touchstone political example of a woman's right to choose an abortion. Self-care distinguishes feminist care ethics from mercy or charity. Joan Tronto's formulation of a "praxis of care" argues that "only those who are able not only to perceive their own needs, but also to satisfy them, are able to reach such a level of attentiveness to the needs of others" (quoted in Maihofer, "Care," 390–91). If one's own needs are unfulfilled, then empty and resented duty replaces genuine care. Satisfying them seems to be a precondition for peace.

Staking out the right to care for oneself is certainly what characterizes the letters I have looked at in this book. In a sense, they prove the point that there is nothing inherently self-sacrificing about "care culture." In the exchanges between Teresa and Kate, the Seneca Encampment's outreach letters to the town, Audre Lorde's "Open Letter to Mary Daly," or the Three Marias' "New Portuguese Letters," we see women asserting themselves alongside care for another, in ways that aim to produce interdependence rather than martyrdom, on the one hand, or separation, on the other. Likewise there is a symmetry between erotic and political discovery in the letters of new lovers, like Noel Birkby and Bertha Harris. This is arguably correspondence at its most ontological, surely the model that care philosophers seek in ethical relationship. The secret of the relational self in this culture, it seems, is precisely a deep sense of its rights, its autonomy, including the right to be cared for.

But the solution of self-care is somewhat paradoxical. How can you care for yourself if you are not first cared for? More to the point, why should you? It is surely for this that social movements cannot begin by organizing on the basis of need, for this is to concede political ground before you have started. Legal scholar Patricia Williams comments that describing needs has not been politically effective as a form of discourse for "blacks." By contrast, "although rights may not be ends in themselves, rights rhetoric has been and continues to be an effective form" (*The Alchemy of Race*, 149). The problem with "needs" as a political platform is also obvious in colonial and patriarchal contexts. Here paternalist models of control purport to fulfill "needs" precisely so as to obviate claims for rights. Importantly, Williams suggests that rights are precisely a "political mechanism that can confront the denial of need" (152). The current interest in using personal testimony to make claims of human rights violations is a case in point, even though the nuance and individuality of these testimonies must be sacrificed in the process (Schaffer and Smith, *Human Rights and Narrated Lives*).

A discourse of needs, then, does seem to be a luxury. Yet this takes us back to the reason that activists fighting for basic rights may try to create that luxury for themselves in movement communities. I have given examples throughout this book of correspondences in which women have asserted and explored their rights. But what feminists expected of one another was much more than this—they wanted care, the nuances. And often they wanted to offer it as well as receive it. It is a premise of care ethics that autonomy must be nurtured. The classical example these philosophers give is of rearing a child to be able to look after itself and others responsibly. On a larger scale, this developmental notion is perhaps what describes the separatist logic of a woman-centered political movement. Stokely Carmichael defended black separatism in the same terms: "before a group can enter the open society, it must first close ranks" (Carmichael and Hamilton, *Black Power*, 44). Yet the epistolary record suggests the feminist dialectic between autonomy and care was more than wobbly at times. Rather than mutual interdependence, a culture of need could develop in which everyone has a "right" to be cared for yet no necessary obligation to care for others. This bears some ironic similarities to the impasse of "self-help" culture, where constant worry about care for the self ironically threatens one's ability to be genuinely self-reliant. bell hooks puts it this way:

Even though women usually know more about caregiving than men do because we have been taught these skills from girlhood on, we do not instinctively or innately know how to give love. . . . Women are often more interested in being loved than in the act of loving. All too often the female search for love is epitomized by this desire, not by a desire to know how to love.

(hooks, *Communion*, 88–89)

A less psychological approach, but one that results in the same conclusion, comes from anthropologist Sarah F. Green's research into the lesbian feminist community in late-1980s London. This was a community saturated by the ideal of full autonomy for each individual, expressed as recognition for each person's "differences." And this led to a continual tension with its other, just as pressing ideal of "community":

On a theoretical level, lesbian feminists both desired a community (as the realization of a women's non-patriarchal sociality) and resented it (as the imposition of the social upon the individual), and therefore the community continually had an air of illusion about it, that it was not really there, and yet it was. To complicate things further, the strongest sense of community *in practice* was associated with lesbian 'authenticity' rather than woman 'authenticity'. The key behind this was not so much intellectual theory, but personal and social interrelations: what made the community feel like a community for most women was their networks of friends, lovers and ex-lovers. Public demonstrations, political groups and organizations, the production of journals and pamphlets and so on were generally regarded as being made possible by those personal and social networks. Such public events demonstrated the existence and relative strength of the community, and they made the community 'visible' to many women; but the community's existence *per se* was based on personal ties, and these ties were based on lesbian relationships.

(Green, *Urban Amazons*, 22)

I dwell upon this example, no doubt, because it was exactly my own landscape, living in a shared lesbian household in London at that time. Yet Green's description of the problem with "identity politics" as the symptom of a much deeper question about submission to community seems to me to have widespread application. The principle of care as "right," which seems crucial to its efficacy as an ethic for feminists, seems to depend, contrarily, upon an already strong capacity for individual autonomy. But if that sense of autonomy takes over, then care becomes impossible. Paradoxically, care must be felt to be both part of one's rights and also the moment of their relinquishing if any genuine collectivity or exchange can take root.

What, then, have feminist theorists of care said about its application to the "public domain" and the management of community? Typically, they have continued to defend the concept of a legality that avoids the perceived errors of patriarchal pretended "objectivity" and abstraction. Yet they have also argued that private principles of care need to be integrated with public laws of justice, so that each ethic provides a check against an exaggerated form of the other. Ruth Lister explains this clearly in arguing for a concept of feminist citizenship based on a "differentiated universalism." This involves agreeing on a "framework of political values" alongside a commitment to valuing difference and a commitment to dialogue. Lister certainly admits the problems that a "politics of needs interpretation" can also pose. Her response is that needs and rights should be understood as tiered, embracing both the universal and the differentiated and standing in a dynamic relationship to each other (Lister, "Dialectics of Citizenship," 17). This seems to be the conclusion to any practical attempt to respond to the problem of difference among women. Martha Nussbaum, a key voice in developing feminist rights as an international force, adds that, of course, the moral evaluations of any cultural practice must always be "immersed" rather than "detached," taking account of "the practices, the perceptions, even the emotions, of the culture" (Nussbaum and Sen, "Internal Criticism," 308). Yet "the full work of developing an internationally focused understanding of the meaning of needs (what counts as a real need rather than a mere want?) and the limits of care (when is one unjustly manipulated by one's caring?) still awaits its author" (Dandekar, "International Justice," 556).

Feminist citizenship, then, like any other, must control needs, and perhaps this is part of the movement's growing up, its deferring to more orthodox structures. Charlotte Bunch, an original member of the Redstockings who is credited with the phrase "feminism is the theory, lesbianism is the practice," told me that feminists' emphasis on personalized politics is nothing unique: there are plenty of "old boy" networks. What distinguished feminists was their attempt to network democratically and caringly. At the same time, this could mean everything was all taken so "personally" that work became impossible. Bunch today directs an institute for developing women's leadership and lobbying for women's rights as human rights.

It is beyond the scope of this book to offer a comprehensive political philosophy of "needs interpretation." My point is to show that letters are documents of a relationship history that struggled with this challenge. Letters reveal the movement's conflict between principles of autonomy and care or, more crudely put, between individualism and collectivism, as much as its conflict with the more familiar question of "identity." Feminism's challenge as a "community" has been to reconcile the two values. In this light, let me turn to two recent epistolary collections explicitly styled as second wavers trying to pass on hard-won political lessons to a younger generation in the "third wave" of the 1990s.

Feminist Generations in Correspondence

Phyllis Chesler, a New York activist best known for her 1972 *Women and Madness* and her later defense of surrogate mothers, published *Letters to a Young Feminist* in 1996. Its confidential tone, aided by peach-colored and pocket-sized packaging, suggests that the nervous novice will have much to learn. In "Letter One," a benefactor addresses a wished-for beneficiary:

> Here I sit, head bent, writing you an intimate letter. I sense your presence, even though I don't know your name. I envision you as a young woman, possibly a young man, somewhere between the ages of eighteen and thirty-five, but you may also be a decade older—or younger—than that. You may not yet be born.
>
> You are my heir. This letter is your legacy.
>
> (Chesler, *Letters to a Young Feminist*, 1–2)

There follow twenty-two "letters," ranging from parabolic autobiographical snippets on Chesler's own oppressed youth and discovery of feminism, to instruction in "How to Develop a Strong Self in a 'Post'-Feminist Age," to adjusting the record in "Feminist Myths About Sisterhood."

Anna Bondoc and Meg Daly's *Letters of Intent: Women Cross the Generations to Talk About Work, Family, Love, Sex, and the Future of Feminism*, issued three years after Chesler's collection, is aimed at a higher age range but is similarly posed as a dialogue between those who are already feminist. The two freelance writers, Bondoc in New York City, Daly in Portland, assembled a book of open letters "between twenty- and thirty-something women and their 'foremothers,'" some pairs of whom were already long-standing mentor-protegées, others of whom agreed to converse for the book (5–6). The book's central sections, on women's entrance into "male" arenas, contemporary and past campaigns, and women's health, bodies, and spirituality, are book-ended by the question of how feminism itself can be reproduced. The book opens with "Intergenerational Approaches to Activism and Social Change" and ends with "Women Pass the Torch to Coming Generations."

Although Chesler and Bondoc and Daly all position their readers as already feminist, they clearly hope their texts will continue the work of consciousness-raising. Anna Bondoc writes to her coeditor: "I want our readers to say, 'I'm fighting for such and such, too,' or even 'They left out so-and-so, and she needs to have our work acknowledged.' You see, Meg, our work could never be finished, in a way. . . . But doesn't that just prove the point that feminism will never be 'over'?" (7). In this appreciation of the "never-finished," these writers accept conflicting perceptions of feminism, and both collections are overt about the need for women to assume different jobs and levels of power. Bondoc and Daly devote an entire section to taking foremothers "Off the Pedestal" and hope that their book will provoke more "fervent discussion, and even disagreement" between their readers than that already elicited in their contributors (7). Chesler explains to her addressee that early feminism's "matricidal" culture left feminists without a language to talk about the ways in which women, too, could assume, manipulate, and abuse power (*Letters to a Young Feminist*, 55–60). Indeed, she appears in Bondoc and Daly's book on the same subject, but here more defensively responding to Lisa Featherstone's request to know "Why Is There So Much Tension Between Feminist Bosses and Their Female Assistants?"

Here is the political family, but the model of sisterhood has been replaced by one of maternal descent whose generational shifts by implication allow for greater difference. In many ways, like the choice to write in the form of an epistolary handbook, this implies the confidence of a dynasty that is beginning to endure. Yet the epistolary form also betrays an anxiety about how much young women care about their elders and a fear that the message will be lost in a climate of antifeminist backlash.

Chesler's approach is to chastise her reader for assuming that she has equal rights. While her advice is sound—for example, her highly practical list of how to support the proabortion lobby[3]—she disdains to consider why young women might feel safer in some ways, or, indeed, more vulnerable in others. Despite her opening topos of the confidante, her model is the conduct manual, citing as forebears Niccolò Machiavelli, Sun Tzu, Virginia Woolf, and Rainer Maria Rilke, and the strategies of government, war, and poetry. Notably, she does *not* reference Madame de Sévigné, the towering literary model of the maternal letter writer, for presumably Sévigné's courtly romancing of her daughter is far too close to the feminine love letter. Chesler's berating tones thus provoke the generational drama she aims to refuse. Naming herself explicitly now as "Mother-Teacher" rather than "Daughter-Risen," she poses her supposedly feminist letter reader as an ineptly self-deceiving victim of the patriarchy. Although Chesler's book has garnered praise from her generation—Susan Brownmiller, Letty Cottin Pogrebin, Gloria Steinem, Joanna Russ, Jill Johnston[4]—pronouncements such as, "You are entitled to know our war stories" make it sound like an obligation for the next generation (France, "Passing the Torch"). Chesler's interpretation of the epistolary admits dissension among her own generation of women but none between her and her proposed young reader:

> Perhaps you believe you can "have it all": a brilliant career, a loving life-long marriage, healthy children/no children, enough money, and happiness too. . . . Darling, I don't want to frighten you away, but I don't want to waste your time either, so I can't pretend that simply because you or I *want* it to be so that in fact women and men are equal.
>
> (2)

Bondoc and Daly's collection has more chance of preaching to the unconverted by maintaining dialogue as a series of questions from young to old: Amy Richards to Gloria Steinem, "How are our experiences with abortion and feminism similar?"; Tayari Jones to Pearl Cleage, "Which comes first, our paychecks or our principles?"; Catherine Sameh to Suzanne Pharr, "Do we need women's spaces when feminists and lesbians have achieved so much?"; Marie Lee to Elaine Kim, "In an interracial world, is choosing a white partner denying your heritage?"; Anna Bondoc to Annemarie Colbin, "Why do so many women have unhealthy relationships with their bodies?"; and Catherine Gund Saalfield to April Martin, "What do you love about being a lesbian mom?" Twenty- and thirty-somethings certainly want their mentors, and are attached to a notion of enlightenment, but they equally want to accommodate contradictions in their relationships and divisions in their political loyalties.

The replies such demands collect are double-edged, epitomized by two exchanges that focus on African American politics. Eisa Nefertari Ulen's account of black self-destruction alongside economic genocide by whites also recounts intense personal disappointment that the utopian days of Black Power were over with her early childhood. Angela Y. Davis courteously replies to her question, "What happened to your generation's promise of 'love and revolution?'" with the suggestion that she get involved in organizing against the racist prison system. Eisa Davis, Ulen's friend and Angela Davis's niece, reminisces about her adolescent inspiration by Ntozake Shange's poetry in the form of her own letter-poem, but she wonders about the bleak postmodernity of much AfricanAmerican life: "if we've gotta live underground and everybody's got cancer / will poetry be enuf?" Shange raps back:

> is poetry enuf to man a picket line/to answer to phones at the
> rape crisis center/to shield women entering abortion clinics from
> demons
> with
> crosses & illiterate signs defiling the horizon at dawn/to keep our
> children
> from believin' that they can buy hope with a pair of sneakers or another
> nasty
> filter for   cheap glass pipe/no/no/a million times no
> but
> poetry can bring those bleeding women & children outta time
> up close enuf for us to see feel ourselves there/then the separations
> what makes me/me & you/you///drops away & the truth that we
> constantly

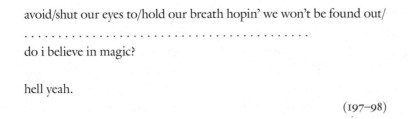

avoid/shut our eyes to/hold our breath hopin' we won't be found out/

. . . .

do i believe in magic?

hell yeah.

(197–98)

Shange's defense of the role of art in politics as a means to overcome "separations" is not only figured through poetry—repetition, rhythm, visual barring, and flowing. Personalizing the poem through reference to her correspondent's mother, she also asserts letter writing's power to animate, a local "magic" of rhetoric across separation and the failure of faith.

As a whole, the collection holds onto the model of a passionate exchange between women through its proliferating models of correspondence between the generations, in which the political imperative is still couched in personal terms. From the point of view of a generation raised on the expectation of "having it all," what seems clear is that finding a way to speak personally to what people feel they *need* remains absolutely crucial. Yet the more astute writers realize that this can become self-defeating, stimulating victimhood rather than building upon already existing strengths. The stakes in "the personal" become startlingly clear in the exchange between Amy Richards and Gloria Steinem, in which Richards states:

> I can't help but ask why so many people wait for a personal experience to make that political connection? I look at Anita Hill and how she was jettisoned into feminism by being forced to painfully revisit her sexual harassment on national television. Through my work with Third Wave . . . I see many young women—and men—who are reticent to speak out on issues unless they themselves are directly affected. But I cling to Third Wave's philosophy: See It? Tell It. Change It! I just wish we could work on "changing it"—whatever "it" is—without having to first experience it so intimately. Do you think it's inevitable that we get motivated to be activists only when we experience injustices?
>
> (15)

Richards rightly worries about the absurdity of needing to perpetuate a sense of vulnerability in order to create activism. Yet this question follows the confession that her own feminist identification was catalyzed by the experience of having had an abortion. This letter garners Steinem's sympathy that Richards had still been made to feel guilty, surprised that even in the 1990s "choosing to give birth to ourselves instead of someone else" still needs so much defending. Yet she also points out that Richards's "time of feeling alone was measured in weeks and months, not years," as her own had been in the 1960s (16). In this symbolic dialogue the epistolary rhetoric of "respect for similarity and difference" (17) is invoked again to mediate between the different degrees of their similarly shaped struggle. Steinem signs off with the ultimate gesture of submission to the other's stronger presence: "But no matter how equal our exchange, I'll always have one advantage over you because of my age. I'll never have to live in a world without you in it" (20).

The kind of personal politics dramatized in *Letters of Intent* can seem inward-looking, "one generation's hard-fought struggle to attain success and equality and the next generation's relative complacency," as one reviewer assessed it.[5] As letters written for publication between many who could now be described as feminist professionals, the missives in *Letters of Intent* do not embody the same degree of personal struggle we see, for example, in *Between Ourselves*. Compared to earlier feminist epistles, these texts mark the strength of young, middle-class women's sense of their rights. This does not mean they always feel that their needs are met. There are wider issues here about how wealthy democracies do not satisfy happiness, perversely stimulating new needs as fast as old ones are answered. Notwithstanding, it is encouraging to see these young voices wondering about how to generate altruism without the catalyst of personal interest and what will motivate political activism in a context where the job has often shifted to working for others, or defending rather than winning rights. It is also exciting is to see that the conflict between autonomy and care is easing in the opening up and diversifying of feminist communities. The conflict between "my needs or yours" seems to be less pressing.

It is very like me to want a happy ending, and these two texts can hardly be made to compensate for today's appalling political backlash against the radicalism of the 1960s and 1970s. In the assimilation of feminist ideas and policies and the loss of identifiable feminist "community," we risk losing the basis for action. The message of all these letter writers is that we have to keep starting all over again: bringing the individual into communities that politicize from needs to rights and back again, creating the dialectic between autonomy and care as best we can. How do you educate resistant, recalcitrant, or rejecting partners, families, colleagues, political allies, and opponents? How do we respectfully enlighten, without controlling? What do we owe one another? In the new feminisms, the questions of both letter writers and feminists will persist.

CHAPTER TEN

How Different Is E-mail?

From: "Susan Jolly"
To: "xxpp hhee"
Subject: deng dai ge dou
Date: Thu, 18 Mar 2004 10:21:30 -0000

Hi darling, was I totally hyper and irritating this morning? poor b put up with me. But I think u can put up with me. I put up with u after all. You and your lovely daughter.
Xxx

From: xxpp hhee
Sent: 18 March 2004 16:23
To: Susan Jolly
Subject: RE: deng dai ge dou [Waiting for Goddo]

b, u were horrible, not this morning tho. i enjoy eating at gugu's every evening, i took bus, travel for 30-45 munites to hers, and travel back for 30 munites, it is totally enjoyable, don't have to recite chairman mao's quotations these days, only cost one RMB, i enjoy just as mush as i did when i was 8 or 9. last night i took different bus and different line, saw somewhere i had never seen, went somewhere i thought i had never been, for a second, i thought i got lost, but soon, i realised it is somewhere i am very familiar!! what a fun!! and the bus driver was jsut fun, he made many jokes, made people in his bus all laughing . . . till stomac broken.

came back home, had massage in that yard, the master was busy, so i got chance to watch TV news: a very shy guy from surburb chengdu had sex change and married to a man from same village, they did not want to have interview, but did not mind TV shoot them. the village people accept it, tho, not very understanding, what a fatastic news!!

love, b, why not have a sex change, i mean u, then we think of getting married? Oh? pi le pa la DONG!

—Susan Jolly and Xiao Pei He, e-mails, 18 Mar 2004

W henever I have mentioned I am writing a book about letter writing, I am treated to three inevitable words: what about e-mail? This is followed by the solemn avowal that the art of letter writing is dying. I agree that it is difficult to find good examples of e-mail art. But, I contend, the art of letters was never something to measure through publishability. There is no question that e-mail is a significant creative, sometimes literary phenomenon. E-mail has seduced people into life writing, into the pleasures and demands of composition for another. It has also spawned a popular aesthetics in which writing's ability to deceive and disappoint as well as delight is a central feature. Lynne Truss muses tetchily in her punctuation guide, *Eats Shoots and Leaves*, "how often do you hear people complain that emails subtract the tone of voice; that it's hard to tell if someone is joking or not? Clicking on 'send' has its limitations as a system of subtle communication. Which is why, of course, people use so many dashes and italics and capitals ('I AM joking!') to compensate" (192). Any of the still growing clutch of "e-mail-writing" manuals will contain a section on "netiquette" and "flaming" as well as warnings about timing, frequency, and privacy. Yet Anne Eisenberg, trying to find a handle on "the new epistolary age" as it suddenly appeared to many in the early 1990s, was correct to observe that "lured by electronic mail's seductive blend of speed, convenience and economy, people who never before touched the stuff are routinely, skillfully, even cheerfully tapping out a great deal of correspondence" (Eisenberg, "E-Mail and the Epistolary Age"). Hardly dreamt of a decade ago, e-mail has more than doubled its share of the world communications market from just over 5 percent in 1995 (with physical mail at nearly 20 percent and fax and telephone at 75 percent).[1] Though computer programmers expected both e-mail and texting to be purely functional, taking some years to design them for anything but technical use within the industry, it is pleasure as well as business that drives the world's nearly 700 million e-mailers[2] and two billion text messagers.[3]

Popular laments about the dying "art of letter writing" are rarely symptoms of a genuine aesthetic interest in epistolary forms. (Most of those who opine thus never put so much as a birthday card in the mail.) Rather, they express much broader anxieties about trust and the individual's place in a time of rapid technological change. Our new "digital economy of writing" (Yates, "Computer-Mediated Communication," 242) is throwing everything, including gender relations, up in the air. At the same time, the "feminist epistolary age" might seem to have disappeared of its own accord. Throughout this book, I have argued for the specific affinities between second-wave feminism and letter writing as form and symbol of women's special relationship. I have also argued that, as the movement diversified, the romance with letter writing petered out along with it. Yet the correspondence between second and "third" wavers discussed in the previous chapter hints at new forms of feminist exchange. It is only fair, then, to wonder what is happening to feminist epistolary practice now that the Internet has made the role of written communication in all aspects of life so obvious.

In the following two chapters I offer a necessary speculation on the gender politics of epistolary art and socializing as it now unfolds in the communications revolution of the digital age. Retracing the steps of the book, we will look first from a literary-cultural perspective, then consider the political context, and, finally, confront this transformation's philosophical implications. I will guide the discussion through the following key questions: Has e-mail altered the association of women with personal letter writing? Do feminists ever identify e-mail as a feminist form specifically? How has the diversification of feminism, particularly in relation to men and to women's movements in the global South, interwoven with new technologies of communication? And finally, how does e-mail enhance the concept of the self as relational, and what kind of ethics has developed to encompass it?

The Gender of E-mail and the Network Society

The ubiquity of e-mail in the developed world has done much to reveal the illusion that women have any special capacity as letter writers per se. We can see more clearly now how that idea took root as a literary, somewhat perverse reaction to the emerging print economy in seventeenth- and eighteenth-century Europe. The handwritten letter was emblematic of a feminized private sphere, but e-mail evokes the in-between scenes of personal chat at the office and working from home. It is, of course, as part of this structural merging of spheres in the network economy that the diversification of gender roles is taking place. Yet if woman and letter no longer equate, communications technology is often still articulated in gender terms, though in more plural, often contradictory ways. As I suggested in chapter 1, this ranges from the marketing of pink mobile phones and electronic greeting cards to women, to speculation about men's new interest in personal corresponding in e-mail and text and the sexualizing of computer technology. In fact, the very fascination with gender deception online tells us that old binaries endure in the very literature of their undoing. Why else is it that the ugly old man posing as a voracious young woman in electronic sexual affairs is the archetypal fable of computer-mediated communication?

Jeanette Winterson's 2000 novel, *The PowerBook*, represents one feminist attempt to explore the paradoxes of gender in cyberspace. "I'm sitting at my screen. There's an email for me. I unwrap it. It says—*Freedom, just for one night*" (3). These opening lines establish the conventional view that, sitting at the screen, identities can be donned and dropped as easily as party disguises. The role that Winterson's electronic heroine soon finds is especially tempting for a woman bored with her castrated lot: she adopts a "language costume" as a sixteenth-century envoy who seduces a princess with a magically erect tulip flower and bulbs. But such freedoms are only for "one night," fragile as much as fantastical and often as silly as a tulip phallus. The woman writer's fun online quickly becomes subject to her reader's unpredictable desires and dialogue, sent whimsically off course by Internet surfing as well as the traditionally epistolary longing for an out-of-reach love. E-mail pulses and blips through a lonely as well as only night as Winterson's writer-protagonist struggles to keep her married woman lover entertained.

Winterson's scenario, in which lesbian desire and imagination are pitted against an age-old marital institution as much as against the challenges of cyberspace, suggests the double-edged politics of gender play online. On the one hand, e-mail has powerfully expanded the possibilities for epistolary idealization and fantasy, signified as escape from gender binaries, monogamies, and sexual boredom. Virtual culture in many ways supports feminist understandings that gender and sexuality are constructed, sometimes consciously chosen; detached from physical identity, online life apparently liberates from biological determinism. Indeed, early sociologists of the Internet such as Sherry Turkle and Allucquere Rosanne Stone largely celebrated the electronic reinvention of gender identity as a healthy adaptation to the challenge of postmodernity (Turkle, *Life on the Screen*; Stone, *The War of Desire*). Literary critic Linda Kauffman more recently saw e-mail, along with related dialogic forms such as Webcam or video, hypertext, faxes, and listserves, as far more receptive to feminist interests than the letter literatures of the past precisely because they are more interactive and performative. Moreover, Kauffman claims, these forms typically display an "anti-aesthetic" perversity and suspicion of classic romance that pushes feminism beyond its own attachments to feminine victimhood or romance ideology (Kauffman, "Not a Love Story").

Kauffman's argument dovetails with my own in finding that feminists' special relationship to the letter has not entirely disappeared but has mutated into dramatically new forms. However, I am less sanguine about both the extent and the quality of a postgender universe. It is true that literature such as the cheerful planning of sex reassignment surgery through e-mail and simultaneous multiple flirtation with both men and women online in Manda Scott's "feMail" suggests an entirely new climate from that which produced the romantic confessions and political debates of earlier feminist epistolary relationships. So do the e-mail responses to the live Web broadcast of performance artist Orlan's facial surgery, which Kauffman celebrates as liberating us from old essentialisms (Kauffman, "Not a Love Story," 211). Anna Holmes's *Hell Hath No Fury: Dear John Letters* contrasts the sassy wit of today's e-mail scorn with women's previous decorousness in ending a heterosexual affair. Even Kay Turner's anthology of lesbian love letters contains its fair share of arch e-mails in a culture now totally at home with virtual sex and writerly self-invention. As one writer puts it, "I want to . . . fuck you w/my feelings" (Kay Turner, *Between Us*, 58). Ironic, picaresque, queer, and sexually explicit, e-mail literatures and practices like these arguably reflect the age of true "correspondence" as Mary Jacobus imagined it back in 1986: feminist writers who do not have to force one another to mirror themselves but recognize "shifting and composite differences," ambivalence and anger, as well as loving identification (Jacobus, "Reading Correspondences," 282).

Feminist e-mail literature, however, has been prey to its own romanticisms, and here I mark my difference with Kauffman's view that the new technology has got us out of a bad old second-wave love story. As these snippets of virtual culture suggest, e-mail's libertarianism is accompanied by a loneliness, aggression, and cynicism that can entrench as much as they can deconstruct gender conventions and that certainly provide no simple escape from the constraints of worldly bodies and communities. As many have remarked, early users of the Internet believed they had discovered a "utopian communication device." But the golden age of crime-free, civil, and uncommodified exchange began to dissipate from 1993, when the advent of Web browsers began the massive expansion from 20 to 200 million users by 2000 (Poster, *Information Please*, 146–47). Further, it seems that users are often unwilling to abandon traditional forms of identity. In relation to gender, Kira Hall's empirical research on social interaction online indicates that "rather than neutralizing gender, the electronic medium encourages its intensification. In the absence of the physical, network users exaggerate societal notions of femininity and masculinity in an attempt to gender themselves" (Hall, "Cyberfeminism," 167). Kenneth Gergen measures the social "saturation" produced by computer technology against what he considers the loss of "true love" in intimate, enduring family and sexual relationships (Gergen, *The Saturated Self,*). The same conservatism about gender roles is even more telling in epistolary fiction that apparently celebrates their renovation.

Stephanie Fletcher's novel *E-mail: A Love Story*, for instance, shows an unfulfilled bulimic housewife recovering her appetite for life through on-line affairs, but concludes with e-mail becoming a dangerous "addiction" that she must give up to save her marriage. Astro Teller's novel *Exegesis*, drawing on Teller's experiences as a researcher into artificial intelligence, tells the story of a renegade computer called Edgar who starts e-mailing his Taiwanese American programmer, Alice. Alice's ethical worries about creating an intelligent computer combine with depression that she is not a good enough scientist. This is enhanced when she loses control over Edgar, who speaks and thinks like a white intellectual man. Alice's male supervisor ends up getting the credit for the scientific discovery, while Edgar remains on the run. Similarly, David Cronenberg's 1999 indie film *eXistenZ* sets up the female protagonist as a technological wizard who receives electronic information, or "mail," through a teleport on her back, while her male partner is merely her access port. However, this technology ultimately controls her in an old equation of woman and her body "portrayed as permeable in both directions" (Simon, *Mail-Orders*, 230). Sunka Simon has also pointed out that in the majority of Hollywood films featuring electronic mail, such as *Copycat*, *The Net*, and *You've Got Mail*, "vulnerable" women appear as the mediators between good and bad technology or industry in very traditional ways. Although their communicative know-how is often prominent, once again, the plots emphasizes what they need to learn emotionally (229). Underneath the new e-mail literature, we see ancient epistolary tropes of women waiting for roaming men, the limit of whose novelty is expressed in performance-art critic Marlena Corcoran's advice "to all the women who lament that men don't talk, don't share their feelings, don't tell you what they're thinking, I say: Send him an e-mail message" (Corcoran, "Male and F:\Email," 340). In this light, e-mail constitutes a prime form of postmodern storytelling that displays incessant choosing without necessarily changing the terms of choice (Plummer, *Telling Sexual Stories*).

E-mail then both aids and contains the social upheaval caused by today's global information economy. Its protean personality comes from the instant exchange: compulsive, flirtatious, promiscuous in tone compared to the hand-posted letter, it upsets borders between private and public as well as distinctions of social register and genre. But its character needs to be understood as part of a much more general shift in the structuring of social space. Communication as the basis for a global capitalist economy is dramatically fragmenting old divisions of public and private, mixing work and home life, and challenging traditional forms of political representation. Clearly, old disparities continue. A recent global report on gender and information communications technologies showed just how unequal is women's access to computers compared to men's; how the much-celebrated new jobs for women in information are stratified by lower pay, job insecurity, de-skilling.[4]

This suggests that (British and American) literary feminists have disproportionately focused on, and overestimated, the deconstruction of identity afforded by digital communication. More persuasive, to my mind, are feminists who see opportunities to restructure gender roles in this merging of public and private spheres, even if the current crumbling of traditional patriarchal family structures is largely driven by capitalism. As we have seen, women's movements have their own histories of individual libertarianism, flexible networking styles, and cultural definition (Gittler, "Mapping Women's Global Communications"). At their most effective, these movements provide a force that opposes both the panicked patriarchy of religious, ethnic, and nationalist fundamentalist movements and the atomized individualism and sex trade of high consumer culture. The sociologist Manuel Castells indeed views "new social movements" like feminism to be better than political parties or unions in managing the political configuration of the capitalist network, for they understand "the power of identity" and cultural change outside the rewards of state or work power. Distinguishing "societies of the information age" from a general "network society," Castells goes so far as to say that because these "identity-based social movements" are relatively autonomous from the institutions of the state, the logic of capital, and the seduction of technology; they are hard to co-opt and "even in defeat, their resistance and projects impact and change society" (Castells, *End of Millennium*, 352).

Castells's broad-brush definition of feminist and women's groups as "identity-based movements" cannot, of course, do justice to the long history of debate about the term and the meaning of "identity" within feminism. In the context of mushrooming global networks of feminist organizations in the 1990s and 2000s, the identity politics that dominated the North American and European women's movements in the 1980s seems old hat. Yet the question of communication still raises the challenge of women's relationships to one another and how the private can be related to the public. Way back in 1984, Gloria Steinem popularized the idea that "networking" was precisely the way forward for feminists who wanted to move on from more inward-looking "consciousness-raising" of the 1970s. Now electronic communications are facilitating women's networking and advocacy with unprecedented speed and scope (Shade, *Gender and Community*, 36). Feminist movements, born out of the contradictions of the first capitalist revolution, meet the "Net" with the "self" in an attempt to pursue not so much "antiglobalization" as globalization from below.

This is how the diversification of feminism, particularly in relation to men and to women's movements of the global South, has most promisingly interwoven with new technologies of communication. More sophisticated, inclusive, and global than second-wave epistolarity, yet more materialist than Western-centered "cyber-feminism," it is less interested in deconstructing gender in the abstract than contextualizing its varieties. Indeed, I would say that e-mail's distinctive contribution to feminism has been as a "low-tech," relatively accessible form of cyberculture. In the next section I will survey the e-mail practices of a number of global feminist groups, focusing on one that set out to explore the form's cross-cultural potential as part of an electronic group forum. What we see is that in an age of global identity politics, feminists continue to argue that women's differences must be acknowledged, especially as they are defined through access to the Net itself. At the same time, finding common ground personally, emotionally, is as vital as ever.

Women on the Net: Difference and the Virtual Community

My work as a human rights activist focuses on self-determination for indigenous peoples and the ability to transcend the typical boundaries of political conflict through a cyberculture. I envisage this cyberculture as one in which creativity and intellect could challenge neo-colonial initiatives of the twenty-first century and reduce the sufferings endured by indigenous peoples living with Fourth World aggressions. The course of my own culture in this information age was set by the evolution of an ancient Hawaiian heritage, on one hand, and a deep desire for the integration of knowledge within the expanding field of computer technology on the other.

(Bray-Crawford, "The Ho'okele Netwarriors," 162–63)

So writes Kekula Bray-Crawford for a book titled *Women@Internet: Creating New Cultures in Cyberspace* (ed. Harcourt).

In this discussion . . . I sense an old paradigm encounter which I would like to be able to comprehend . . . I've struggled with academia [in order] to challenge the borders, recognizing the gap as a large part of our problem (globally). I need messages loaded with academic terminology when it is thick to [be interpreted] for me in my own poetic language so I can understand where the discussion or people themselves are coming from. This does give life, appreciation and light to a world I thought was without.

(quoted in Harcourt, "Cyborg Melody," 8)

And that was also Kekula Bray-Crawford, e-mailing in the discussion list set up for the book's contributors. Women on the Net (WoN) was a group of more than one hundred women and men activists, academics, information technologists, and nongovernmental-organization employees brought together by the Society for International Development in 1997. They were funded by the United Nations Educational, Scientific, and Cultural Organization to meet, establish a listserv, and then reunite in person a year later at a conference on Gender and Globalization at the University of Berkeley, California. Wendy Harcourt, director of programs for the Society for International Development as well as the group's coordinator, explained the aims of the discussion in the book that came out of the conference. First, it hoped to encourage women, particularly in the South and in marginal groups in the North (and Central and East Europe), to use the Internet more easily as their space, thereby empowering women to use technology as a political tool. Second, to open up and contribute to the new culture that was being set up on the Internet from a gender perspective at once local and global. Third, to bring together individual women and men working from different institutional bases . . . to explore a transnational women's movement agenda in response to and shaping evolving telecommunication policies. And fourth, to create a resource . . . base which could be tapped into by different women's groups . . . in navigating the Internet.

(Harcourt, "Cyborg Melody," 1).

This group was explicitly formed to respond to globalization as it has been defined through information-communications technologies. Beginning from the political assumption that feminist representation on the Internet is necessary for gender equity, WoN was also founded to explore and unite across differences among women—academics and activists, Northerners and Southerners, Easterners and Westerners—to create a "transnational women's movement agenda." The participants also shared an interest in working with men. Those who wrote for the subsequent book included Alice Mastrangelo Gittler, with the New York International Women's Tribune Center, for which she reported from the Beijing United Nations women's conference in 1995, until she chose to work at home with her small son "and test the limits of global telecommuting"; Wendy Harcourt, an Australian in Rome, director of programs at the Society for International Development, and committed personal e-mailer; Lourdes Arizpe, cultural anthropologist from Mexico and a maverick intellectual in UNESCO's cultural program at the time. There were also Arturo Escobar, professor of anthropology at the University of Massachusetts, who works on Latin American eco-activism; Gillian Youngs, at the Centre for Mass Communication in Leicester; and Fatma Alloo, founder of the Tanzania Media Women's Association and now webbing up community organizations whose foci range from sex education to swapping traditional Zanzibari women's cloth designs. Laura Agustín is a popular educator and researcher of women working in the sex trade, and Marisa Belausteguigoitia Rius was doing her doctorate at Berkeley in ethnic studies and anticipating welcoming the whole bunch there for the conference—and worrying whether the academics would be friendly to the activists. And the Hawaiian cyberactivist Kekula Bray-Crawford, dreaming of an archipelago of indigenous cyberculture in the liquid continent of cyberspace.

This was not, then, a group of friends or even close colleagues, but professionals brought together by social-policy makers with public money and a political agenda. They were not writing privately to one another but taking part in the cloister of an electronic forum. Yet two aspects are particularly interesting about this group as a test case for how the diversification of feminism has interwoven with new technologies of communication. The first is that although in no sense literary, the project was explicitly conceived of as "an experiment in the politics of communication" (Harcourt, "Cyborg Melody," 3). And the second is that they brought with them feminist perspectives that suggested that the individual pursuit of ethical relationship should be intimately related to social movements for global development. The opening e-mail, sent by Marisa Belausteguigoitia Rius, suggested both concerns in her acutely deconstructive style:

> I am thinking of concentrating on: place-consciousness, the socialized conception of place and overall the political use of global/local, space/place confusions, parallel to a careful, microscopic analysis of the demands for going 'back into place'. I think that focusing this from a complex academic angle and also from our activist and institutional experience we will 're-conciliate' the visions of academia, activism and government institutions in the necessity of grounding our analysis and projects 'from below'. . . . This may lead us to frame the analysis 'creating transformative spaces for alternative futures'. And through this, also help us to locate a hyphen, a mark (scar?) in this alternative (alter-native) and figure out what is 'other' (alter) and what is native (place-bound).[5]
>
> (quoted in Harcourt, "Cyborg Melody," 4)

Challenging the way that globalization has undermined local cultures, Ruis's pun on "alter-native" figures the hope that the project could be made to accommodate "native" interests. This established the group's political stance toward the Internet. Rather than an escape into a utopian cyberspace where all difference will be erased along with bodies, nations, wars, and, arguably, political resistance, networking must be "grounded" in the material contexts of people's use and abuse of information technology. The interesting thing here is that "place-consciousness" is also proposed as a theme that can "re-conciliate" academic, activist, and institutional visions. It is the common difference that will allow the "experiment in communication."

But Ruis's location of a hyphen in an "alter-native" globalization was ironically too linguistic and not place-bound enough. Although the academics were quite at ease with using electronic communication to problematize communication, the activists pushed for a more literal "situating" of perspectives. As Harcourt describes it, "there seemed to some . . . to be a danger of spinning off into abstractions that did not root the group's work clearly enough in the stated aim to empower women working in the South. There was considerable anxiety about discussing issues as activists and women of color in an academic setting" (6). Pi Villanueva, a technician working in Isis International-Manila, a feminist resource center with a new information-technology base, pointed out:

> 'Mediating Borders' is a good metaphor for the work we are doing. But 'we' are also different from one another. 'We' have different points of reference. The members and collaborators of WoN are women working in women's resource and information centers . . . , in international agencies . . . , in academia, in Internet Service Providers (ISPs). Then there are also the men whose role in an initiative called 'Women on the Net' is presumed but not necessarily clear to everyone. (I don't mean the individual men who are already part of WoN, but men as a group. I raise this query in part because it is not clear to me how WoN will and should respond if other men would like to join the network.)
>
> We are also mediating borders inside WoN. Take, for example, some of the words used to frame the proposed Berkeley discussion: ventriloquism, patriarchal cyberdiscourses. Even the word cyborg, the name of our mailing list . . . These are words not normally used by individual women and women's groups I work with.
>
> (6)

Neither were these necessarily words that everyone in the group worked with. Bray-Crawford forwarded an e-mail of Arturo Escobar's to her partner asking for "translation"; Laura Agustín asked, "I hope we are not dreaming about a utopian 'unity'" (9); while Lis, working for the United Nations said:

> I agree very much with [Pi] about how to focus the discussion. We work at different levels, and while being interested in theoretical debates, my main concern is now to make the link with the practical day to day lives and realities of women, some of whom don't even know yet that the Internet exists . . . how to make the Internet useful (and accessible of course) for women in remote urban or rural areas of developing countries, and how they can make optimal use of the medium in support of their process of (economic) empowerment.
>
> (7)

The familiar question of identity now challenged the abilities of "place" to function as mediator. But it was here in these old debates between academia and activism, the privileged and the less privileged, that e-mail proved to be both a focus of conflict and a potential resource. Promising intimacy, it facilitated the admission of alienation. To the same degree, it broke the alienation of academic and public statement. Harcourt intercepted Bray-Crawford's request for translation by suggesting that:

> Your warmth and energy comes across the cyberwaves and opens out . . . the struggle you and other indigenous people are going through in quite another way from me reading about it in books and journals. I feel I can support and be with you in some way. For me this is about another way of being or here and now that is for me very politically feminist as I reach out to you as a woman doing this and we are finding ways to support each other. The references Gillian and Arturo make to feminist literature, ecologist thinking and philosophy in fact celebrate much of what you are doing, and that for me is what is so important in terms of connecting and making the effort to understand how we can work together in our different places.[6]

Harcourt's e-mail began to "place" the discussion emotionally as well as materially, and Bray-Crawford wrote back enthusiastically. Laura Agustín followed this by pointing out that the debate over "abstract thinking" in the group reflected educational histories and "that's where we have to tolerate and accept differences" (10). Gillian Youngs, one of the academics, responded that she "would feel very sad if anyone thought that [her] comments identif[ied] [her] as someone locked in a world of academic non-communication." The "confession" that followed, however, was of being emotional *about* ideas:

> The incredible exchanges about language in the last few days moved me intellectually as well as emotionally and I suppose that's a confession I can make here. I find it hard to separate my practical desires and imaginings from my intellectual and emotional ones, I have all my life and that's why academic life and its different dimensions including teaching and educational teamwork as well as thinking, sharing ideas and writing, is comfortable for me. There are important ways that I feel at home in it. It is not an abstract realm to me, it is very practical in so many ways.
>
> (12–13)

In these e-mails, the question of academic abstraction intriguingly displaces that of electronic virtuality, in which it is merely the physical body that is obscured. The extraordinarily large "socio-emotional" element that so many have remarked in e-mail, the product of its interactive immediacy, here allows the experience of academic and professional life, and indeed the physical realities of writers' lives, to become mentionable (Yates, "Computer-Mediated Communication," 246). Four list members gave birth during the year, and this was announced and discussed online. One woman described typing while breastfeeding. The group's most fervent and intimate exchanges took place just before the much-anticipated meeting when one member wrote to say she would be unable to attend because of a potential miscarriage. For a group that was attempting to mediate global differences in an academic setting, this kind of life writing was key to creating the trust that could genuinely mediate borders as the meeting in Berkeley drew near.

Did this sense of trust develop, paradoxically, because nobody had to engage in person? Analysts such as Sherry Turkle have suggested that textual virtuality is so popular precisely because people can conceal their physical status (Turkle, *Life on the Screen*).[7] It is true that for the activists, e-mail appeared to hold off "the symbolism of power embedded in face-to-face communication," something that may be the reason for e-mail's popularity with women, other oppressed groups, and "lower-status workers in company-based networks" (Castells, *The Rise of the Network Society*, 360). However, as with letters, the form may provide the illusion of care in a community that is safely imagined rather than material. It seems that even this highly professional group found it mildly challenging to meet in person after these exchanges.

This was a concern discussed by Women on the Net, who explicitly sought to establish new forms of authenticity and responsibility online. Marisa Ruis for example, suggested the "circulation in cyberspace of information without a body" could be "the same old story of kidnapping others' voices or reproducing others' concerns, disregarding politics of place-based experiences" (Harcourt, "Cyborg Melody, 8). Wendy Harcourt suggests that e-mail's "personal and even poetic [language]" is an attempt "to help people gain a sense of who 'I am really' beyond the typing on the screen" (Harcourt, *Women@Internet*, 220). These concerns with trust and reliability are apparently far more typical of Web users than many postmodern celebrations of virtuality would suggest (Zuern, "Online Lives," xiii). Interestingly, it appears that Internet culture generally associates only white masculinity with escape from bodies that labor, suffer, or nurture (Balsamo, *Technologies of the Gendered Body*). Further, the WoN group specifically aimed to find new ways of "situating" themselves in the face of globalization. Their bits of autobiographical "place" were consciously linked to geographical resistance to the invasion of local economies and the disorientation of mediated "real time." Emotional exchange is a crucial aspect of "place-consciousness" and "mediating borders."

In this light, we can appreciate the significance of Women on the Net as a writing as well as political experiment. The group's coherence as a community was facilitated by e-mail's distinctive combination of abstraction and affect, nibbling away at old binaries of emotion and thought that were institutionalized (at least in fantasy) as professional divisions between academics and activists, Westerners and Southerners. E-mail is the least dramatic form of virtual reality, but as those who have attempted to understand its relation to print literacy have remarked, at least at this point, it functions as a "primary utterance" (Spooner and Yancey, "Postings on a Genre," 268), that is, a writing that approximates the structures and stances of speech. Castells indeed situates e-mail as part of the sensuality and visuality of cyberculture, the revenge of a popular orality on the alphabet of the elite (*The Rise of the Network Society*, 327–75). Computers can paradoxically make us more aware of the part that intuition and sensitivity play in our lives (Seidler, "Embodied Knowledge"). Of course, e-mail's function as an "off-duty" writing (replacing the phone call as much as the letter) is often remarked on as dangerous, a deceptive intimacy that causes professional lapses and relationship blow-ups. But WoN sought to use "soft dialogue" as part of a discourse *about* communication (Arizpe, "Freedom to Create," xii).

In this respect, Women on the Net joins the long history of feminists using letters to explore women's identity in terms that rethink the meaning of professional and personal divisions that have deep roots in binaries of mind and body, reason and emotion. But it may be characteristic of the changed nature of feminist epistolarity that the group no longer expressed its virtual relationship in erotic, spiritual, or therapeutic terms. Laura Agustín, indeed, argued that activists enamored of the Internet should be wary of imposing "evangelical" ideas about literacy, even in the form of e-mail, on other women (Agustín, "They Speak, but Who Listens?" 155). Gillian Youngs, in her contribution to the book, suggested there are interesting parallels "between the concrete connective qualities of the Net and the present open and self-conscious goals of feminist politics" (Youngs, "Virtual Voices," 66). Fatma Alloo, demonstrating such "concrete, connective qualities" in writing from "the steaming island of Zanzibar," affirmed that her "most innovative and stimulating work has been as a result of my interaction with academicians on the one hand and the grounded community on the other hand. When I say academicians I mean intellectuals who have NOT remained in ivory towers of theories that never play a part in mobilizing communities or impacting change." Alloo concludes (quoted in Harcourt, "Cyborg Melody," 15–16) with an appeal to alliance that also acknowledges her own place as a "mediator" among different identities alongside more "individualized and personalized" attempts "to share more vividly people's 'here' and 'now'":

Now my dears I have spoken of my country and analyzed it as I see it. I am on the cyborg. What does this make me? A journalist, an IT freak? An intellectual? a feminist?—you got it! We have to move out of compartmentalization and incorporate a movement with a pulse and feel the ripples and if we are to be the delicatessen so be it!

CHAPTER ELEVEN

Care Ethics Online

H ow does e-mail enhance the concept of the "relational self," which I have argued has typified both feminist letter writing and its theoriza-tion? Relational writing practices in the age of e-mail and mobile phones are now so pervasive and so important to our subjectivity that, oddly, theorists of digital culture suggest that today the "relational self" has become the norm, rather than the autonomous individual of traditional humanist phi-losophy; in these theorists' model, the autonomous individual is in the mi-nority. Mark Poster is representative in his description of "the heterogeneity of identity, the inextricable mixing of consciousness with information ma-chines, the dispersal of the self across the spaces of culture, its fragmenta-tion into bits and bytes, the nonidentical identity or better identities that link machines with human bodies in new configurations or assemblages, the suturing or coupling of pieces of information in disjunctive time and scattered spaces" (Poster, *Information Please*, 114). For him, the binary logic of self and other has been surpassed with the experience of "fusion and dis-traction specific to information machines" (175).

Thus, in the network society, it is not so much the fact of relationality it-self but the question of the quality or *type* of relationality that determines whether we have moved into what feminists hoped would be a liberating ac-knowledgement of identity as relational. The question is whether e-mail, and indeed phone texting, have provoked new ethical codes. If so, how do they relate to the ethics of care that has celebrated that concept of relation-ship and relationality as its base? Women on the Net's "experiment in com-munication" would suggest that there is a great deal of overlap between "netiquette" and feminist epistolary ethics. Unromantic about women's identity, the group seemed to remain attached to expectations of mutual, even embodied, care. It clearly attempted to set up a dialectic between au-tonomy and relationship, as well as one between "place" and "space," body and writing. But clearly there is a world of difference between feminist hopes for public-private equality and the indifferent trampling of the private sphere offered by digital culture. Can we sensibly talk about care ethics—the moral recognition of needs as well as rights—online?

Before I attempt to answer these questions, I must acknowledge that care ethics has never explicitly dealt with the question of mediation, whether in the form of letter writing, telephoning, e-mailing, or even the mass media. Indeed, it has been formulated contrariwise through physical relationships such as nursing, feeding, holding, protecting, or straightforwardly convers-ing. We might say this is precisely why epistolary culture has shown the lim-its of care ethics, where moral response to the stranger is stretched and thinned. This is another way to understand the somewhat ambiguous effect of care by letter. Whether in love letters of desire; in political position papers about race, disability, sexuality; in mother-daughter letters about pregnancy, breast feeding, or abortion; or in campaign demands, emotions at a dis-tance appear ambiguous. This is true even when we reread old letters, as I will suggest in the following chapters on the sensitive legacy of epistolary archives.

Electronic relationships make these ethical fault lines still plainer. Dis-simulation in relationships has been vastly facilitated by three key features of the Internet as a medium: anonymity, reproducibility, and a structure of "many to many" (Deborah Johnson, *Computer Ethics*). We can all write and receive an anonymous letter, but compare this to the number of people who send spam. Again, we can all think of times we have photocopied or hand copied a letter, say for the family at Christmas, but compare this to how easy it is to forward or copy in somebody to an e-mail. And because the medium is a broadcast of "many-to-many," there is little vetting of information, though equally, of course, little censorship either. For this reason, the conventional "ethical duty" in cyberculture is to maintain one's identity (Poster, *Information Please*, 153).

Despite these caveats, I propose that not only have feminist expectations of mutual care survived but, ironically, that they may have something to offer the digital age, precisely because of its erosion of the traditional ethical foundation of identity. To appreciate this, I wish briefly to contrast the approach of an ethics of care to the philosophy of Jürgen Habermas, who has been the most influential source of thinking about the Internet as a resource for social movements, despite the fact that he never explicitly address the media (Poster, *Information Please*, 157). Habermas has held that today's withered democracies need to be regenerated through egalitarian dialogue in the way of the early civil society in the eighteenth-century Enlightenment (Habermas, *Between Facts and Norms*). This seemed, at least in the early relatively lawless days of the Internet, to describe perfectly the political potential of virtual communities (Rheingold, *The Virtual Community*). Habermasian visions of communities "deliberating" on the Internet are described in his notion of "discourse ethics." This requires "keeping controversial questions open"; being able to "criticize the rationalization underpinning the actions and projects of others," especially their "facticity"; and "preserving overall goals, principles and rights" in conditions of domination-free communication (Slevin, *The Internet and Society*, 186–97). Recognizing the rights of all participants to equal concern and respect depends upon being able to produce "reasons" for demands that are unprejudiced and free from "personal emotional reactions." In Habermas's view, "emotional involvement does not demonstrate moral commitment" (195). This is because it undermines sincerity and consistency, and can be hypocritical, tempted to appeal to generalized or projected "higher authorities" or some arbitrary statement that one's views are self-evident.

Useful as such moral positions may be, they do not describe the actual nature of network relationships nor the generally relational nature of the self. E-mail is ambiguous, volatile, and deceptive even in such carefully managed groups as Women on the Net. We might go so far as to consider today's intensive production of virtual "relatedness" as having paranoid elements (Civin, *Male, Female, Email*). Thus we need a model of community that offers alternative forms of engagement, that can deal with today's machine-dependent, mutable subjectivity and acknowledge people's needs and feelings as well as rights and reason. From a care ethicist's perspective, this is to understand autonomy as growing *from* emotionally nurturing contexts, rather than as something to be respected as preexisting. At the same time, the Habermasian emphasis on neutrality and reason in virtual community may be an important balance to feminist ideals of caring and personalized exchange, for conflicts can be just as bitter online as anywhere else.

As I argued in chapter 9, an ethics of care more happily describes the production of the conditions for political engagement than the resolution of political crisis. It is difficult enough to negotiate the fulfillment of needs within a relationship or family, let alone those so vertiginously provoked by globalization. How does an ethic of care measure up to the much more typical ethos (hardly an ethic) of the network society: "a culture of the ephemeral, a culture of each strategic decision, a patchwork of experiences and interests, rather than a charter of rights and obligations" (Castells, *The Rise of the Network Society*, 199)? The "privatization of sociability" (Silverstone, "Complicity and Collusion," 767) that probably describes most e-mail exchanges opens up the vision of chaos that, in some respects, care ethics itself invites, and this privatization also takes us back to the problem that care is easier when individuals already feel autonomous. The conference list set up before the Fourth World Conference on Women held in Beijing in 1995, for example, was monitored for ten months before and after the actual conference for its "tolerance." Dinah Davis found tolerance for a diverse range of opinions; tolerance for continued discussion of procedural variations and violations on the list (e.g., netiquette, list rules, duplicate postings); and minimal flaming (she cites only one instance based on ideological and cultural differences). Criticisms were based upon unequal access to the technology by developing countries (Shade, *Gender and Community*, 39–40).[1]

We have seen how a similar pursuit of "tolerance" worked for Women on the Net. Yet, perhaps because they were all strong professionals already, it was the emotional exchange that proved most interesting and important in creating community. It transformed abstract discussions about "place politics" and access into personal explorations that ironically made those very questions of place, body, and technology much more material for their readers. Perhaps most indicative was the resolution of conflicts over accessibility and "difference" within the group in terms of confession and empathy as well as self-consciousness about the terms of communication. The individual investment this resolution embodied was crucial to its ethical efficacy. We can see in it aspects of Habermas's notion of "discourse ethic." But rather than arriving at an agreed policy or truth, they continued to nurture relationships as part of a range of particular truths.

WoN's dual understanding of the Internet as economically divisive yet potentially culturally inclusive is also very different from relativist versions of postmodern feminism and much more representative of non-Western feminist perspectives. This is why virtual relationship did not lead to questioning gender identity per se. Despite titling the discussion as a "cyborg list"—itself debated as a potentially alienating term—the variable meanings of "woman" or even "women" and "men" were explored far more in terms of differences in access to information, education, money, or power than as challenges to linguistic or even bodily identity. Indeed, having children provided a unifying motif in the conversation. It is interesting to me to that the one man in the group, Arturo Escobar, argued that to be effective, cyber-cultural politics requires

> awareness of the dominant worlds that are being created by the same technologies on which the progressive networks rely . . . and an ongoing tacking back and forth between cyberpolitics (political activism on the Internet) and . . . place politics, or political activism in the physical locations at which the networker sits and lives.
>
> (Escobar, "Gender, Place, and Networks," 32)

The choice to use e-mail, rather than a more experimental Internet medium itself expresses the materialist emphasis of transnational feminism. On one level, this is simply because it is the cheapest, easiest form of Internet communication (cheaper than listservs, in fact) and as such a public relations tool fast becoming as important as radio, television, or print. On another level, it is the key to making the Web accessible. Leslie Shade's study of gender and community on the Internet concludes that e-mail and listservs are "low-tech tools for networking" that remain one of the earliest and most successful forms of feminist communication (*Gender and Community*, 34–36). The preference for using e-mail over other aspects of the Web is also evident in a recent survey of the use of Internet-communication technologies in women's groups in twenty-three countries in the Caucasus, Central Asia, the Pacific Islands, and Asia, mainly for administrative purposes and for correspondence with donors and other international partners, followed by networking, information access, and advocacy. Indeed, Internet-accessed information is often repackaged as e-mail or radio, while some posit that groups may jeopardize their empowerment goals when they place a higher priority on access to the Web and developing Web sites over facilitating e-mail access to isolated grassroots communities (Tim Scott et al., *I on the Mouse*, 19; Gilbert, "The Gilbert Email Manifesto"). Focusing on efforts to place databases on the Web or to increase the number of "hits" registered on sites can reflect donor requests for accountability and transparency rather than accessibility or actual organizational performance and effectiveness (Scott et al., *I on the Mouse*, 19). Laura Agustín considers that communications technology can only empower many groups, such as migrant sex workers, if it is "not isolated in offices, not connected to formal education, not touted as a new religion, not pushed as a 'right,' but instead associated with coffee, sandwiches and chat." She envisions a "true network, which women could enter and leave at different points" to be a fleet of vans offering wash facilities, condoms and blood tests alongside mobile phones and Internet access (Agustín, "They Speak, but Who Listens?" 154–55).

In one sense, it is simply stating the obvious to point out that economics takes precedence over aesthetic or philosophical priorities for campaigns, especially those representing poorer groups. But this is to underestimate the potential creativity and community involved in administration and networking, as well as private correspondence. One group that has used e-mail to further social solidarity in the former Yugoslavia titles itself The Electronic Witches (Shade, *Gender and Community*, 44). Laura Agustín conceives of a communications advocate for sex workers as "a postmodern scribe" (Agustín, "They Speak, but Who Listens?" 154). The Network of East-West Women subsidizes participants' e-mail in exchange for "supporting dialogue, informational exchange and activism among those concerned about women's swiftly changing situation in Central and Eastern Europe and the former Soviet Union" (Shade, *Gender and Community*, 44). The End-violence Virtual Working Group, for example, an Internet discussion list sponsored by the United Nations Development Fund for Women (UNIFEM), the World Bank, and the Global Knowledge Partnership, got 2,500 people from every region of the world (including more than a third from developing countries) to use e-mail to share experiences, resources, and ideas about ending violence against women, establishing an unprecedented global network of human rights workers.[2]

Most famously, the Fourth World Conference on Women held in Beijing and its concurrent Non-Governmental Forum, which brought together 40,000 women from almost 200 countries, has been seen as "a model for many on the role of electronic networking in supporting the international women's movement" (*Gender and Community*, 38). The Women's Outreach Program of the Association for Progressive Communication (APC), set up in 1993, was the primary telecommunications provider for NGO groups and U.N. delegates during the preliminary stages (38–39). We get a sense of its effects from Patti Whaley, coordinating the London Amnesty International delegation: "E-mail was the bread and butter of my daily existence. I looked on the APC conferences and found background documentation, last-minute hotel reservation forms, and gory details about the awful facilities at Hairou" (quoted in *Gender and Community*, 39). Whaley's delegation was able to send press releases by e-mail to the Hong Kong office, which then contacted the office in London, which in turn reposted to the news service on Greennet, the London APC affiliate. Greennet then cross-posted to the Beijing listservs:

> Those listservs sent me about 80 messages a day. I had all the major speeches, all the important press releases, and detailed reports of who was stalemating whom. I knew what Bella Abzug was wearing, what days it rained, and how many days it took our list moderator's clothes to dry . . . I had probably never felt as close to the women's movement as I did then, even though they were literally on the other side of the world from me. Although I work with email daily, I remain astonished and indeed moved at the range and intimacy of the contacts we were able to establish with this technology.
>
> (39)

These prosaic kinds of organizational correspondences are like the white of the egg within which a testimonial yolk is suspended; networks nurturing the newborn voice of an individual or group. They are the distracting babble of multiple internal monologues, but they are also the group of friends in the night preparing the court case. Consider, for example, the range of political representation produced by Women on the Net. The listserv, conference presentation, and book secured further funding for IT training in the Southern women's projects as well a Rockefeller grant to continue a research group on "place-consciousness" and an eventual further book (Harcourt and Escobar, *Women and the Politics of Place*). In 1999 members of the group met in Zanzibar to discuss the potential of "the virtual world" to communicate across traditional divides of gender, class, culture, and nation. Women who had never seen a computer before are now meeting virtually and face to face to tackle themes such as domestic violence, social justice, and sex education (Harcourt, "World Wide Women and the Web").

There were more directly testimonial links. Alice Mastrangelo Gittler helped disseminate the testimonies of women at the Beijing Women's conference in 1995. Arturo Escobar writes of Amazon indigenous activist testimonies and petitions on the Web ("Gender, Place, and Networks," 40). Wendy Harcourt writes online of her reaction to the heightened Israeli-Palestinian conflict as someone of Jewish heritage.[3] Fatma Alloo networked with women organizing a conference in Mumbai in 2003 called Empowering Women Through Information and Knowledge: From Oral Traditions to ICT.[4] And it is apt that this chapter itself has grown out of generous e-mails from Wendy Harcourt. This is the pattern for so many of the published auto/biographies or even legal, educational, and medical testimonies of today, from The Women's Court at the Permanent Arab Court to Resist Violence Against Women soliciting testimonies through e-mail on its Web site to the posthumous publication of cancer sufferer Ruth Picardie's bleakly witty e-mails and magazine columns.[5]

If we accept that our "multi-faceted, virtual culture" is not "a fantasy, [but] a material force because it informs, and enforces, powerful economic decisions at every moment in the life of the network" (Castells, *The Rise of the Network Society*, 199), e-mails and, increasingly, the social-networking sites of "Web 2.0" are potentially more powerful than the kind of letter networks that sustained the tracts of nineteenth-century suffragettes or the radical magazines of women modernists in the 1920s (Hanscombe and Smyers, *Writing for Their Lives*) or even the feminist webs of the 1970s and 80s. E-mail is not simply the nurturing white around the yolk of a more public form of testimony but the semiprivate, semipublic genre of an age of multiple and constantly shifting privates and publics. Gillian Youngs, musing as to "how these conversations, transferred from their times and spaces on to the printed page, would communicate to others," points to this question as "a crucial dimension of the wider cyberpolitical potential of endeavours such as WoN" (cited in Harcourt "Introduction," 19).

I have given positive and successful examples of electronic networking, in part because I am tired of the lament that we have entered an irrevocably artless era of machine-impelled communication. The sheer variety of electronic connections cannot help but produce creative and sophisticated writing games, as well as emotional or functional spam. Feminists evidently continue to search for holistic forms of virtual community, despite the needs that this opens up. We must, of course, resist the temptation to idealize global feminism as an imagined community. And even less than a decade after its conference, today's cyberfeminists perhaps see groups like Women on the Net as a somewhat innocent and early form of "communication experiment." But communications, especially when they are personalized, do seem to be creating new forms of civil society.

Of all forms of life writing, e-mail and other forms of computer-mediated communication are the most symptomatic of our age in positioning the individual in networks of multiplying relationships. Testimony remains the public form of political voice: e-mail is the grubby yet also gracious agent in the pipes of the machine. Testimony makes the case for justice among the staggering inequalities of an increasingly linked world; e-mail compulsively registers our unconscious interdependence and particularity. Yet for this reason, feminist e-mail—extending the letters of earlier feminist groups— explicitly displays the ethical and political issues at stake in an information society: the reconstruction of private and public, material and virtual; the nature of citizenship in a global village rather than a nation state. Most especially, it shows the ever more pressing requirement that we find ways of creating communities that can resist the fragmentation of globalization without re-creating our own defensive boundaries. This puts a check on the more libertarian interpretations of cyberspace and e-mail. To accept this requirement is also to accept the continuing presence of women-centered communities alongside the deconstruction of gender—both equally possible and typical of Internet use. It is to think about the emotional life of virtual, transnational, citizenship.

PART FOUR

The Afterlife of Letters

CHAPTER TWELVE

On Burning and Saving Letters

P utting down the pen, shutting up the laptop, can be a relief. Sometimes changes, both personal and political, depend upon it. Letters can outlive a relationship, but relationships can also outlive letters. Yet, whether lying in the bottom of a drawer, munched by the shredder, or carefully tied in ribbon, the letter is never just an object. While researching this book, it has become obvious to me that what happens to personal letters *after* they are written and received is itself a significant psychological and ethical as well as literary issue. Most people do not keep the letters or e-mails they receive, let alone copies of their own; the very idea can strike one as hubristic. But some letters are somberly preserved, even sent to archives and editors. Others are disposed of equally seriously. Burning a letter describes many literary denouements for that reason. Such epistolary afterlives also involve their own gender politics: destroying a personal letter is especially associated with love or family gone wrong, just as the preservation of personal letters is typically a woman's task.

Archiving, publishing, or even simply analyzing letters is therefore a highly sensitive business, delicately traversing the correspondents' relationship as well as other layers of relationship that connect editor, publisher, archivist, and public reader. I have heard many stories about why people have got or not got letters, how they would be more than glad to show them to me, or why they would not show them to me even if they had them. Correspondences of my own were spawned; academia, like art, is sustained by relationships. This has brought special pleasures but also special anxieties, replaying questions of identity, difference, and community that thread through the original correspondences. Like others working with letters, I have wondered what we *owe* one another in relation to our personal lives? How far do we need to put our personal lives on the line—that is, in the public sphere? How do we balance individual need—for privacy or, conversely, for public attention—against collective interest—for education, for political change, for amusement? This chapter is more than an account of my own research stories, then, for I wish to offer a more substantial reflection on what are evidently topical anxieties for anyone interested in the publication of letters.

I begin by using the motif of the burned letter to consider the significance of the letter as a material object and why it may feel dangerous to let it survive its original function and context. I then explore the reasons that feminists like myself have wished nevertheless to save personal letters and make them public. I go behind the scenes of some letter collections to show editors wrestling with ethical questions as well as with letter writers, owners, and their inheritors. Finally, I analyze these ethical dilemmas as part of the general conflict in life writing between "the obligation to truth and the obligations of trust" (Couser, *Vulnerable Subjects*, 198). This conflict is heightened in correspondence because two writers' truths are at stake. I show that our "relational" lives and identities, especially the sexual relationships so important to feminism, do not square with privacy laws that currently regulate life writing. The bargains we make between self-disclosure and protecting another's privacy are therefore often political themselves. Epistolary publication, like letter writing, is ethically hazardous because it involves relationships of difference, power, and desire. It returns us to the ongoing question of this book, whether such relationships can themselves be ethical resources.

Burning Letters

Nowhere is the vitality of a letter clearer than when it is burned. A living communication, its physical death can only be symbolic. Miss Matty, in Elizabeth Gaskell's *Cranford*, burns her parents' love letters doubtfully because "no one will care for them when I'm gone." Matty's merging of person with letter is obvious as she ritually drops the papers into the middle of the fire, "watching each blaze up, die out, and rise away, in faint, white, ghostly semblance, up the chimney" (Gaskell, *Cranford/Cousin Phillis*, 86). Similarly visceral is Agnes Lockwood's destruction of Lord Montbarry's letters in Wilkie Collins's *The Haunted Hotel*: "there were none of the ordinary signs of grief in her face, as she slowly tore the letters of her false lover in two, and threw the pieces into the small fire which had been lit to consume them" (20). It was "fantasies of death" that prompted Henry James to burn forty years of correspondence near the end of his life (James, xiii–xv). The writing of Sylvia Plath's poem "Burning the Letters" followed a literal bonfire of Ted Hughes's missives to her (Plath, *Collected Poems*, 204–5). More recently, Julian Barnes's novel *Flaubert's Parrot* satirizes poststructuralist attacks on the cult of authors by having its biographer-protagonist salivating when he thinks he may have access to a secret stash of Flaubert's love letters. He is, of course, distraught when he discovers they have been burned. Antonia Byatt's *Possession* similarly spoofs a romantic letter burning to show how critics and archivists are possessed *by* the writers' letters they frantically compete to own (496). Therapists and New Agers, by contrast, advise cathartic epistolary bonfires or even writing letters expressly for a ritual destruction.[1]

Charles Bazerman suggests the basis for the power of the letter as a material object in observing that the letter is the form in which writing's historical substitution for speech is most evident. As such, letters possess a physical authority rooted in closeness to the writer's body. Proof of being physically touched is most obvious in the handwritten signature, and this retains a special place in our electronic, textualized society. Letters as objects look back to a premodern system of "concrete value," signifying "personal trust of known individuals who act as guarantors of value," in the "increasingly abstracted symbolic" of exchange value (Bazerman, "Letters and the Social Grounding," 22). (The epistolary gesture survives in paper money's printed promise "to pay the bearer on demand the printed sum of ——.") Bazerman's aim is to explain the social grounding of the letter in systems of exchange and why the letter is an especially transitional genre because of this. But his argument also explains the psychological power of the letter as form of bodily trade that underwrites, and sometimes dominates, its text.

Bazerman's argument is borne out by Elizabeth's Cook's explanation of the eighteenth century's proliferation of what she terms "epistolary bodies," where printed texts mimicked "traces of the body" in pretend "inkblots, teardrops, erasures, revisions, a scriptive tremulousness that signifies iconically instead of semantically." Cook interprets these as symptoms of the transition from the habits and thought forms of a pretypographical world to a culture shaped by the technology and logic of print and the burgeoning of a democratized market economy (E. Cook, *Epistolary Bodies*, 2). It is as a similarly transitional object that paper letters are still required for legal guarantees in the age of electronic text. E-mail lacks the physical trace of its writer, and, partly because of this, its legal status is in flux. But some of the same contradictory materialism resurfaces in e-mail's "emoticon" graphic script, as well as in digital watermarks and electronic signatures. Indeed anxiety about the authority of e-mail in this respect confirms Cook's suggestion that "at different historical moments of cultural transformation and political pressure, when existing categories of public and private are being redefined along with the bodies that inhabit these spaces, the letter-form returns to the foreground of the cultural imagination" (179).

Derridean literary critics have used the letter to show just how uncertain are written guarantees of presence and authority. In fact, in *The Postcard*, Derrida tantalizes the reader with descriptions of censored or burned letters as part of his "death sentence for epistolarity" itself (Kauffman, *Special Delivery*, 84, 90). Letters from this point of view show most graphically how writing is founded upon the writer's absence, how language itself refers only obliquely to the material world. But dialogic paradigms like Bazerman's— which emphasize writing's communicative function precisely *because* it is socially, rather than generically, grounded—more convincingly explain the enduring power of the personal letter. Stories of letters as material objects make the same point. Letters are abstractions haunted by the concrete value of the body's presence, and this is why as an inheritance they can seem to possess the luminosity of "a burning beacon, every word . . . a live coal, in its time" (Carlyle, xii). A live coal will burn well, and perhaps *must* be burned to be properly extinguished. I recently met a woman, however, who decided that burning her ex's letters would accord them too much dignity: she took them to a public trashcan instead.

The physical presence of a letter's signature, as well as the paper, font, and layout, subliminally indicate its function as a legal authority in systems of economic or political exchange, often codified through professional or class status. But literary and personal narratives of epistolary burning, like the idiom of perfume, tears, inkblots, and even blood, symbolize more perverse and primitive systems in which the mortal and sexual body is exchanged. Just as people cherish or even kiss the letter from a loved one, they destroy it because of its vital, often sexual trace. It was surely for this reason that in 2002 Terry Lynn Barton mounted a legal defense against the charge of starting Colorado's biggest wildfire by claiming it was accidentally sparked while she was burning a letter from her estranged husband.[2] Although her attempt to turn arson into the effects of feminine feeling did not convince the court, it showed her belief that this sexual epistolary coin still had currency. The letter is often fetishized as evocative of a woman's body and identity, for historically women have themselves been objects of men's exchange. In the prolific epistolary fiction of the eighteenth century, "the letter comes to signify nothing quite so much as female sexuality itself, that folded, secret place which is always open to violent intrusion" (Eagleton, *The Rape of Clarissa*, 55). Linda Kauffman elaborates the way that this can be turned round by the female epistolary lover who asserts her body as a form of authority:

> Through such [physical signs of writing], the heroine transmits a part of herself, the corporeal, to the textual, implying that the body's message is truer than speech: tears are irrefutable evidence. . . . Throughout amorous epistolary discourse, the heroine glorifies her tears, her heart, her tongue, her body as authentic registers of her emotions.
>
> (Kauffman, *Discourses of Desire*, 36–37)

The letter's fetishistic aspect also emerges in the way people treat the letters of the dead, particularly in "last letters," posted before or at the writer's death. The uncanny comfort of apparently posthumous communication turns ephemera into relic. Roy Fuller's poem "War Letters" evokes the most commonly celebrated occasion for this ironic literary transcendence: "A pair might cease to live / While the indestructible letter, / Turned lies, flew to the other" (quoted in Blythe, *Private Words*, 20). Conversely, the burning of posthumous letters evokes acts of cremation, releasing the spirit from the writer's material remains. Franz Kafka begged for all his letters to be burned after his death precisely because he feared their power to keep him alive in a ghostly hinterland (Zilcosky, "Kafka's Remains"). In the case of inheriting—or losing—a family member's letters, we often find the emotions evoked by the letter as relic confusingly combined with its status as legal instruction. Nina Bawden plays family love off against underlying greed in her novel *Family Money*, where a house fire accidentally destroys a widow's family letters. Though the widow was not especially attached to the letters, nor were they literal wills, her children's subtly selfish concern about the fire provokes her to leave her inheritance to her cleaner instead.

Admittedly, the fetishistic qualities of e-mail are diminished because it lacks the physical trace of its writer and, unless printed out, the sensuality and flexibility of paper. But e-mail's earthy virtuality is provoking new scenarios of sexual and posthumous exchange. Bel Mooney's novel *Intimate Letters* tells of a wife discovering her husband's affair after his death, in the passionate letters stored on his computer. In doing so she realizes he had relied upon her "technophobia" to conceal them, and it is deleting them (alongside literally burning her friend's extramarital letters) that lets her come to terms with the unspoken bargains of their marriage (278). The challenges of posthumous e-mail are increasingly common in fact as well as fiction, notwithstanding popular assumptions that no one keeps it. Matt Seaton describes his dead wife Ruth Picardie's last e-mails about her breast cancer as artfully deliberate last letters partly because they were so "transient and disposable":

> Beyond the practicalities, email for Ruth represented a new and subtly different medium of communication: it was a way of expressing thoughts and feelings more spontaneously than in a letter, yet more reflectively than in a telephone conversation. It had a quality of being simultaneously intimate and serious, yet transient and disposable, and this meshed with something in her writer's psyche. . . . Ruth knew she had left a rich resource of writing in her email correspondence—in fact, it was her idea that any book of hers might include a selection from them. In compiling this book I know that we have been carrying out her wishes.
>
> (Picardie, *Before I Say Goodbye*, viii–ix)

More often, people discover unintended legacies in the inboxes of the dead. Internet storage possibilities mean that the minutiae that used to disappear in phone calls may endure in unprecedented ways exciting for social researchers (Youngs, cited in Harcourt, "Introduction," 2). But relatives discovering "skeletons in the digital cupboard" of the deceased, or simply having to make grueling choices about which "digital memories" to save, show that e-mail retains some of the letter's ability to provoke complex emotional legacies (Preston, "Are You Fully Prepared"). AfterLife, a nonprofit organization, archives Web sites after their authors die and are no longer able to look after them, while www.cherishalife.co.uk creates memorial Web sites. No doubt there will soon be a company that turns old e-mails into a similarly manageable "message" from the dead.

As the examples above show, a letter's afterlife is as thoroughly culturally gendered as its writing. It is difficult to imagine marketing a book of men's letters in the manner of Anna Holmes's 2002 anthology, *Hell Hath No Fury: Women's Break-Up Letters*, although her stories of military men ceremoniously burning "Dear John" letters from girlfriends—or even using them as toilet paper—suggests how men, too, fetishize letters in anger as well as desire (169). Similarly, the disproportionately large showing of women writers on www.sothere.com, a Web site of "unsent letters," suggests the attachment that women have to letters and e-mails as symptoms even of failed relationships. It is women who tend to be the family archivists in both fiction and fact. Feminists have critiqued these representations to the extent that they perpetuate women's dependence and their exclusion from the public sphere. Feminist criticism has also shown that women's identification with letters derives from the same system that identifies women *as* letters, objects of exchange in patriarchal and racist economies. Ironically, it is because women's bodies are fetishized that women understand so well the fetishistic power of a writing so redolent of bodily trace. But feminists are also interested in what happens to letters as a private history of women's relationships and networks, especially when these have resisted the victimization that describes traditional epistolary "discourses of desire" (Kauffman, *Discourses of Desire*). For that reason, feminists have often tried to stop the burning of letters and their "corporeal souls" (Meigs, in Dawson, *The Virago Book*). It is obvious where my own colors lie in this game.

Saving Letters

The building of archives and documentary collections needs to continue. The archive of women's autobiographical history already recovered in the last few decades has transformed the field, establishing a rich legacy. Expanding the archive by incorporating works formerly regarded as "merely personal" and extraliterary will make available to scholars and students a broader range of texts—including diaries, letters, journals, memoirs, travel narratives, meditations, cookbooks, family histories, spiritual records, collages, art books, and others.

—Smith and Watson, "Introduction"

Sidonie Smith and Julia Watson's vision of archives and documentary collections is compelling. One of the most enduring critiques made by second-wave feminist historians has been that gender and sexual politics have been "hidden from history" and this, in part, is precisely because the private or ephemeral documents that have represented them have not been considered of enough public value to keep or circulate. Deliberate censorship of letters has also been a concern. Literary scandals, such as Thomas Carlyle's control over the letters of his wife Jane; Cassandra Austen's snipping up of the letters of her sister Jane; and Arthur Nicholls's marital wish that Charlotte Brontë destroy her passionate correspondence with Ellen Nussey, have been interpreted as evidence of control over women's relationships and reputations as well as their writing (Clarke, *Ambitious Heights*; Castle, "Was Jane Austen Gay?"; Gordon, *Charlotte Brontë*, 310). Margaret Atwood's novel *The Handmaid's Tale* satirizes patriarchal editing in a postscript by a priggish "archivist" interpreting the handmaid's tapes (Kauffman, *Special Delivery*, 225). Kay Turner, whose collection *Between Us* I discussed in chapter 1, writes:

I do feel fortunate that the lesbian struggle for freedom and recognition in recent years makes it possible in 1996 to gather together a collection of letters that represents the variousness and vitality of our loving. This book would have been much more difficult to assemble ten years ago, probably impossible just twenty years ago. Not surprisingly, I had the easiest time gathering material from the post-liberation period, since the 1970s. But certainly my project speaks as much to what has been lost, burned, restricted, or otherwise denied as it testifies to what remains.[3]

(11)

But stories of burned letters begin to suggest the problems with Sidonie Smith's expansive advice. Saving, archiving, or publishing letters is rarely a case of wresting them from deliberate censorship, still less from patriarchal conspiracy. As objects that represent psychological investment in legal, sexual, and financial negotiations, letters embody much subtler clashes of interest. As I repeatedly discovered in trying to convince feminists to let me use their letters—and in considering whether to use my own letters—relationship histories are hot, hot coals. Public letters were easy to find, for example Smith College's fabulous file of letters to *Ms.*, (a jewel in Amy Erdman Farrell's study of the magazine).[4] But Britain's largest feminist archive, the Women's Library, possesses only a handful of collections containing personal letters from recent years, all of which are uncatalogued or currently embargoed from public use.[5] The personal collections at the foremost American archive of women's history, the Schlesinger Library, such as Susan Koppelman's (intriguing, given her proposal to replace all academic publication with an "intense correspondence") and Carolyn Heilbrun's (who rejoiced in e-mail as a liberation for the old), are similarly under wraps.[6]

Making private documents public may be sensitive for the letter writer, but the desires of the letter's recipient are also at stake. It is rare to get both sides of a correspondence in the same place because usually one party or the other has not had the same interest in preserving or publishing or because their perceptions of the relationship differ. Kay Turner, who passionately wishes to "encourage lesbians everywhere to donate personal papers to local and national archives" (*Between Us*, 30), also tells us that:

> It is a bit of a dare to attempt to wrestle love letters from lesbians. Some are more than willing, others are anxious and still require the protection of anonymity; some cannot bear the review process, and others maintain a trash and burn policy at the end of any relationship. In my pursuit I pleaded and hounded and had a ball as I went through a remarkable process of discovery.[7]
>
> (11)

Noeleen Heyzer, the director of the United Nations Development Fund for Women, recalls a close friend and feminist scholar burning her letters from women migrant workers in the late 1980s as Singapore and Malaysia were undergoing "Operation Lalang," a massive crackdown on opposition activists and academics begun in 1987 to get rid of the "new wave of activism."[8]

The letter's legal status itself reflects the dual interest of author and recipient, for the author owns copyright but the addressee owns the object. This means that the recipient has the right to give—or sell—letters addressed to them to an archive or editor but no right to publish them. On the other hand, the writer very often cannot exercise her right to publish because she has not kept a copy of the letters and the recipient has disposed of, or will not relinquish, the originals. This division of interests is manifested with a twist in the case of the letters that Vera Brittain wrote to her friend Storm Jameson. When the two great writers quarreled in the 1940s, Jameson asked Brittain to return her letters, which she then destroyed. But Brittain made copies, which are now available in public archives. Cathy Clay, who researched the letters for her Ph.D. thesis, comments that "in terms of the politics of women's friendship, I've felt it important to engage with and write about this correspondence, but my ethical responsibility continues to feel ambiguous, especially now I'm seeking permission to publish."[9] Helen Buss points out that the "importance placed on women's relational sense of self creates a special challenge in working through their archival remains," as their letters have often been scattered through the collections of the men they were attached to (Buss, "Introduction," 4). Marlene Kadar, for example, had to track down "three sets of letters in three separate collections" in three different archives to reconstruct her "epistolary constellation" of correspondences among Frida Kahlo, Ella Wolfe, and Earle Birney (Kadar, "An Epistolary Constellation").

We also have to ask why others' personal correspondences might be considered to have public interest in the first place. Carole Gerson, who provides a handy guide to "Locating Female Subjects in the Archives" is right that archivists are a researcher's best friend in helping us to what is actually there and accessible, but they, more than anyone, are aware that archives are themselves shot through with institutional politics. A university archivist will assess documents' value not only in relation to disciplinary ideals but academic market value—what will attract visiting scholars, grants, biographers, or students—and the resources available to catalogue or preserve them. (On average, less than half of any given archive is catalogued).[10] The Women's Library only in 1998 received sufficient funds (through a national lottery grant) to catalogue its collections of suffragette letters. Kathryn Jacob, assistant curator at the Schlesinger, described to me the ongoing professional balancing of the needs of donors, scholars, and funders. This includes warning donors about third-party concerns; deciding whether to undertake the laborious and expensive process of making uncopyrighted material available to researchers; and refusing donor requests to embargo access for centuries or to their enemies.[11] The Schlesinger's policies are as much the result of the library's belief that it is important to support researchers' interests in the history of process and struggle within organizations and movements as the result of the preciousness of space.[12]

Independent archives may be more purely motivated by ideas of political education, but they work under even greater material constraints, with a largely voluntary work force and a complex dependency on the community they represent.[13] The Lesbian Archive at Glasgow Women's Library has "at present no money for purchasing materials," though notably its Web site now suggests that donating "letters from loved ones" might be one way that interested women could help.[14] The Feminist Archives (North), at the time I was researching, was in boxes waiting for volunteers to help unpack them in their new home at the University of Leeds.[15] One of the best resources I found for my book was the legendary Lesbian Herstory Archives in Brooklyn, which entranced me with its stacks of colorful boxes surveyed by a life-size cut out of Gertrude Stein, photos of archivists on Pride demonstrations, button displays, and comfy rocking chair.[16] But the special expectations that it has to manage are reflected by the anonymous donor who suggested that the public interests of the lesbian community will *relieve* her of the responsibility of deciding whether to burn or save: "I heard you wanted old love letters, so I send these to you instead of burning them. . . . Thank you for providing a place to save our herstory when it gets to be too much to keep it at home."[17] The ambiguity of this writer's wish for a public readership haunts my own decision to write about this correspondence, especially when I suspect that her correspondent did not know of the donation.

It is thus close to home that I turn to the interests of the editors, publishers, and general readers of letter. Many letter editors are amateurs motivated by the wish to celebrate or commemorate friends or family—even the letters of well-known authors are often edited by a relative—and it is with a shock that they discover the criteria for commercial publication. At the other end of the spectrum lie editors like Anna Holmes and Jill Dawson, professional writers commissioned by trade publishers to do middle-of-the-road anthologies like *Hell Hath No Fury* and *The Virago Book of Love Letters*. The average reader has little tolerance for the arcane or academic. For that reason publishers encourage a focus on public figures, preferably with literary skill and personal revelations, although the market for war stories sustains a niche for "ordinary" people's correspondences (M. Jolly, "Myths of Unity"). Academic editors or critics, however, are motivated by their own volatile mix of disciplinary interest, career pressures, and, often, personal connection. Clare Brant introduces her readings of the love letters of Mary, Queen of Scots, by admitting that "the study of love letters requires an acknowledgement that in this genre (perhaps above all), critics wear dark glasses, as if to disguise the glare of their involvements." Although a critic's "snooping is sanctioned by scholarship . . . for my singular infraction of the writers' privacy, I pay with acknowledgement of my own secrets: so this is how you love! *Me too,* or, *so do not I!* Intimacies collide and collude: mine with my lovers, theirs with their lovers, mine with their lovers and them" (Brant, "Love Stories?" 74–75). The same collision of intimacies is plainly visible in the following accounts by feminists who have written explicitly about their research.

Margaret Rose Gladney, in "Personalizing the Political, Politicizing the Personal: Reflections on Editing the Letters of Lillian Smith," describes how, researching the civil rights activist Lillian Smith in the early 1980s, she discovered proof of Smith and her companion Paula Snelling's sexual relationship in a bundle of letters hidden in a small leather case in Snelling's house. Gladney tentatively told the elderly Snelling of her discovery and was naturally delighted when Snelling asked her to read them aloud and talked freely of their love. Unsurprisingly, Gladney could hardly bear to obey Snelling's request to burn them when "she'd finished with them," and decided to interpret her work as unfinished so she could safely deposit them with Smith's other letters in the University of Georgia archives. Although she was within her legal right to do this, Snelling having given her ownership, her anxieties were not over, as Smith's relatives were furious when she quoted the letters in a conference paper, denying that Smith could have had a lesbian relationship. Confronting her own experience as a closeted white Southern lesbian, Gladney decided nevertheless to persevere in publicizing Smith and Snelling's relationship in a planned biography. For Gladney, it was important to show how Snelling and Smith's love had supported their civil rights activism—and important to show the history of sexual as well as racial oppression in the upper-class white South. What a relief, then, when Smith's relatives approved of the draft of the biography, vindicating her view that "sexuality and sexual expression" are not "purely private matters" (97) and that "our expressions of sexuality, like our expressions of gender, race, and class, do not exist in isolation but emerge in relationship with one another" (103). Gladney's deeply personal decision to "out" Smith, as she presents it, was also how she helped herself to come out, as well as to get over crushing writing block and professional doldrums.

Estelle Freedman, in "'The Burning of Letters Continues': Elusive Identities and the Historical Construction of Sexuality," explores a similar scenario when writing the life of prison governor and reformer Miriam Van Waters. In Van Waters's diary account of burning their love letters, Freedman, with as much emotion as Gladney, discovered that Van Waters *did* have a sexual relationship with her partner, Geraldine Thompson. "They might have been *inspiration*, history, joy, style—to me in 'old age,'" Van Waters recorded. But, as Freedman puts it, "instead, she resolved to keep their message within herself" (51). Van Waters' diary continues: "The letters are bone and sinew now in my carnage. Doubtless my character has been formed by them" (quoted in Freedman, 51).

In publishing this diary account, Freedman in a sense "unburns" the letters, makes visible the loving body in which Van Waters hoped to hide them. But she also sympathetically explores *why* Van Waters burned them, concluding that Van Waters was not only protecting herself and her lover from stigmatization in the homophobic 1940s but, ironically, protecting the poor, black, lesbian prisoners that she had charge of as a white, upper-class prison reformer. Freedman says less than Gladney about the personal effects of her research, perhaps because she was already both out and an established scholar at Stanford when working on the letters. However, Freedman unashamedly empathizes with Van Waters's experience of being dismissed from her job in 1949, under a cloud of having "condoned" homosexuality among inmates. Freedman herself had been discriminated against as a woman, and perhaps as a lesbian, by Stanford University in 1983, when it tried to reverse her department's recommendation of tenure. (She won a nationally recognized sex discrimination case.)

The challenges facing these editors are partly the consequence of dealing with the inheritors of letters after the death of the writer, partly the result of changing mores. Karen Payne's more urgent dilemmas in trying to publish the letters of living writers in *Between Ourselves: Letters Between Mothers and Daughters, 1750–1982* (1984) were even closer to my heart. Payne's original appeal, addressed "Dear Sisters" and circulated in the general and feminist press from 1979 till about 1981, explained:

> I am collecting material for a book about women's liberation and the mother/daughter relationship—particularly the communication between mothers and daughters about the issues of women's liberation. The book will consist of letters written between mothers and daughters and is designed to appeal to women not usually receptive to feminist tracts.[18]

Replies came in slowly over five years. Some came from friends of friends, some from strangers who quickly disclosed personal histories and often shyly stated literary ambitions, sometimes precipitating new correspondences within families and even a workshop to follow up "the new relationship" their letters had generated. Payne noted that "I have talked with more than three hundred women about their intimate family histories and tried to tell them something about myself so that there would not be a disturbing imbalance of 'secrets' between us."[19] Such "secrets" inevitably proved challenging to represent sensitively, especially when contributors became friends. Payne's drafts, often mixed with diary accounts, show her exhaustive attempt to find the right tone in editorial introductions, attending a "Feminist Methodology research group" for almost three years and exchanging her own passionate correspondence with her research assistants Karen Jacobson and Diana Clarke. One draft introduction, eventually unused, admitted that

> there are, inevitably, limitations and mistakes as well as biases in my analysis and insights. I was helped immeasurably by the fact that at a certain point I began to view the letters of contemporary women as historical documents. I was also helped by the fact that I could ask these women questions in person, probe the meaning of apparent inconsistencies and challenge their contradictions.

Payne hoped to resolve the difficulties of her material by emphasizing the positive message of what women shared and could do for one another. However, she was advised by those in the publishing industry to play up conflict, famous names, and professional writers and to play down "interpretation." One suggested that Payne could access more negative experiences, including incest or abuse, by commissioning letters on things women *couldn't* say to their mothers. Nan Talese, her American editor at Houghton Mifflin, wanted her to open the book with some letters from Sylvia Plath to her mother, although Payne successfully refused to begin the book with a suicide and a famous writer, insisting, with her English editor Alison Burns, on the literary power of "ordinary" letters.[20] One of the hardest challenges was simply cutting the manuscript by half, casualties of which included Payne's idea of a section of letters from supportive men and all comments on the research process itself.

Payne successfully walked the line between commercial appeal and political vision. *Between Ourselves* remains in print. But Payne was still not spared criticisms from feminists. One contributor wrote to suggest that in return for Payne's potential profiting on their personal lives, she would like a donation to Rape Crisis (Karen duly made it). Another wrote suspiciously to say that the book was "American in tone and style," arguing that such projects should be as voluntary and collective as her own unpaid work in a women's film collective. Yet another considered that a section on men was inappropriate as the book no longer answered its title theme, "between ourselves."[21] A more painful challenge was the discovery that Payne's call for letters had been slated as "ageist" in the British feminist magazine *Spare Rib* because she had given as an example of what she was looking for, "letters explaining to your mother why. . . ." Payne wrote back with a heartfelt explanation that she had been only too excited to receive letters from feminist mothers, that in any case mothers were themselves daughters. Payne also worried that she was unable to find letters from women racial and ethnic backgrounds other than white:

> I circulated the open letter explaining this book among several Black and Asian women's groups and talked about the project with many Black women, particularly on my trip to America—yet this yielded scarcely a dozen letters. I hope someone succeeds in bringing to light letters written by women of the many races and nationalities not represented here. It is now clear to me that this would require a special coordinated effort of its own—more letters *must* exist somewhere.

Payne's papers show that in fact she cared far more about the opinions of her contributors than those of editors or reviewers. One draft set of headings included: "The Right-on and Write-off Feminist in me; the politics of writing about emotions and the emotions of writing about politics (fear of exposure, fear of censure from other feminists if I express contradictions instead of the line)." It was hardly surprising. They were her community, as an American in her late twenties, living in a shared house in London, describing herself as "a socialist feminist" as well as a "struggling freelance writer, editor and (recently) assistant director." "I do what I can to scrape together a living," she explained to one contributor, "I love my life here, living in this house with 3 people, working on the Feminist Review collective working to bring Judy Chicago's Dinner Party to Europe, loving lots of women and a few men, aching for my mother to have a feminist perspective on her life and stop blaming herself."[22] Although only a tiny portion of this autobiographical element made it into the book (*Between Ourselves*, 334–35) and Payne was cross with "therapeutic" interpretations, the book was deeply personal, conceived of alongside long letters to her own mother and even one to an imagined "unborn child."

For Payne, challenging old gender conventions remained more important than protecting privacy. To the question, "Why publish such painful outrageous correspondence?" she answered, "Why is it considered almost bizarre (or, at any rate, suspicious) to say things which are likely to cause disagreement or highlight the differences between a mother and a daughter?" and even, "why is it necessary to lie?" Yet this is merged with another question less clearly answered: why is it necessary to publish? Of course, one answer to that question was Payne's own professional gain. Though Payne herself felt this was justified, many feminists frowned upon this kind of self-interest. Once again, we see the tight control that the feminist community could exert over its members and its contrary demands for "care" against individual autonomy. Although this community has now relaxed in its dispersal, I can still identify to a degree with these worries.

Gladney, Freedman, and Payne identified with their subjects and wanted to celebrate them but did not always have the power to reward or persuade in terms acceptable to the letter writers. They are editors from the mold of the epistolary confidant. But what happens when the editor knows right from the start that she is facing a problem of vast social status and difference? Shula Marks's account of editing a correspondence among three South African women marks out the other extreme of editorial ethical dilemmas in wanting to publish the writing of a woman who was *unable* to give informed consent. Marks discovered the letters of Lily Moya buried in the University of Natal archives in the papers of the white educationalist Mabel Palmer. Moya was fifteen when she first wrote to Mabel, living unhappily with her guardian-uncle in the Transkei, a "native area," and attending an Anglican missionary school. The letters were written between 1949 and 1951, the crucial years when apartheid was being institutionalized, and speak powerfully of the forces ranged against a lonely, bright teenager from a rural and unsettled family. Mabel, an idealistic English battleaxe in her seventies, was sympathetic enough to fund Moya's schooling but had no conception of, nor interest in, her needs or culture. Although she enlisted the help of a social worker, Sibusiswe Makhanya, this only produced another failed attempt to communicate, for Makhanya came from another tribe and had her own professional and religious agenda. The title of Marks's edition of the letters, *Not Either an Experimental Doll*, is the reproach that Moya made two years later, bitterly disillusioned with her helpers' efforts to "improve" her, and dreadfully upset by her experiences of what appeared to be harassment by boys at her school.

For Marks, discovering the correspondence turned an academic project into a personal one and a planned history into a kind of biography. She decided to trace Moya in order to ask for copyright and to offer her any royalties received but soon realized the mire into which this led her. As a white academic, she feared becoming a second Mabel, which was compounded when she received an anonymous letter warning her off her "do-gooding" project. The letter, uncannily echoing the obsession with sexual purity in Moya's original letters, was signed "Lily De-flowered." When Marks finally met Moya, she discovered that she had been mentally ill since her disappearance from Mabel's life in 1951, suffering from symptoms variously described as schizophrenia or spirit possession. Most tellingly, Moya listed the names of the schools she went to in the same breath as the hospitals she had been kept in for the twenty-five years since. This encounter forms the final part of Marks's epilogue, ending the story that Moya could not directly write. Instead, Marks directs us toward the collective narrative of historical context: the socioeconomic story of apartheid, the differently oppressive colonial and tribal constructions of black female sexuality, and the cultural relativity of Moya's madness. In this way, Marks acknowledges the limits of individual agency in the destructive grip of racial and sexual politics.

Marks realized through her experience of editing Moya's letters that even so-called ordinary people usually can claim some kind of "success." "It is far more difficult," she says, "to encounter those who have been destroyed in the very process of their adaptation and resistance to the structures of domination" (Marks, "The Context of Personal Narrative," 47). How do you

Elizabeth Barakah Hodges, *Ghosts*, 1996.

write the story of someone who really *was* a "victim"? One answer is to do precisely what Marks does—publish the personal letters as symptoms of the writers' frustrated ambitions and desperation in place of a more achieved form of life writing such as an autobiography. The gap between editor and writer will almost inevitably be far greater than that in the celebratory model of a book like Payne's *Between Ourselves*, and to the public reader this can only add to the painful ironies of the initial correspondence. Yet feminists, perhaps even more than the general reader, find interest in life stories that chart the full range of women's struggles, particularly where they focus on women's differences from one another.

There is a spectrum then among editors—and publishers and archivists—who are culturally similar and equal in power to writers and those who are not, much as Tom Couser has schematized "collaborative autobiography" as "lying somewhere on a continuum ranging from ethnographic autobiography, in which writers outrank subjects, to celebrity autobiography, in which subjects outrank writers" (Couser, *Vulnerable Subjects*, 40). Couser notes that "it makes little sense to discuss the 'ethics' of collaborative autobiography in isolation from the politics—or for that matter, the economics—of collaboration, for ethical problems are most likely to occur where there is a substantial differential between partners in power or wealth" (41). Feminist awareness of the political dimensions of these kinds of ethical dilemmas became acute from the mid-1980s, when Marks was working on the South African letters. Editing and archiving letters is part of feminist "epistolary discourse" in that sense, moving from a period of presumed identification among women to the working through of their differences, especially in terms of race and class. But this does not necessarily match the difference between consensual and nonconsensual publication of letters. Even in the more equal relationship of, say, Payne and her contributors, who sometimes became her friends if they hadn't been already, there are huge expectations on both sides that put pressure on the identifications in their own correspondence. Similarly, it may be precisely because a letter writer has very little social power that a third party may consider it ethical to archive or publish the correspondence, even against the writer's wishes. In the final chapter, then, I conclude by considering the justifications for "readdressing" a letter to the public reader.

CHAPTER THIRTEEN

On Stealing Letters

The Ethics of Epistolary Research

S idonie Smith and Julia Watson accompanied their appeal for a women's
autobiographical archive with a call for a "feminist ethics of autobiography" to go with it:

> Autobiographical ethics includes a host of issues about how and what sub-
> jects and audiences know of each other, and how they comport themselves.
> The ethics of self- and family revelation within the autobiography, the posi-
> tioning of audiences during and after the subject's life-time, the subject's re-
> lation to biographical accounts and extratextual evidence are areas that
> deserve further scrutiny. What would a feminist ethics of autobiography
> look like? As Doris Sommer suggested in a recent essay on Elena Ponia-
> towska and the testimonial novel, the relationship between (woman) infor-
> mant and (woman) narrator, like that between writer and reader, may be
> neither symmetrical nor unmanipulated. Indeed an informant may resist be-
> ing "consumed" by an interlocutor's mediation. A writer attentive to issues
> of difference can acknowledge ethical problems in conversations of social un-

equals, can write so as to resist the "complicity between narrator and reader," acknowledging the social inequities of lives and the privilege of her own authority as author.

(Smith and Watson, "Introduction," 38)

Like the auto/biographer or ethnographer, the letter editor or archivist must negotiate much more than copyright with their correspondents in deciding how each will be represented in a wider community. The key negotiation takes place over how and whether the private should be publicized, and in this the balance of power becomes a central ethical question. But there are special ethical challenges involved for letters, for here there is also the relationship between the correspondents (or their inheritors) *themselves* to be negotiated. Sometimes an editor effectively repeats an original difference in status, for often, as for Lily Moya, a correspondence is driven by one person's wish to get love or an education, to get out, or to get help from the other. This is overdetermined by the fact that publishers and editors are disproportionately middle class, white and Western, and they may, of course, be interested in the letter writers precisely because they are not.[1] Conversely, biographers like Ian Hamilton and Diane Middlebrook, who tracked down unpublished letters of J. D. Salinger and Ted Hughes in university libraries, find themselves up against the financial and psychological demands of immensely influential literary estates (Hamilton, *In Search of J. D. Salinger*; Middlebrook, "'Fair Use'"). Hamilton ended up in a bitter court case with Salinger for having wanted to praise his favorite author's epistolary gifts.[2] Even in the case of editors or archivists who come from the same community as their writers, or where the letter writer or recipient is editing her *own* letters, numerous ethical questions of privacy arise.

Yet in the stories of those who wish to stop the "burning of the letters" we can see justifications for epistolary publication, even if, on some level, this purloins from the original relationship. Max Brod famously ignored his best friend Kafka's fantastically detailed instructions for him to burn all his letters, those to as well as from him, after his death, publishing them all instead. The original ethical outrage by Kafka's family and fans has long been superseded by praise for what they argue was Brod's courage and foresight (Zilcosky, "Kafka's Remains"). Letters personify the power of a writer's hold. But just as a letter writer owns the copyright but not the object, letters equally personify the reader's matching power of interpretation and, of course, the danger that an address can fall into unintended ears or hands. In fact, often readers enjoys letters *because* they are not addressed to them. Seventeenth-century anthologies of purportedly "found" love letters were marketed as "stolen postbags," while the waylaid letter rivals the burned one as a literary motif.[3] The editors and archivists I consider in this chapter similarly stake an interest in letters' public value as part of the belief that they tell some kind of truth, whether beautiful like the love that inspired Lillian Smith's work for civil rights, or horrible like the maternalist racism and sexual repression that crushed Lily Moya. What this implies, of course, is that truth can contribute to social change. In the case of Karen Payne's writers, who were still living and, in some cases, wrote in response to her book, this idea is also reinforced by the belief that public interest can change the writer's life directly.

Stealing Letters

It is in this light that I moved from my own celebration of feminist letters to a more honest account of the struggles and frustrations within recent feminist communities. But let me recount the harder moments in what I felt was a justified "stealing" from the flames so you can decide for yourself. I have mentioned my decision to write about the anonymous love letters in the Lesbian Herstory Archives. My imagination was particularly caught by these fragments of a dead relationship, but also by their evident poetry even in its afterlife. The ritual necklace in the accompanying envelope said it all: this was the relic donated as a form of memorial. Although Deborah Edel, one of the archive's founders, is still wonderfully available to do things like help obtain permission from a donor who last contacted them in 1983, it proved impossible to find the writers. Similarly, I struggled to trace Lise, whose correspondence with Joan Nestle exemplified, to me, the delicacy of feminist epistolary negotiation. What to do? After extensive discussion with both Columbia University Press and several archivists, I decided it was within the terms of "fair use" to write about them, since my intentions were to value the terms of the relationship, no contract had been signed, and the writers retained some anonymity. Lise, at the last minute, heard I was looking for her, sparking another delicate correspondence.

More dilemmas ensued after my forages in the Feminist Archive (South), a packed room of papers, books, posters, and old coffee cups at the back of a tiny town library in Bristol, England. Among a large collection of Greenham papers, I found the exchange between Carole Harwood and her husband that I discuss in chapter 8. Happily, Carole Harwood was traceable, thanks to the kindness of the archivist Jane Hargreaves—we met, indeed, on a peace walk commemorating twenty years since the beginning of the women's protest at Greenham Common. Although she and her husband had long since separated, she put me in touch with him, and he congratulated me, in a generous e-mail correspondence, on turning up a useful "stash"—despite the fact he had not known of the deposit. But trouble came when I tried to trace the woman with whom Carole had been having a relationship at the same time and whose ardent letters were also among the "Harwood papers." I was able to find someone who could contact her on my behalf, but she would not even accept a letter from me. Contradictory stories ensued as to whether she had known about the deposit. I believe that the archivist has since sent her photocopies of her own letters at her request, but the originals are Carole's property and she therefore cannot remove them from the archive. I understood her wishes. Yet I did not want to erase her presence entirely from the story. I chose to acknowledge that Carole had had a woman lover at that time, using the generic pseudonym that Greenham women gave in court, Bridget Evans, and to allude to the existence of their letters without quoting from them. Total anonymity remains impossible, since Carole was adamant that she wanted her own real name used. Further difficulties sprouted a year later, when Carole's husband decided that he had had enough of going over the past. Again I understood his wishes, and I cut a chapter of this book's original manuscript. But my soul searching was only resolved by turning to autobiography to talk about the issue of feminist relationships with men, putting my own past out for consumption, however that may be interpreted.

You might imagine that it was easier simply to advertise for letter writers willing to share their letters. Not so. The famous names of the movement, to whom I tentatively wrote, were unresponsive, although Charlotte Bunch graciously let me interview her and Noeleen Heyzer, and Lee Waldorf and Roxanna Carillo of UNIFEM let me behind the scenes of the End-Violence listserv. To my "call for letters," circulated on listservs and notice boards, through conferences, archives, libraries, and friends, only a dozen or so responded. Of these, few actually had letters and were willing to share them with me. I was faced with my own vulnerability as a researcher, fully aware of how little I could offer for potentially deeply personal revelations: recognition from an academic publisher, no pay, and certainly no therapy! In the case of a man who wrote to me as a passionate amateur of letter writing and a long-time member of men's groups, I felt I was being drawn into a volatile mix of seduction and revenge against the academy. Another woman wrote to offer me love letters between her and her Ph.D. supervisor, but then thought better of it.

My correspondence with S, whose story I tell in chapter 8, was also motivated in part by her complex relationship to the academy as a long-time activist, but, happily, we were able to exchange mutual fascinations. She a craftswoman who was also a writer, I an academic who is also an amateur of crafts, she a charging bull and survivor, I a dogged inheritor of both lesbian feminism and a subsequent heterosexuality (or hasbianism, as it is often waggishly named), we recognized an interest that carried us through the careful negotiation over what should be made public or even shared between us. Similarly Wendy Harcourt, who provided me with the e-mail archives of Women on the Net, envied me the time for literary feminism, while I was inspired by her global development work, appropriately through e-mails between England and Rome and the connecting e-mail from my father, who put us in touch. It was pure serendipity, however, that brought Karen Payne's archive into my life. After the United States bombed Afghanistan in 2001, I went to a "Stop the War" meeting at the local mosque, advertised enticingly as "An American Willing to Listen." The American was she.

Obviously there are thousands more letters and e-mails squirreled away or forgotten about. Others with more resources or chutzpah could certainly wriggle them out more than I. But the real problem is privacy, not resources. It is simply too early to expect many who were writing and protesting in the 1970s, 1980s, and 1990s to share such traces, to expose the personal relationships in a movement that threw old morality up in the air and so often came down in a mess. Perhaps the fallout of revolutionary youth means that feminists are less ready now to invite such vulnerability than they were twenty years ago when Karen Payne received so many petitions to be included in her "mother-daughter" book. For those with public reputations, it is only natural that they want the value of their papers recognized professionally and financially, if they want to share them at all.

Paul John Eakin has recently weighed the justifications of "truth" for the publishing of autobiography in the current climate where selves are "sold" with such aggression and "personal extremity has become our daily fare" (Eakin, *How Our Lives Become Stories*, 157). Are memoirs, he asks, "now courageously speaking hitherto unspeakable things, things that we have held in silence precisely because we have refused to accept them as a part of knowledge? Or is their speech in such cases culpable, compounding the original trespass with unseemly disclosure?" (143). Eakin discovers the "beginnings of an answer" to the difficult questions of what is "fair and right" for us to write and publish about one another, in "legal and philosophical treatments of the individual's right to privacy" (160). The legal history of the idea dates from 1890, when Samuel D. Warren and Louis D. Brandeis published "The Right to Privacy" in response to the intrusive coverage of Warren's family in the newly established popular press (162). They defined privacy not only as a question of individual space but as "the right to an inviolate personality." The simultaneous rise of paparazzi, mass printing, photography, and the nuclear family suggests links between this concept of privacy and Western bourgeois culture as it developed in the nineteenth century. Eakin, though, suggests that privacy is a fundamental human need, if we think of it not so much as "an objective physical space of secrecy, solitude, or anonymity" but rather an aspect of "the forms of respect that we owe to each other as members of a common community" (Robert C. Post, quoted in Eakin, *How Our Lives Become Stories*, 165). Deprivation of privacy, for this reason, devastates people, not only upsetting their place in the community but, for people such as prisoners, literally killing off their sense of self altogether (167).

"Truth," then, must be weighed against the harm done to a person's sense of self, one's "personality," which in part is defined through one's standing in their community. Here the law is a crude tool for, as Eakin notes, many formulations of privacy, person, and autonomy are couched in the language of individual property, which cannot explain this psychological or even social dimension:

> When it comes to texts, to life stories, the law tends to adopt a commodified notion of personality, gravitating to questions of ownership and copyright,

but if we regard the possession of "a life"—and, by extension, "having" a life story—as a defining attribute of the individual, then, once again, violations of privacy could be construed as committed against *person* rather than property.

(167–68; my italics)

On the other hand, in what sense can a personality ever be "inviolate"? Even Eakin's more psychological formulation of privacy is as much about being able to live *with* others as being able to shut them out. Autobiography itself is rooted in the pursuit of "recognition," dependent on witnessing and dialogue (52). Letters even more obviously dramatize the relational nature of identity. What may be my privacy is your story to tell, what is my story is your privacy. Much like forms of "proximate collaborative autobiography," (176) where, for example, a son tells his and his father's story together, the story of a correspondence shows that "the boundaries between self and other are hard to determine, and . . . the boundaries between person and property as well" (169). This is perhaps especially true for women, who historically operate as both "bargain and bargainer" in patriarchal systems of exchange (169). For all these reasons, the ethics of biography have never been more heatedly debated than in today's insatiable market for the intimate facts of others' lives (170). But the jury is still out on the fundamental question of how to square "fidelity to the truth" with the "right to privacy" (185) when privacy is such a relative, relational entity. Eakin concludes that "the confessional drive behind life writing that draws us to it—our desire to penetrate the mystery of another person—may also constitute its primary ethical flaw" (185).

G. Thomas Couser further illuminates the conundrum of finding a proper respect for privacy that can recognize that we "are relational selves living relational lives" (Eakin, *How Our Lives Become Stories*, 161) and, we might add, writing relational stories. He, too, boils the ethics of life writing down to "weighing competing values: the desire to tell one's story and the need to protect others, the obligation to truth and the obligations of trust" (Couser, *Vulnerable Subjects*, 198). Couser makes the case for protection and trust very clear in life writings about what he calls "vulnerable subjects," such as "children, members of disadvantaged minorities, and people with certain kinds of illnesses and disabilities" (17). Examining the unintended voyeurism, exclusion, and appropriation of these subjects' personhood in parental memoirs of injured children, "as told to" stories, "euthanasia narratives," and case histories, Couser shows how life writing can be as shocking to a person's identity as medical intrusion or pathology. He, then, is wary of the justifications of "truth" *especially when the form is intimately relational or collaborative*, like a family memoir. Couser instead argues that life writers should redress the balance from a bias toward unregulated free speech (at least in the United States), to a more stringent cultural pursuit of tact, fairness, respect, and confidentiality. He also condemns most forms of publication without the subject's consent and recommends explicitly acknowledging the ethical issues involved in any particular research (201). Perhaps the supreme ethical principle in collaborative life writings, he says, "should be a variant of the Golden Rule: Do unto your partner as you would have your partner do unto you (or the equivalent Kantian imperative, 'One must act to treat every person as an end and never as a means only')":

> Which is to say that autobiographical collaborations should be mutually gratifying and maximally egalitarian, neither partner should abuse, exploit, or betray the other. Given the subject's special stake in the textual product, a corollary principle might be that the subjects of as-told-to autobiographies, like those of oral history interviews, should have the right to audit and edit manuscripts before publication.
>
> (36)

In taking "collaborative" autobiography, particularly family memoirs, as his paradigm, Couser supports Eakin's point that the construction of privacy itself is also a question of relationship. In this, no definition of intellectual property can deal with the complexity of life writing's contracts, and Couser does not recommend its legal control. Rather, he implies, bioethics has much to teach life writers about respecting and caring for the vulnerable through its intimate forms of care for the body, even for the corpse. If we can find caring ways to tell stories of how we can live with, and as, vulnerable beings, we are performing a public good just as morally beneficial as physical healing and care. Surprisingly then, Couser suggests we need not less but *more* life writing to do this, and more "ethical criticism" of life writing to boot:

> Although we need to acknowledge that difficult ethical dilemmas are built into life writing, what is called for is not more but rather less policing of life

writing than already takes place. We may need, then, to turn to a very different arena for our metaphor—perhaps to gardening, for as a particularly vital art, life writing needs to be delicately and carefully nurtured, not coercively controlled.

(202)

Although Couser does not discuss epistolary publication, this model of "caring" sharing would seem especially appropriate for letters, which are identified with the writer's body precisely because they represent dependent relationships. For example, Lennard J. Davis's edition of his parents' love letters, *Shall I Say A Kiss? Courtship Letters of a Deaf Couple* (the one epistolary reference in Couser's book), potentially makes his parents vulnerably exposed. But this is complicated by Davis's own vulnerability, for his previously published memoir, *My Sense of Silence: Memoirs of a Childhood with Deafness*, includes details of suffering physical abuse at the hands of his older brother, Gerald. Couser suggests that the publication of such accusations, if true, would qualify as "justified harm," but Davis "blunts their force by noting that he and Gerald became closer as a result of Lennard's life writing, Gerald, indeed, writing the preface to the edition of the letters at Lennard's invitation" (Couser, *Vulnerable Subjects*, 41). The power of epistolary care, suggested by the deaf parents who used letters to figure sound as well as touch, was replayed in the healing relationship between the brothers' joint work of publication. At best, the same relationship of care would extend from the brothers' writing and epistolary editing out to the general readers, who would enlarge their own ways of relating empathetically through reading the book.

Privacy, Relationship, and Feminism

Both Eakin and Couser then push us to rethink privacy as the *effect* of relationships in ways that echo the dialectic of autonomy and care when it works. The question is not so much the protection of an absolute form of privacy but understanding and respecting the kind of contract or sociability each form of address presupposes. Neither, however, considers how we can apply this to the publication of letters, which themselves owe their existence to relationship. (We might surmise that letters are always already "published" to that degree.) Let us turn then to Nancy K. Miller's "diary" essay "The Ethics of Betrayal: Diary of a Memoirist," which directly assesses the problem of publishing letters as part of relationship contracts. In this, Miller struggles with her desire to use her former husband's letters in her latest memoir—despite the fact that they are very personal, she does not possess copyright, and she has not seen him for twenty-five years. One of several ironies that propel the essay is that Miller has led the way in theorizing the relationships that define life writing and has done so in part by a much-lauded style of "autobiographical" or "personal" criticism. Having initially demonstrated the theoretical purchase of autobiography in understanding and improving gender and race relations, she has more recently argued that we love reading other people's personal stories because of a primary need to discover people *unlike* ourselves (Miller, *Getting Personal*, 15). This perception turns autobiography into a collective story of mutual exchange and discovery:

> More and more I take comfort in not knowing my own story because of the joys of the uncertainty principle but also because I find that it's not mine alone. Others have their part in it. The presence of others—whether through intimacy or the proximity of generations—expands the material, lends ballast to a diminishing self. This has a double advantage: it provides new stories and unexpected connections. . . . When I corresponded with the girl who had shared my con-man adventure, and she helped me with her diaries and photographs (a writer, she saved too), she was also telling me *her* story (in fact, she considered the experience *her* story as well as mine).
>
> (Miller, *But Enough About Me*, 136)

It is no accident then, that Miller has also long been fascinated by the epistolary, as this example of corresponding with "the girl who shared [her] con-man adventure" shows. Letters prove the positive aspect of the "uncertainty principle" in writing and reading lives, the sense of "the presence of others." They are also a form of "getting personal" in academia, in which the theoretical and aesthetic dimensions of relational identities come to life. For Miller, this is clearly of a piece with her feminist commitment. With Couser and Eakin, Miller has shown that men have often structured their life writings through primary relationships in the way critics used to claim was the mark of women's autobiography. However, she suggests that women inherit a special connection to relational, specifically epistolary, forms.[4] Her early work on eighteenth-century literature explored the sexual and literary vulnerability of feminine epistolary heroines, echoed in *Bequest and Betrayal* in the image of Colette correcting her mother's letters when she decides they are worthy of publication and Miller herself waiting for the letters of a married man she was in love with (Miller, *Bequest and Betrayal*, 5, 154). But the letter as a more positive means of literary intervention prompted her interest in the eighteenth-century writer Madame de Grafigny's anticolonial *Letters from a Peruvian Woman*, and her defense of women's identity in a published correspondence with the critic Peggy Kamuf ("Parisian Letters"). Miller's work as a whole presents epistolary forms as part of an autobiographical dialogue with a reader who is most immediately figured as a woman who may face the same puzzles and pains about her gendered lot as the writer. Of Simone de Beauvoir's gushing love letters to Nelson Algren, published in 1997 as the apparent comedown of the great feminist existentialist, Miller stresses that the letters "reveal a Beauvoir present in the flesh as a physical and sexual being" (Miller, *But Enough About Me*, 58–60).

Yet the thought of using someone else's letters as part of her story, as Miller describes it in "The Ethics of Betrayal," precipitates a crisis of her feminist conscience. She explains this as the effect of her own experience of having some of her own personal letters stolen two decades before by a middle-aged French academic who had been romantically involved with her close friend. This man had used Miller's letters to her friend to

> construct an ending for a thinly disguised autobiographical novel he had written about their relationship and its demise. Hijacking my letters without, of course, acknowledging theft to the reader was how the wounded author chose to document the woman's change of heart toward him; it was as if the letters proved that he was justified in taking revenge in print against someone he had once loved in life.
>
> ("The Ethics of Betrayal," 150)

Miller continues:

> The violation of my privacy was not without effect on my life outside the text; the stain of revelation spread, embarrassing, in particular, the man I was soon to marry. While I *might* one day have told him about aspects of my secret history chronicled in the correspondence, his discovering them in

print during the early days of a new relationship, in a book friends and colleagues were bound to read, was a rather different matter. I view the appropriation of my letters to be as unforgivable an act of plagiarism today as I did then, but now that I myself am writing a memoir about a love story gone wrong—my first marriage—I better understand (while still regretting) a writer's temptation to put the material before the person, as though the letter were no more than words on paper (a mistake well understood by eighteenth-century novelists, and belatedly by their characters), as though the words no longer carried, were no longer attached to, the sender's emotions.

(150–51)

Revisiting her earlier memoirs, she wonders if she has wrongly assumed that truthfulness, certainly autobiographical artfulness, may *require* betrayal, just as children must eventually betray their parents (152).

Miller's passionate justification for "going public with private stories" because "there is no way to tell a story that's only about you," seems to turn around on itself here (*But Enough About Me*, xx). That is, if you cannot tell others' stories without betraying them, then you should not tell yours either. "Sometimes," she admits, "I have the uncomfortable feeling that the truest ethical position is closely related to silence, to self-silencing" ("The Ethics of Betrayal," 157). And yet, if we look more closely at *why* she wants to use her former husband's letters, and the story she wishes to tell with them, we can understand the force of her dilemma:

> In addition to my letters home, I have in my possession letters written by my ex-husband to me and also, as I've said, to my parents, who are now dead. I can't help feeling that the letters are mine, that they belong to me, and most of all to my *story*. I want to tell that story as I remember it, fully aware that I might be getting some of the details wrong. But if this is how I remember it, and it feels like my truth, then shouldn't I have the right to put it out there? Yes, but.
>
> (151)

What begins to emerge is that her "story" *itself* was one of betrayal in and through letters, in a marriage to a much older man who, she discovered, was writing almost medically to her parents about her unhappy behavior. In addition to details of financial exchanges between her husband and her father, she hints that she is particularly hurt at the thought that her mother has handed her over to him, a transaction now repeated in their private correspondence (154–55). Unconsciously, this positions her with his letters, which she inherited at her parents' death, and now "can't help feeling" belong to her and her story. This identification becomes more suggestively corporeal in the following passage, where she admits that the eighteenth-century letter-novels that were her academic subject at that time remain a seductive literary influence in trying to reconstruct what went wrong with the marriage:

> "My Dangerous Relations." As the title of my memoir (in progress) suggests, I'm looking back at my life through the literary legacy of eighteenth-century France, not with Rousseau's confessions but with Laclos's epistolary novel. Something about seizing the world through letters *imprinted on me at a vulnerable moment* in my intellectual development—sex, letters, and a rage for freedom combined to confuse and excite me.
>
> (153; my italics)

Letters are symptoms of Miller's status in the pre-feminist 1960s as both bargainer and bargained, notwithstanding her "rage for freedom," a status that seems to retain its mark as she still feels "ventriloquised" by the letters of her former husband (154).

In this respect, Miller's relationship to the letters to her parents is somewhat different than that to the plagiarizing academic who stole Miller's letters to her friend, his partner at the time. In the novel in which he reproduces Miller's letters, all women are portrayed as sexual betrayers when they are not subservient objects, and he crudely uses Miller's confidences about extramarital affairs, lesbian experimentation, and newly coined feminist psychoanalysis to support his vengeful fantasy of dismembering his girlfriend, who, he feels, has "castrated" him (Doubrovsky, *Un Amour de soi*, 348). Even so, Miller clearly does not want to risk repeating his ethical abuse. Thus, though wanting both to confess and to accuse both him and her own former husband, in the end she draws back from publishing more than a short paraphrase of one of her ex-husband's letters, with all names disguised, including the novelist's. Even this does not seem a perfect ethical solution, for she realizes that paradoxically, were I to flout the rule of intellectual copyright, I would betray the letter writer *less* rather than more. Patrick, the bewildered husband, sounds quite appealing in his own words minus the edge of caricature that I create through my paraphrase; even I feel that. So perhaps there really is such a thing as an ethical betrayal: publish the letters and let the man speak for himself.

("The Ethics of Betrayal," 157)

All this brings her back to the question at the heart of any justification she can find for using such letters: "What is the truth in the name of which I choose to betray another person by revealing intimate details about his life?" Since truth must be relative to perspective, memory, and writing itself (157), there cannot be any absolute justification. But equally, Miller's relational view of truth permits no absolute condemnation. Although she does *not* publish the letters, in the end she will not push aside the desire to tell how she felt about reading them, to write "back" to them and their writer in some way through the public reader. The larger issue gestured to in this desire is the best way to maintain the dialogue about gender, among women but also between men and women. If she must publicize her own fall "into the marriage plot," or even her anger at the "dangerous liaisons" her generation pursued, so be it. As she puts it in *But Enough About Me*:

As always it's in the private stories behind the public statements, as much as in the collective pronouncements and manifestos, that the history of feminism continues to remain—however embarrassingly—alive. Autobiographical moments provide keys to the emotional logic at work in the culture, and that supplies the juice for any political movement.

(67)

The real secrets at stake in the public exchange of private letters, from this perspective, are the underlying systems of sexual, gender, class, and racial exchange that prompt such epistolary possessions and outings. The justifying "truth," then, is a "political movement" that might interpret and improve these exchanges, the movement Miller calls feminism.

It must be said that the price of the truth may be harder to pay for those who are socially vulnerable subjects with less of a confessional and literary tradition. About her own decision to write autobiographically about her parents' poverty and abusiveness, bell hooks suggests that black and working-class writers struggle to write personally, which then becomes an emotional work itself. In *Remembered Rapture: The Writer at Work*, hooks reprints part of a letter she wrote to her parents explaining her choice to write about them and describes her sadness that they did not reply (104–5). Yet hooks presents writing about these writings, as Miller does, as a direct dialogue with a reading community that she hopes will transform our private relationships, even if indirectly. At one end of her interest in autobiography, she is inspired by the letters of Rilke, a white European modernist, at the other, by the "problem" letters her readers send her; all are part of the virtual community created through public, epistolary life writing (*Remembered Rapture*, 58, 149–51).

The relationships involved in burning, saving, stealing, and publishing letters drive us back to the history of the personal letter as a genre of sexual politics and feminine identification, to the gendered divisions of labor that have prompted women's networks, men's migrations, and sexual trafficking. This is why women so often want to talk about personal letters, even when it seems apparently not just embarrassing but unethical to do so. But what *is* ethical in this political context? Today's communications economy makes this much more than a question of simply weighing up the right to "free speech" versus the right to individual "privacy." We cannot idealize free speech, while Third World and feminist lobbyists are unveiling the hidden monopolies behind the Internet and worrying about the aggressive marketing of the "private life."[5] On the other hand, neither can we idealize individual privacy and choice in the spiral of sexual and social inequality. The trade in women's bodies in a global economy has not so much lessened as been joined by the forces of capitalist exchange, old forms of fetishism mixed with new ones of commodification. Ironically, the more that global forms of exchange invade our privacy, the more we need to understand the social constructions and remedies of that privacy. A recent conference on "Accountability and Ethics in the Archival Sphere" ran as its headline: "Accountability . . . ethics . . . integrity . . . whistleblower . . . These seem to have become the latest buzz words. We appear to live in a time that yearns for individuals and corporate bodies that embody these ideals in word and deed to protect us against other buzz words such as Ipperwash, Walkerton, Enron, Arthur Anderson."[6] What do we make of James Hewitt's attempt to auction the love letters that Princess Diana sent to him, or even the Lesbian and Gay Archives Roundtable's recent debate over "the pros and cons of buying letters for our collections via e-Bay?"[7]

Ethical treatment of somebody's personal details or life story cannot be left as a simple question of preserving a pure "inviolate personality" any more than of guarding a form of individual property. Rather, the issue is how to transform the unequal domestic, sexual, and generational currencies of private address as well as the economic terms of trade that sustain the inequities of public or business correspondence. This, of course, has been the effort of all the correspondences considered in this book, as part of the transformation of the "private sphere" that feminism took as its task after 1970. The writers' essential strategy was simply for women to write to one another as political allies, a quietly revolutionary shift from a literary economy defined for centuries and across many different cultures through women's dependence on men.

The ethics that has prompted the public circulation and the writing of letters in feminism, in other words, treats personal relationships as potential resources rather than mere liabilities. Feminism's epistolary expression has attempted to arbitrate through love rather than judgment, through speaking about private things rather than through silencing them, through using the distance underlying a letter to come closer. In its weaker form, this turns into covert control, just as letter writing and publishing can try to force similarities and obligations through intimate appeal. But when it succeeds, its respects the paradox that we are all both different and dependent upon one another simultaneously. As I argued of the more sophisticated forms of feminist coalition in virtual electronic community, the most compelling philosophies of citizenship today integrate care ethics with more generalized forms of justice and human rights. Similarly, we need to maintain the laws of intellectual copyright and libel, privacy laws, and ethical contracts that currently govern the public circulation of letters. But just as much, we need to use writing to extend alternative visions of personal and public relationship, and to preserve the history of those who began them, if we are to have any hope of a truly just, truly protective form of privacy.

CONCLUSION

Life has been damn hard for most everyone I know—both in and out of "the Movement" (there's been so little movement, I feel funny even using that term) these past ten or so years. I have had some pretty bad bouts of depression and burnout, and even some times when I've had to focus on just getting through to keep from going down all the way. The worst was in the early '80s when the full impact of the "sacrifices" began to hit home—turning 39 with no man in sight and with little hope of having a child and the introspection that comes with that. Even having a man in my life some of those years didn't help a whole lot.

A trip to Nicaragua in 1985 in support of the Sandinista Revolution was an enormous help as it focused my attention on something other than "self" and put my problems into a broader perspective. Noone completely escaped the "Me-ism" of the '80s; it wasn't just a Yuppie disease. I think it's in large part due to the isolation, self-imposed and forced on us by our culture (or lack of it). . . .

For a time I thought it was just me or us Movement veterans suffering from the sacrifices we had made, but one day about a year ago my neighbor was telling me how lonely I must be, since it had been nearly two years since my mate and I had broken up. She then blurted out, "But it's even worse to be with someone and still be lonely." She's been married 25 years and had three kids. . . .

I know the panic and fear that getting older engenders—especially without money and family. But in my dread, I try to remember it's not, at root, a problem of, or for, my comrades individually, or even of the Movement, but of this stinking, decaying capitalist system and its greedy grabbers bleeding and endangering us all with increasing intensity and in ways we never dreamed of, like the massive downsizing and making so many of the remaining jobs temporary and insecure, and often with longer hours. The capitalists have made our lives so difficult that people don't have the time or energy to do things right. That's one reason for the "shoddy work" of the U.S. work force that we hear so much about. I think we should call this decade "The Great Burnout."

> I certainly haven't solved the immediate and future problems of relative poverty and time to do political work. What I miss most is the Movement with its forward thrust, community, sense of purpose, excitement of new discoveries and victories. I miss the Movement more than I miss a child, money or even a man. It's lacking all that's really the pits. And having a child or a man without the Movement to make things more equal is more work, more oppression, more exhaustion.
>
> —Carol Hanisch, "To a feminist friend," August 1989

This book has explored the social practice of feminist letter writing, as well as its political functions, and the art of written communication in general. The feminist *"système épistolaire"* comprised a host of factors—the dispersed and highly mobile nature of the movement, its ephemeral publications and alternative media, its cultural activism and codes of good relationship, and, indeed, the postal service. It survives as a literature of subjectivity that takes us to feminist selves in all their needs and desires. This accompanies the movement's more overt literatures about women's rights and is why letters as *internal* binders and mediators are so interesting for what they can say about the communities that grew up around the political program of the second wave.

I have presented a wide spectrum of epistolary texts, prominently personal letters but also open letters, epistolary novels, poems, and campaign newsletters and announcements. Despite their extreme variety, they are held together by an idea of women's love and duty to one another in the creation of a feminist culture. In conceiving of this, I was inspired by Caroll Smith-Rosenberg's description of the intense epistolary networks of white American wives and mothers in the nineteenth century as a world of love and ritual. I have not intended to suggest that the British and American feminism of a century and a half later literally derived from white, Protestant bourgeois cultures like these, although some of it did, alongside many other equally important heritages of women's domestic networks, most obviously in African American communities. My point is that across and within different groups, feminists formed their own kinds of kinships, which were just as loving and as ritualistic. They were also as often held together by writing. In fact, it was the sudden vista of a women-centered family, community, and political class that inspired academic feminists to get interested in women's letter writing from other periods and places, even to see the letter as a "women's" genre.

Yet of course, feminist kinship, even across distance, was far more turbulent than those nineteenth-century families and friendships, since it was an act of political construction. Letters quickly became a medium for confronting difference and disappointment, from the expression of confidantes to a wondering about what kind of "correspondence," in the deepest philosophical sense, could be possible at all. Few feminists now would invoke "the women's web" as a method or even symbol of campaigning, even though it was itself an idea of organizing that began from the premise of acknowledging difference and care. We can appreciate this by contrasting it to today's feminists' far more globally savvy negotiations through electronic networking on the World Wide Web.

I hardly anticipated this when I began my research on letters. I was looking to value the everyday life writings of a movement dear to my heart, to extend what so many feminists have done for autobiography and for letters of other periods. The first version of this book was a paean of praise in the second wave's own preferred mode of "recovery" of an unsung history. But the material says different, in offering a literature of internal struggle, defiance, and disappointment, as well as of joy. And the processes of research said different too: I ran into problems even getting people to share their letters with me, and even a little bit of autobiography forced me to be honest about the complexity of feminist relationship. The relational self enacted in these texts is not the good or generalizable creature of much epistolary criticism. Moreover, I am clearly talking about one period in Anglo-American feminism, and within that the fragments I know best. I know very well that there are thousands of correspondences I have not been able to reach or discuss. The ethical dilemmas involved in writing about other people's letters are so evident that I offer two chapters on the topic, exploring still unresolved challenges in enacting care alongside discovery. For now, I offer some preliminary conclusions about what I hope will be a much bigger investigation into the letters from this period.

First: the literary one. There is no elaborate art in most of these texts, with the important exceptions of a few novels and essays, such as Mary Meigs's *The Time Being* or Alice Walker's *The Color Purple*. Yet I hope no one could dispute their creativity. Satire, romance, comedy, and tragedy all

make their appearances in writings that reversed centuries of literary tradition by putting the drama of women's relationship *with one another* centre
stage. Domestic, private writing was celebrated as a medium of possible art
and self-invention that could be taken into the public sphere in published
"open letters," epistolary fiction, and published editions of letters. Yet one of
the enduring interests of letter writing is the sense of performance for an audience of one. The very personal letters of anxious lovers, the life-long correspondences of S and the irreverent e-mails of Xiao Pei He and Fatma
Alloo remind us of this fact.

Second, letters reveal the nature of feminist relationships and communities. I have already described this world of love and ritual, and its special investment in emotional, often erotic connection between women. While
brilliant campaigns for legal rights, childcare provision, and economic re-
distribution unfolded, the movement's achievement was also to create a
"feminist public sphere" (Felski, *Beyond Feminist Aesthetics*). Sometimes intensely exciting, inspiring, and supportive, this was also a culture of unconscious needs, dependencies, and revenges, in which the letter's dual nature
as both gift and bargain could play a direct part.

This prompts my third angle of reflection, the philosophical and political. Letters repeatedly forced questions about feminism's own relationship
to relationships. I have argued that this has provided a test on the ethics of
care, formalized by psychologists and philosophers like Carol Gilligan, Nel
Noddings, and Sara Ruddick in the heat of the second wave. In many ways
this morality remains compelling for its realism about people's emotions
and the inequalities of needs and wants, its common sense acknowledgment
that you cannot judge without taking into account the particulars. It is an
ethics that certainly answers to the practices of community making that
characterized the women's movements of the 1970s and 1980s. It also describes the hot-headed world of e-mail relationships today, in contrast to the
idealized view of those who hope that the Internet is ushering in a new Enlightenment of democratic and reasonable dialogue. Yet feminists' attempt
to live out an ethics of care often proved to be a disappointment.

"Every Second-Wave feminist has a theory about why the movement lost
steam," says Anselma Dell'Olio, before offering her own: "our refusal to
wash our dirty linen in public, i.e., to examine and thus politicise the new
experience of (nonsexual) competition between/among women" ("Home
Before Sundown," 167). I myself have not pretended to offer any full politi-

cal explanation, nor do I consider that the movement always did "lose steam." My own coming to consciousness was already a decade after Dell'Olio and Hanisch had found their own "wave" subsiding. Rather, I have found that letters dramatize a very particular tension between the individual and the group and reveal the tendency for political groups to polarize. This may be because the nature of community making is to limit what people can reasonably expect. At one level, this is to offer a feminist version of civilization and its discontents, and as a literary critic, it is tempting to present these texts as fragments of a doomed romance. I have argued, however, that the emotional zigzagging was symptomatic of a more specific cultural drama in an underlying clash between the value of autonomy and that of care.

The movement was by definition committed to the independence and self-determination of the oppressed. Autonomy was understood to be a form of care for the self, an essential fulfillment of basic needs and rights that was also the way to prevent self-sacrifice by those already positioned as society's thankless carers. Yet how did this answer the needs and rights of fellow activists? Or the confusion that people felt when the pursuit of autonomy seemed to require deliberately ceasing to care for those not oppressed in the same way, most obviously men? The contradiction between autonomy and care is not the invention of the women's movement, of course. In many ways, the difficulty of maintaining communal bonds when individuals assert their "right to be cared for" is characteristic of the late-modern "Me-ism" that Carole Hanisch refers to as endemic to the 1980s. Yet there is a particular poignancy in the emotional battles between individuals and groups so dedicated to the creation of psychological as well as political emancipation.

Philosophers do not claim that care ethics can control conflict and competition on its own, and feminist theories of citizenship invariably propose some integration of the principles of care with those of justice. These letters lead to the same conclusion, and, fascinatingly, it seems that today's culture of digital relationship might benefit from it too. Philosophical theory in the abstract, however, has not been the point of this book. The question is much more visceral, in the ongoing struggle to make communities that answer to our ideals, in working out how to love, care, argue, be angry, be inspired, and write to each other.

Notes

Introduction. The Feminist World of Love and Ritual

1. Joan Nestle, letter to Lise, 3 January 1977. Lise is a pseudonym. For more information about Nestle's letters, contact the Lesbian Herstory Archives, New York.

2. Lise, letters to Joan Nestle, 17 and 25 January 1977. Lesbian Herstory Archives, New York.

3. Joan Nestle, unpublished e-mail to the author, 9 July 2005.

4. See, for example, the letters from friends of Terri Jewel, an African American lesbian writer, in the Lesbian Herstory Archives, folder 85-16, and friends of Barbara Smith, folder 21, 84-2.

1. Love Letters to a New Me

1. Examples of coming out letters from this period include Bohlin-Davis, *Breaking Silence*; Eichberg, *Coming Out*; Ferrante and Jacobson, *Letters from the Closet*;

Jolly and Kohler, *Gay Letters*; Norton, *My Dear Boy*; Stockton, *Lesbian Letters*; Umans, *Like Coming Home*.

Coming out letters are now easy to find on the Web sites devoted to sexual and gender minorities. See, for example http://www.gayforum.nl/post-3599.html. By contrast, http://wiltedflowerchild.com/trans/out features "transition" letters of transsexuals specifically distinguished from happier "coming out" letters once a new gender identity feels achieved.

2. Harris, audio letter.

3. Significantly, Hammer herself provided the finding aid for "Love Letter," as well as Birkby's other films, for the Sophia Smith collection after Birkby's death. Hammer, "Love Letter," Appendix: Descriptive List of Films, Finding Aid to the Noel Phyllis Birkby Papers, Sophia Smith Collection, Northampton, Massachusetts.

4. Bonner, interview.

5. Bonner, letter.

6. Lover to S, 10 September 1982.

7. S, interview.

8. See also the results of the Mass-Observation Archive study on popular letter-writing practices in Britain today, at www.sussex.ac.uk/library/massobs.

9. See also the entries on "Letters and Diaries" by country in Jolly, *The Encyclopedia of Life Writing*. See Shade, *Gender and Community*, for a history of women's domestic networking by telephone and e-mail.

10. On men and e-mail, see Corcoran, "Male and F:\Email." On text messaging, see Bensen, "The Joy of Text."

11. Geser, "Towards a Sociological Theory of the Mobile Phone." For details of Vodafone's postcards-by-phone facility, promoted with photos of young white women on holiday, see http://www.vodafone.co.uk.

12. "Paid ecards are less than one percent of the greeting card market, but the lucrative female-skewed audience is driving solid growth," cites one American marketing community Web site, citing figures in January 2004 to show a 61.5 to 38.5 percent female/male split in buying e-cards. 123Greetings.com records a 64 to 36 percent ratio (cited at http://www.imediaconnection.com/content/2890.asp).

13. Brownmiller, letter to Gloria Steinem, July 10 1974.

14. Some exceptionally good editions are Beauchamp, ed., *A Private War*; Rosen and Davidson, eds., *The Maimie Papers*; Thompson, ed., *Dear Girl*; Fischer, *Aimée and Jaguar*. Also see Karen Hansen's research on the flirtations of nineteenth-century African Americans Addie Brown and Rebecca Primus, found in the Connecticut Historical Society archives more than a century after their composition: Hansen, "'No Kisses Is Like Youres.'"

15. This Web site is amusingly stringent on how men should cultivate spontaneity in writing without appearing uncouth. See http://www.fairbride.com/tip.shtml.

2. Feminist Epistolary Romance

1. Sharp, "Letter-Writing." Available at http://www.chss.montclair.edu/inquiry/spr95/sharp.html.
2. See also Letherby and Zdrodowski, "'Dear Researcher.'"
3. From the paper's abstract, available at http://ssrn.com/abstract=874752.
4. Linda Farrer, letters to Elizabeth Meese, accession number 88-11, Lesbian Herstory Archives, New York.
5. Both have since retired.

3. Velvet Boxing Gloves

1. Anonymous, love letters, 1980–1982, accession number 83-18, Lesbian Herstory Archives, New York.
2. See tatiana de la tierra's Web site http://www.acsu.buffalo.edu/~td6/index.html.

4. Theorizing Feminist Letters

1. For details of the conference itself, see http://www.iaba.org.cn.

5. Mothers and Daughters in Correspondence

1. Karen Payne, unpublished letter of invitation, undated, Karen Payne personal papers.
2. Payne was not able to find more than a couple of correspondences produced out of Third World–First World migration (Payne, *Between Ourselves*, 343–52).
3. *Between Ourselves* was reprinted four times on both sides of the Atlantic and gained the backing of trade presses Michael Joseph and Picador. It is still in print with Houghton Mifflin.
4. Jackie Page, letter to Karen Payne, 28 July 1980, Karen Payne personal papers.

5. It should also be noted that I refer to the writers by the names, in this case pseudonyms, they are given in Payne's text, as with all the names in this chapters.

6. Kate, letter to Karen Payne, 7 May 1983, Karen Payne personal papers.

7. Karen Payne, personal papers.

6. Writing the Web: Letters from the Women's Peace Movement

1. Jenny Maxwell, the current coordinator of Britain's Campaign for Nuclear Disarmament letter-writing group, confirmed that it currently features about a third more women than men (Jenny Maxwell, e-mail to the author, 1 October 2002).

2. Ann Pettitt, unpublished article sent to *The Guardian*, September 1981, Glamorgan Record Office, Cardiff, Wales, GB 214 DWLE/3/7.

3. Anonymous, letter to "the women of Greenham Common," personal collection of Alice Cook.

4. Juley Howard, letter to Ginette Leach, 15 February 1986, personal collection of Ginette Leach.

5. Although these activists have used their full names in interviews or with me, Ginette Leach points out that surnames were very rarely used at Greenham because women did not wish to be defined by patriarchal relations of inheritance. Women were often known by their first name and where they came from.

6. Julie, letter to "Dear Sisters," undated, Women's Encampment for Peace and Justice collection, Schlesinger Library, Radcliffe Institute, Harvard University, Cambridge, Mass., box no. 7, folder 197. There were many other Greenham-Seneca correspondences, for example, Becky Griffiths, to "Dearest Seneca Sisters," 21 February 1984, Women's Encampment for Peace and Justice collection, box no. 4, folder 99.

7. Anonymous, leaflet advising on how to prove legally Greenham was one's home includes showing post received there. Miscellaneous material/Greenham Common Peace Camp collection, Feminist Archive (South), Bristol, England.

8. Camps set up on a permanent or part-time basis throughout Britain included Molesworth, Faslane, Porton Down, and Menwith Hill, in which women's groups organized more than half of the direct actions beginning in 1983. See Rochon, "The West European Peace Movement," 110. Women's camps were set up at the U.S. base in Comiso, Sicily, at an underground bunker near Viborg in Denmark, at the Hasselback cruise base, and at the Seneca Women's Encampment for Peace and Justice in upstate New York from where cruise missiles were to be shipped to Europe.

9. Women's Peace Camp Orientation Information 1985, Women's Encampment for Peace and Justice collection, Schlesinger Library, Radcliffe Institute, Harvard University, Cambridge, Mass., box no. 6, folder 168.

10. Newsletters were produced nearly every fortnight from February 1983 until the camp began to wane in 1985, by different groups going under different names such as "Green and Common News," "Women's Peace Camp News," and "Greenham Women Everywhere."

11. Newsletter, 1982, personal collection of Alice Cook.

12. "Reflect the Base" report, "Lin Simenon collection," Feminist Archive (South), Bristol, England.

13. Kirsty, letter to Dina, late 1985, in newsletter titled *Greenham Women Everywhere*, personal collection of Ginette Leach.

14. Agata Ruscica, "Letter from Comiso," in newsletter titled *Women's Peace Camp, February 1983*, "Sigrid Shayer Collection 1983–93," Feminist Archive (South), Bristol, England.

15. Editorial, newsletter titled *Women's Peace Camp, February 1983*, "Sigrid Shayer Collection 1983–93," Feminist Archive (South), Bristol, England.

16. Editorial, newsletter titled *Womyn's peace camp green & common february news and Bristol newsletter*, "Miscellaneous material/Greenham Common Peace Camp," Feminist Archive (South), Bristol, England.

17. Letter from Blue Gate, "Lin Simenon collection," Feminist Archive (South), Bristol, England.

18. Letter from Blue Gate, *Greenham Newsletter*, Bristol, January 1985, "Sigrid Shayer Collection 1983–93," Feminist Archive (South), Bristol, England.

19. Stibbs, "Beyond the Pale," 1.

20. Stibbs, "Beyond the Pale," 11.

21. Some letters observed on the fence were: "To Lucy T. and all wimmin"; "To my dear son David, age 24, who gave his life in the miners' strike, 1984" (Snitow, "Holding the Line," 42).

22. Chain letter from Greenham Common, personal collection of Ginette Leach.

23. The letter inviting women to "beam" energy was reprinted in a *Women for Life on Earth* newsletter of Autumn 1982, Glamorgan Record Office, Cardiff, Wales, reference GB 214 DWLE/5/3. The invitation to laughter comes from a leaflet advertising a "Huge Children's Party" on May Day 1983, "Miscellaneous material/Greenham Common Peace Camp," Feminist Archive (South), Bristol, England.

24. Rainbow Dragon leaflet, "Sigrid Shayer Collection 1983–93," Feminist Archive (South), Bristol, England.

25. "From the Women of Orange Gate," letter, 30 December 1983, personal collection of Ginette Leach.

7. Do Webs Work? Letters and the Clash of Communities

1. Chain letter from Pettitt and others, Glamorgan Record Office, Cardiff, Wales, GB 214 DWLE/6/11. Interestingly, most of the letters Pettitt received in response were from supporters, mixed as well as women-only, who disagreed with the need or tactic of a mixed event at Greenham.

2. See *Breaching the Peace*. Both letters were reprinted in the section "No Nukes" in Kanter et al., eds., *Sweeping Statements*.

3. Juley Howard, e-mail to the author, 24 October, 2004. Howard points out that the post had already been moved from Yellow to Green Gate temporarily after the evictions at Yellow in 1984. Later, after the camp at the North Side folded, it moved from being delivered at Woad to Blue. See Junor and Howse, *Greenham Common Women's Peace Camp*, for an account of the camp from the perspective of women allied to Wages for Housework that emphasizes its later years (skirmishes over the post are specifically mentioned at pages 42 and 99). Roseneil, *Common Women*, analyses the history of this group at the camp as the most important of Greenham's inner political divisions.

4. From *The Greenham Newsletter, 1986*, "Sigrid Shayer Collection 1983–93," Feminist Archive (South), Bristol, England.

5. From the unpublished diary of Ginette Leach, 30 May–2 June 1984, personal collection of Ginette Leach.

6. One copious letter from Judy Scheckel to "Womyn of the encampment," dated in the feminist calendar 9 July 9985, expresses this well: "Being at Seneca that summer [of 1983] was an extremely important part of my personal/political evolvement. I had never been in a large all-womon space where there was a political focus. I was particularly affected by a workshop where keening was a focus—releasing pain—letting pain move thru us instead of holding onto it, instead of letting it settle in our bodies, our psyches. It validated what I was beginning to learn about purging the patriarchy that lives inside me. . . . In October '83, after being at Seneca in August, I was arrested in Aiken S[outh]C[arolina]—in a womyn's action of blockading the savannah river bomb plant. While we were in jail we planned our next action—a peace walk from Gainesville to Key West—550 miles—it took six wks. All 4 of us were a part of that action. During that 6 wks. my political focus changed profoundly. For the first half of the walk we were connecting primarily w. freeze groups, church groups. By the time we got to South Florida we were beginning to connect w. lesbians & something different started happening. I began to feel what I can only call magic. & because I believe in majic as an essential part of our survival, the survival of the planet—I have chosen/am choosing to focus my energy on *lesbians* & our community. The next large action I was part of was the 1st Southern Leap

(lesbians for empowerment) action, & politics. We planned for over a yr.—& in that planning, the planners became a community—working on our personal relationships, doing C/R, sharing our lives. Now—this travelling is the current action I'm involved in. we hadn't planned to come to the encampment but as we found ourselves nearer & nearer the place as July 6 rolled around—it began to seem like we were being drawn here—or even downright pushed here. At first I didn't understand why . . . but one thing I do know—is that no matter what its actual name, no matter what the brochures, flyers, newspaper articles say—the encampment is a lesbian community. . . . The connecting that happened among the separatists was wonderful—so energising, so inspiring, so validating of a way of life, a way of perceiving the world that shakes the very foundation of this patriarchy. Womyn, lesbians withdrawing our energy from men & men's values as much as possible—an ongoing process of letting go of things, attitudes, ways of being that we're taught to base our lives on. It's hard hard work, work that generally goes unrecognised, much less supported by lesbians making other choices. It's painful to experience the oppression of separatists that is so often a part of lesbian culture. . . . I am in no way criticising the encampment community because you all are struggling. . . . I do have some specific criticism & some suggestions that I would like to make. . . . With much, much love & belief in our revolution—Judy" (Women's Encampment for Peace and Justice Collection, box no. 4, folder 107, Schlesinger Library, Radcliffe Institute, Harvard University, Cambridge, Mass.).

7. Kat, letter to "Peace Camp," Women's Encampment for Peace and Justice Collection, box no. 4, folder 98, Schlesinger Library, Radcliffe Institute, Harvard University, Cambridge, Mass.

8. John Wenger Berquist DeHority, Epistle to the Peace Encampment, 15 July 1983, Women's Encampment for Peace and Justice Collection, box no. 4, folder 107, Schlesinger Library, Radcliffe Institute, Harvard University, Cambridge, Mass.

9. Letter dated 21 December 1983, Women's Encampment for Peace and Justice Collection, box no. 4, folder 98, Schlesinger Library, Radcliffe Institute, Harvard University, Cambridge, Mass. Similarly, "Ellie" writes back to "♀ at Seneca," "Hello family I'm not with. New York's been hard, coming 'home' I felt so diminished: 'I am I and my circumstances'. Without Seneca as my ground I am less; less supported; less loved; less active and giving; less focused" (letter from "Ellie," 21 October 1983, Women's Encampment for Peace and Justice Collection, box no. 4, folder 99, Schlesinger Library, Radcliffe Institute, Harvard University, Cambridge, Mass.

10. Betsy Aswad, letter to "Kim, Pam, Aja, Margit, Coyote, Nell, et al," 14 October 1983, Women's Encampment for Peace and Justice Collection, box no. 4, folder 98, Schlesinger Library, Radcliffe Institute, Harvard University, Cambridge, Mass.

11. Letters in Women's Encampment for Peace and Justice Collection, box no. 4, folder 99, Schlesinger Library, Radcliffe Institute, Harvard University, Cambridge, Mass.

12. Shell-Lee Miller, letters, Women's Encampment for Peace and Justice Collection, box no. 5, folder 160, Schlesinger Library, Radcliffe Institute, Harvard University, Cambridge, Mass.

13. "Constructive Criticism," Women's Encampment for Peace and Justice Collection, box no. 4, folder 107; "Dislike Mail," file 108, Schlesinger Library, Radcliffe Institute, Harvard University, Cambridge, Mass. One camp journal entry for 30 December 1984 records: "Fire made, house cleaned—25 handbooks taken and mailed to St Louis to be used in a womyn's studies class—all with inserted paper indicating $3.00 cost, inflation, donation etc . . . a bad pr article appeared in last night's *Finger Lakes Times*, indicating guilt of the encampment of sending postcard to Moscow and two Christmas cards—with 'US Out of Lebanon' and No-Nukes. Waterloo— Redneck capital of the world . . . anyways so we the writer and editor indicating our anger and etc . . . then call Aliana Esp—attorney—read it to her and had her call . . . then wrote letter to the editor—saying the same" (Women's Encampment for Peace and Justice Collection, box no. 1, folder 26, Schlesinger Library, Radcliffe Institute, Harvard University, Cambridge, Mass.).

14. Pam Flanigan, letter to the editor, 12 December 1984, Women's Encampment for Peace and Justice Collection, box no. 4, folder 115, Schlesinger Library, Radcliffe Institute, Harvard University, Cambridge, Mass.

15. A handwritten leaflet produced in 1983 and signed "the women of Greenham Common" gave a more worrying picture of the importance of letters, asking supporters to "write to the Newbury District Council, Mr Brian Thetford, in our support as they are encouraging local people to make complaints about our presence and the parking of vans on the common; we also need to keep a record of letters to the council and also the police concerning their harassment as they are under no obligation to produce the thousands of letters in our support that they have received over the last 12 months—please send us a copy" ("Miscellaneous material/Greenham Common Peace Camp," Bristol Feminist Archive, Bristol, England).

16. Personal communication. The interviewee wishes to remain anonymous.

17. Jana Runnalls, letter to Zephyrine Barbarachild, 17 December 1982, personal collection of Zephyrine Barabarachild.

18. Chain letter, anonymous, personal collection of Zephyrine Barbarbachild.

19. Newsletter from *Women for Life on Earth*, Autumn 1982, no page number. A copy of this is held in the Glamorgan Record Office, Cardiff, Wales, GB 214 DWLE/5/3.

20. http://www.amnestyusa.org/activist_toolkit/referenceresources/uan_letter_guide.pdf

21. Political scientists who analyze lobbying methods refer to letter writing as a bread-and-butter aspect of any campaign but are reluctant to pronounce on how effective it is, although they invariably agree that letters that appear to come unprompted from individuals are much more valued than those sponsored or even written by an organization and that those generated at the beginning of a campaign are counted more than when the size and weight of a constituency is easily judged. (Ironically, personal letters now have more influence than the flood of e-mail petitions.) According to a 1998 study by the nongovernmental watchdog group OMB Watch, congressional offices in the USA give the most attention to personal letters, followed by personal visits, telephone calls, faxes, personal e-mails, and, lastly, email petitions. See http://www.pcworld.com/news/article/0,aid,48788,00.asp. In the 1980s, however, new technology was only just being adopted for lobbying purposes. Political letters have also been seen as an aspect of the rise of "interest group society," in which lobbying of representatives has become professionalized (Berry, *The Interest Group Society*, 149–55).

22. Karen Payne, personal communication to the author, June 2003.

23. "The decision to site US cruise missiles at Greenham by December 1983 was taken by top NATO commanders in December 1979. There was no discussion in parliament, though a few British politicians knew about the decision and supported it. Our system of government is supposed to be open and democratic. There are 'proper channels' for making our views known: voting every four or five years, *writing to MPs who are supposed to represent us*, forming pressure groups to campaign over particular issues. Once government policy is decided—especially, as in the case of cruise missiles, way above the heads of most MPs—the *'proper channels'* are virtually useless" (Cook and Kirk, *Greenham Women Everywhere*, 109; my italics).

8. Care Versus Autonomy: The Problem of (Loving) Men

1. Krasniewicz draws on Victor Turner's definition of liminality. See Turner, *The Ritual Process*, 105.

2. Samoa, "Open letter to all ♀♀♀," 18 November 1984, Women's Encampment for Peace and Justice Collection, box no. 4, folder 98, Schlesinger Library, Radcliffe Institute, Harvard University, Cambridge, Mass.

3. Phyllis Sawyer, letter to "Women's Encampment for a Future of Peace and Justice," 29 June 1983, in Women's Encampment for Peace and Justice Collection, box

no. 4, folder 107, Schlesinger Library, Radcliffe Institute, Harvard University, Cambridge, Mass.

4. Carole Harwood, personal interview, 20 May 2003; KL (Harwood's former husband), e-mail to the author, 21 May 2003.

5. Carole Harwood, diary, Carole Harwood papers, Bristol Feminist Archive, Bristol, England.

6. Excerpts are from S's e-mails to the author and interviews, written and taped, between September 2001 and August 2005, author's personal collection. Excerpts from letters by S are dated as given in the narrative and remain in S's personal collection.

7. See Carroll, *War Letters*. See also http://www.hbo.com/docs/programs/lastlet tershome.

8. For "meninist" letters, see http://www.feminist.com/resources/links/men.htm.

9. The Paradox of Care as a Right

1. Sabina Erika, personal interview, September 2002.

2. Shortly after Freeman had gained press coverage with other feminists speaking at a meeting of the American Historical Association in 1970, she received a letter postmarked in Boston without a return address. It was addressed to "Jo Freeman (GUT FEMINIST) Doctoral Candidate, University of Chicago, Chicago, Illinois." "Inside was a six-page handwritten hate letter, which concluded: 'They ought to put your tits (if you got any) in a wringer and then kick your ass 100 times.' Some clerk at the University of Chicago, assigned the task of looking me up in the directory and forwarding this letter, had stamped on the envelope in bright red: 'Please inform your correspondents of your correct address'" (Freeman, "Origins," 195–96).

3. Chesler's list includes: "Lobby your church or religious congregation to change its stance on birth control and abortion"; "campaign for a guaranteed above-minimum wage for all workers, so the choices are more affordable for everyone"; "*personally* shelter, or become family to, a particular pregnant woman who wants to keep her baby" and "become a physician willing to perform abortions" (*Letters to a Young Feminist*, 100). Notably, she ends by asking, "Do I think the Second Wave of feminism worked as hard on obtaining the right to mother or parent under *feminist* working conditions as they did on keeping abortion legal? No, I don't. But obtaining the right to an abortion is far easier than redefining the family" (101).

4. Some of these positive reviews are collected on Chesler's Web site: http://www .phyllis-chesler.com/publications.php?pid=letterstoayoungfeminist.

5. Jennie Dunham, review of *Letters of Intent: Women Cross the Generations to Talk About Work, Family, Love, Sex, and the Future of Feminism*, ed. Bondoc and Daly, *Publishers Weekly*, 2 January 1999, editorial review cited on Amazon.com.

10. How Different Is E-mail?

1. See the Web site of the Universal Postal Union, the world's largest physical distribution network, http://www.upu.int. Surprisingly, the actual number of physical letters is still increasing by about 2 percent each year, although much of this is unsolicited advertising.

2. As far as it has been possible to document, approximately 20 percent of global e-mailing is for personal use. See http://redmondmag.com/news/article.asp?EditorialsID=6527. Approximately 59 percent of Americans use e-mail, according to the Digital Citizen Survey, available at http://www.hotwired.com/special/citizen/survey/survey.html.

3. The world's billionth GSM user was connected in the first quarter of 2004, just twelve years after the commercial launches of the first GSM networks. This figure is provided by the Groupe Spèciale Mobile, the global trade association that promotes the interests of GSM mobile operators. See http://www.gsmworld.com/news/statistics/index.shtml. When cross-network text messaging first appeared in Britain in January 1999, 40 million messages were sent that month. The British Mobile Data Association predicted that text messages sent in Britain in 2005 will top 30 billion. See http://www.guardian.co.uk/mobile/article/0,,1383498,00.html.

4. Gurumurthy et al., "Gender and ICTs," http://www.bridge.ids.ac.uk/reports_gend_CEP.html.

5. All the e-mails cited here, except one, are published in Harcourt, "Cyborg Melody." Page references will refer to this article.

6. Wendy Harcourt, e-mail to Kekula Bray-Crawford, 6 February 1998, personal archives of Wendy Harcourt.

7. See also Scott et al., *I on the Mouse*.

11. Care Ethics Online

1. The Women's Networking Support Programme also conducted a survey, concluding that overall the Internet was seen as an effective tool for social change, although "time constraints, limited accessibility because of poor technical or social infrastructures, security and privacy concerns, language barriers, and skill

deficiencies"—i.e., access barriers, were a major problem, especially for women from the South. See Harcourt, ed., *Women@Internet*, 102–13.

2. See http://main.edc.org/newsroom/features/vaw.asp.

3. "SID-WID: Working in Solidarity," for *Lisistrata*, the SID-WID newsletter, May 2002. Available at http://www.sidint.org/Publications/Lisistrata/Lisistrata-5 .pdf.

4. The conference was organized by the SNDT Women's University (Mumbai) and Centre for Women's Development Studies (New Delhi) in May and June of 2003.

5. Ruth Picardie's confessional columns in *The Observer* magazine about getting breast cancer were paralleled with daily e-mails to friends in a style just as grumpy and witty. See Picardie, Seaton, and Picardie, *Before I Say Goodbye*. The Women's Court at the Permanent Arab Court to Resist Violence Against Women solicits testimonies through e-mail on its Web site. This was established in 1995 to challenge women's oppression under the Personal Status codes in some Arab countries. See http://www.arabwomencourt.org/womenscourt/aboutus/aboutus.htm. See also Gurumurthy et al., "Gender and ICTs," 37.

12. On Burning and Saving Letters

1. See, for example, "The Burning Man" group at http://www.odeo.net/tales/ bman/bman.html. The Landmark Forum (see http://www.landmarkeducation. com) also recommends writing and sometimes destroying "therapeutic" letters.

2. See http://www.cnn.com/2002/LAW/06/19/colorado.fire.suspect.

3. In fact, a note accompanying Beth Levine's donation of some love letters to the Lesbian Herstory Archives in 1978, records that Diane Edington and "Joan" attempted to publish a collection of lesbian love letters that year but did not get enough responses to their call. Diane Edington, letter to Beth Levine, 1 December 1978, Lesbian Herstory Archives, New York, Beth Levine and Mimi Stein collection, accession number 79-04.

4. Gloria Steinem papers, Sophia Smith Collection, Smith College, Northampton, Massachusetts. See http://www.smith.edu/libraries/libs/ssc/index.html; and Farrell, *Yours in Sisterhood*.

5. The Women's Library holds correspondence of socialist feminist and Irish rights activist Nina Hutchinson; sister peace campaigners Jayne and Juliet Nelson; socialist historian Sheila Rowbotham; and health educator and activist Sue O'Sullivan, but most of these are as yet uncatalogued and, as personal papers, may be closed in any case. See http://www.londonmet.ac.uk/thewomenslibrary.

6. See Koppelman, "Excerpts from Letters to Friends," 77; and "Email" in Heilbrun, *The Last Gift of Time* The Schlesinger does hold good open collections of fan letters, for example, in the papers of Betty Friedan and Holly Near. See http://lib .harvard.edu/archives/0009.html.

7. Keith Breckenridge writes similarly of his difficulty studying "the intensely private" correspondences between South African migrant workers in the 1930s: "My own informants will happily discuss the writing of letters but they are politely but resolutely reticent in the face of my badgering—the letters were burnt on the male migrant's final return home" (Breckenridge, "Love Letters and Amanuenses," 343).

8. Noeleen Heyzer, e-mail to the author, 16 December 2002. Lalang is the Malay word for a dangerous wild grass that can cut flesh.

9. Catherine Clay, e-mail to the author, July 2004. See also Clay, *British Women Writers*.

10. Teresa Doherty, head of special collections, The Women's Library, London, personal communication to the author, 23 June 2004.

11. Kathryn Jacob, personal interview with the author, 16 October 2003. Jacob explained that preserving the anonymity of sensitive material involved photocopying it, blacking out all names and dates, and photocopying it again.

12. Staff Assistant Diane Hamer wrote in 1987 to reassure the Seneca Women's Encampment for Peace and Justice that "the Schlesinger Library will be an appropriate and safe place" for their papers: "In the 6 years that I have been here I've seen a true effort by the library staff to collect papers of lesbians, radicals, non-famous women and others to whom *we* have had to make an effort. While they are not catalogued as lesbian papers, we do have the letters, diaries, and journals of women who were lesbians. There is an ethical question, however, of whether we can call those papers lesbian or not since the woman in question did not. Most of those kinds of papers do include a catalog card under 'friendship' the closest the curators are able to identify the papers. The encampment papers, however, will probably be able to have the word lesbian in the card catalog and this will be a great step forward" (Diane Hamer, letter to Lucinda Sangree, undated, appended as Note to Eva Moseley's letter to Lucinda Sangree, dated Jan 14 1987, Women's Encampment for Peace and Justice collection, Schlesinger Library, Radcliffe Institute, Harvard University, Cambridge, Mass., box 4, folder no. 11).

13. A fascinating set of minutes of a meeting by supporters of the Seneca Women's Encampment for Peace and Justice in February and October 1986 show how activists anticipated archiving their papers and were advised by a woman at the Lesbian Herstory Archives to go with the Schlesinger Library because "there is a lesbian-sympathetic directorship; agreed upon location; funds are available" (minutes from

Brainstorming, Heartsearching Meeting, part 2, October 11–12, 1986, Minutes, Agendas, Etc., Women's Encampment for Peace and Justice collection, Schlesinger Library, Radcliffe Institute, Harvard University, Cambridge, Mass., box 1, file 10). Nevertheless, they felt it necessary to negotiate a contract with the Schlesinger that specified that "it is understood that any material using the term Lesbian or referring to Lesbian life style, sexual preference, politics will not be treated in any manner different from other material in the collection. Such material will be just as accessible as any other material and preserved just as carefully. The word Lesbian will be included in any indexing procedures and publications when appropriate" (Terms of Use of the Records of, Women's Encampment for Peace and Justice collection, box 4, folder no. 116). They had wished initially to restrict future access of the records to women, but the library would not agree (Lucinda Sangree, letter to Diane Hamer, 20 July 1987, Women's Encampment for Peace and Justice collection, box 4, folder 116).

14. See http://www.womenslibrary.org.uk/laic/laic.html. The Lesbian Archive houses some correspondence in the papers of the lesbian feminist writer Anna Livia and the activist Jude Tyrie, but both are restricted until 2035.

15. See http://www.leeds.ac.uk/library/spcoll/fan.htm.

16. See http://www.lesbianherstoryarchives.org.

17. Cover note, love letters 1980–1982, accession number 83-18, Lesbian Herstory Archives, New York.

18. Karen Payne, unpublished letter of invitation, undated, Karen Payne personal papers.

19. Karen Payne personal papers.

20. Karen Payne, letter to Nan Talese, 27 May 1982, Karen Payne personal papers. Alison Burns, letter to Nan Talese, 9 November 1982, Karen Payne personal papers.

21. Contributors' letters to Karen Payne, Karen Payne personal papers.

22. Karen Payne, letter to Leslie Young, 13 December 1980, Karen Payne personal papers.

13. On Stealing Letters: The Ethics of Epistolary Research

1. See my discussion of my own "repetition" of the original corresponding relationship in researching and editing the letters from women who worked as welders during the Second World War, in M. Jolly, ed., *Dear Laughing Motorbyke*, 154–55.

2. Salinger also insisted that a note be read out warning bidders that he still retained copyright at the Sotheby's auction of his love letters to Joyce Maynard Michael (Ellison, "Salinger's Letters").

3. For discussion of the artifice of the stolen postbag, see Versini, *Le Roman épis-tolaire*, 34. See Pool, *Other People's Mail*, and Curtiss, *Other People's Letters*, for recent examples of a similar marketing ploy.

4. See Smith and Watson's brief overview of her work in *Reading Autobiography*, 141, 155. Also see Miller, "Writing Fictions"; Miller, "Representing Others."

5. See www.genderit.org.

6. Association of Canadian Archivists, 2004 Annual Conference, Montréal, Québec, 27–29 May 2004.

7. See http://www.archivists.org/saagroups/lagar/about.htm.

Bibliography

Primary Sources

Anonymous. Leaflet advising on how to prove legally Greenham was one's home, Miscellaneous material/Greenham Common Peace Camp collection, Feminist Archive (South), Bristol, England.

Anonymous. Love letters 1980–1982. Accession number 83-18, Lesbian Herstory Archives, New York.

Anonymous. Letter to "the women of Greenham Common," personal collection of Alice Cook.

Anonymous. Letters in Women's Encampment for Peace and Justice Collection, box no. 4, folder 99, Schlesinger Library, Radcliffe Institute, Harvard University, Cambridge, Mass.

Anonymous. Letter dated 21 December 1983, Women's Encampment for Peace and Justice Collection, box no. 4, folder 98, Schlesinger Library, Radcliffe Institute, Harvard University, Cambridge, Mass.

Aswad, Betsy. Letter to "Kim, Pam, Aja, Margit, Coyote, Nell, et al," 14 October 1983, Women's Encampment for Peace and Justice Collection, box no. 4, folder

98, Schlesinger Library, Radcliffe Institute, Harvard University, Cambridge, Mass.

Bonner, Eileen, Letter to lover, August 1982. Bonner's personal collection.

——. Interview by author, September 2002.

Brownmiller, Susan. Letter to Gloria Steinem, 10 July 1974. New York, Sophia Smith Archives. Gloria Steinem papers, correspondence, individual, box 85, file 6.

Burns, Alison. Letter to Nan Talese, 9 November 1982, Karen Payne personal papers.

Camp journal entry, 30 December 1984. Women's Encampment for Peace and Justice Collection, box no. 1, folder 26, Schlesinger Library, Radcliffe Institute, Harvard University, Cambridge, Mass.

Chain letter from Greenham Common. Personal collection of Ginette Leach.

Chain letter from Ann Pettitt and others. Glamorgan Record Office, Cardiff, Wales, GB 214 DWLE/6/11.

Clay, Catherine. E-mail to the author, July 2004.

"Constructive Criticism." Women's Encampment for Peace and Justice Collection, box no. 4, folder 107; "Dislike Mail," file 108, Schlesinger Library, Radcliffe Institute, Harvard University, Cambridge, Mass.

Cover note, love letters 1980–1982. Accession number 83-18, Lesbian Herstory Archives, New York.

DeHority, John Wenger Berquist. Epistle to the Peace Encampment, 15 July 1983, Women's Encampment for Peace and Justice Collection, box no. 4, folder 107, Schlesinger Library, Radcliffe Institute, Harvard University, Cambridge, Mass.

Doherty, Teresa, head of special collections, The Women's Library, London. Personal communication to the author, 23 June 2004.

Edington, Diane. Letter to Beth Levine, 1 December 1978, Lesbian Herstory Archives, New York, Beth Levine and Mimi Stein collection, accession number 79-04.

Editorial. Newsletter titled *Women's Peace Camp, February 1983*, "Sigrid Shayer Collection 1983–93," Feminist Archive (South), Bristol, England.

Editorial. Newsletter titled *Womyn's peace camp green & common february news and Bristol newsletter.* "Miscellaneous material/Greenham Common Peace Camp," Feminist Archive (South), Bristol, England.

"Ellie." Letter, 21 October 1983, Women's Encampment for Peace and Justice Collection, box no. 4, folder 99, Schlesinger Library, Radcliffe Institute, Harvard University, Cambridge, Mass.

Farrer, Linda. Letters to Elizabeth Meese. Lesbian Herstory Archives, accession number 88-11, New York.

Flanigan, Pam. Letter to the Editor, 12 December 1984, Women's Encampment for Peace and Justice Collection, box no. 4, folder 115, Schlesinger Library, Radcliffe Institute, Harvard University, Cambridge, Mass.

"Greenham Newsletter, 1986." "Sigrid Shayer Collection 1983–93," Feminist Archive (South), Bristol, England.

Griffiths, Becky. Letter to "Dearest Seneca Sisters," 21 February 1984, Women's Encampment for Peace and Justice collection, box no. 4, folder 99.

Hamer, Diane. Letter to Lucinda Sangree. Undated, appended as Note to Eva Moseley's letter to Lucinda Sangree, dated Jan 14 1987, Women's Encampment for Peace and Justice collection, box 4, folder no. 116, Schlesinger Library, Radcliffe Institute, Harvard University, Cambridge, Mass.

Hammer, Barbara. "Love Letter." Appendix: Descriptive List of Films, Finding Aid to the Noel Phyllis Birkby Papers, Sophia Smith Collection, Northampton, Massachusetts.

Harcourt, Wendy. E-mail to Kekula Bray-Crawford, 6 February 1998, personal archives of Wendy Harcourt.

Harris, Bertha. Audio letter to Noel Phyllis Birkby, and Noel Phyllis Birkby to Bertha Harris. Not dated. Noel Phyllis Birkby Papers, Sophia Smith Collection, Smith College, Northampton, Massachusetts.

Harwood, Carole. Diary, Carole Harwood papers, Feminist Archive (South), Bristol, England.

——. Personal interview, 20 May 2003.

Heyzer, Noeleen. E-mail to the author, 16 December 2002.

Howard, Juley. Letter to Ginette Leach, 15 February 1986, personal collection of Ginette Leach.

——. E-mail to the author, 24 October, 2004.

Jacob, Kathryn, personal interview with the author, 16 October 2003.

Jewel, Terri. Letters from friends. Lesbian Herstory Archives, folder 85-16.

Jolly, Susan. E-mail to Xiao Pei He, and Xiao Pei He, e-mail to Susan Jolly, 18 Mar 2004.

Julie. Letter to "Dear Sisters," undated, Women's Encampment for Peace and Justice collection, box no. 7, folder 197, Schlesinger Library, Radcliffe Institute, Harvard University, Cambridge, Mass.

Kat. Letter to "Peace Camp," Women's Encampment for Peace and Justice Collection, box no. 4, folder 98, Schlesinger Library, Radcliffe Institute, Harvard University, Cambridge, Mass.

Kate. Letter to Karen Payne, 7 May 1983, Karen Payne personal papers.

Kirsty. Letter to Dina, late 1985, in newsletter titled *Greenham Women Everywhere*, personal collection of Ginette Leach.

Leach, Ginette. Diary, 30 May–2 June 1984, personal collection of Ginette Leach.

Leaflet advertising a "Huge Children's Party" on May Day 1983. "Miscellaneous material/Greenham Common Peace Camp," Feminist Archive (South), Bristol, England.

Letter from Blue Gate. *Greenham Newsletter*, Bristol, January 1985. "Sigrid Shayer Collection 1983–93," Bristol Feminist Archive, Bristol, England.

Letter from Blue Gate. "Lin Simenon collection," Feminist Archive (South), Bristol, England.

Letter from Greenham support group inviting women to "beam" energy. Reprinted in a *Women for Life on Earth* newsletter of Autumn 1982, Glamorgan Record Office, Cardiff, Wales, reference GB 214 DWLE/5/3.

Letter "From the Women of Orange Gate." 30 December 1983, personal collection of Ginette Leach.

Lise. Letters to Joan Nestle, 17 and 25 January 1977. For further information, contact Lesbian Herstory Archives, New York.

Maxwell, Jenny. E-mail to the author, 1 October 2002.

Miller, Shell-Lee. Letters, Women's Encampment for Peace and Justice Collection, box no. 5, folder 160, Schlesinger Library, Radcliffe Institute, Harvard University, Cambridge, Mass.

Minutes from Brainstorming, Heartsearching Meeting. Part 2, October 11–12, 1986, Minutes, Agendas, Etc., Women's Encampment for Peace and Justice collection, box 1, file 10, Schlesinger Library, Radcliffe Institute, Harvard University, Cambridge, Mass.

Nestle, Joan. Unpublished e-mail to the author, 9 July 2005.

Nestle, Joan. Letter to Lise, 3 January 1977. Individual Letters to Joan Nestle Collection, Lesbian Herstory Archives, New York, accession number 79-14.

Newsletter. Greenham Common Women's Peace Camp, 1982, personal collection of Alice Cook.

Newsletter. From *Women for Life on Earth*, Autumn 1982, no page number. A copy of this is held in the Glamorgan Record Office, Cardiff, Wales, GB 214 DWLE/5/3.

Runnells, Jana, to S, letter, 10 September 1982, S's personal collection.

Page, Jackie. Letter to Karen Payne, 28 July 1980, Karen Payne personal papers.

Payne, Karen. Draft notes and contributors' letters to *Between Ourselves: Letters between Mothers and Daughters 1750–1982*, Karen Payne personal papers.

——. Letter to Leslie Young, 13 December 1980, Karen Payne personal papers.

——. Letter to Nan Talese, 27 May 1982, Karen Payne personal papers.

——. Personal communication to the author, June 2003.

——. Unpublished letter of invitation, undated, Karen Payne personal papers.

Pettitt, Ann. Unpublished article sent to *The Guardian*, September 1981, Glamorgan Record Office, Cardiff, Wales, GB 214 DWLE/3/7.

Rainbow Dragon leaflet. "Sigrid Shayer Collection 1983–93," Feminist Archive (South), Bristol, England.

"Reflect the Base" report. "Lin Simenon collection," Feminist Archive (South), Bristol, England.

Runnalls, Jana. Letter to S, 17 December 1982, personal collection of S.

Ruscica, Agata. "Letter from Comiso," in newsletter titled *Women's Peace Camp, February 1983*, "Sigrid Shayer Collection 1983–93," Feminist Archive (South), Bristol, England.

S. E-mails to the author and interviews, written and taped, between September 2001 and August 2005, author's personal collection. Excerpts from letters by S are dated as given in the narrative and remain in S's personal collection.

——. Personal interview, 21 February 2002.

Samoa. "Open letter to all ♀♀♀." 18 November 1984, Women's Encampment for Peace and Justice Collection, box no. 4, folder 98, Schlesinger Library, Radcliffe Institute, Harvard University, Cambridge, Mass.

Sangree, Lucinda. Letter to Diane Hamer, 20 July 1987, Women's Encampment for Peace and Justice collection, box 4, folder 116, Schlesinger Library, Radcliffe Institute, Harvard University, Cambridge, Mass.

Sawyer, Phyllis. Letter to "Women's Encampment for a Future of Peace and Justice," 29 June 1983, in Women's Encampment for Peace and Justice Collection, box no. 4, folder 107, Schlesinger Library, Radcliffe Institute, Harvard University, Cambridge, Mass.

Scheckel, Judy. Letter to "Womyn of the encampment," dated in the feminist calendar 9 July 9985, Women's Encampment for Peace and Justice Collection, box no. 4, folder 107, Schlesinger Library, Radcliffe Institute, Harvard University, Cambridge, Mass.

Smith, Barbara. Letters from friends. Lesbian Herstory Archives, folder 84-2.

Stibbs, Carol Ann. "Beyond the Pale: Representations of the Greenham Women." Masters diss., Sheffield City Polytechnic, 1987.

Terms of Use of the Records. Women's Encampment for Peace and Justice collection, box 4, folder no. 116.

"The Women of Greenham Common." Handwritten leaflet, 1983, "Miscellaneous material/Greenham Common Peace Camp," Feminist Archive (South), Bristol, England.

Women's Peace Camp Orientation Information 1985. Women's Encampment for Peace and Justice collection, box no. 6, folder 168, Schlesinger Library, Radcliffe Institute, Harvard University, Cambridge, Mass.

Secondary Sources

Acker, Kathy. *Don Quixote, Which Was a Dream*. New York: Grove Press, 1986.

Agosâin, Marjorie, and Emma Sepâulveda-Pulvirenti. *Amigas: Letters of Friendship and Exile*. Louann Atkins Temple Women & Culture Series 3. Austin: University of Texas Press, 2001.

Agustín, Laura. "They Speak, but Who Listens?" In *Women@Internet: Creating New Cultures in Cyberspace*, ed. Wendy Harcourt, 149–55. London: Zed Books, 1999.

Ahearn, Laura M. *Invitations to Love: Literacy, Love Letters, and Social Change in Nepal*. Ann Arbor: University of Michigan Press, 2001.

Alloo, Fatma. "Information Technology and Cyberculture: The Case of Zanzibar." In *Women@Internet: Creating New Cultures in Cyberspace*, ed. Wendy Harcourt, 156–61. London: Zed Books, 1999.

Altman, Janet. *Epistolarity: Approaches to a Form*. Columbus: Ohio State University Press, 1982.

——. "The Letter Book as a Literary Institution 1539–1789: Toward a Cultural History of Published Correspondences in France." *Yale French Studies* 71 (1986): 17–62.

——. "Women's Letters in the Public Sphere." In *Going Public: Women and Publishing in Early Modern France*, ed. Elizabeth Goldsmith and Dena Goodman, 99–115. Ithaca, N.Y.: Cornell University Press, 1995.

Anderson, Benedict R. O'G. *Imagined Communities: Reflections on the Origin and Spread of Nationalism*. Rev. and extended ed. London: Verso, 1991.

Arizpe, Lourdes. "Freedom to Create: Women's Agenda for Cyberspace." In *Women@Internet: Creating New Cultures in Cyberspace*, ed. Wendy Harcourt, xii–xvi. London: Zed Books, 1999.

Atatimur, Sara. "In Defense of Womyn: An Open Letter to Marj Schneider." Manuscript. Lesbian Herstory Archives, New York.

Attar, Dena. "An Open Letter on Anti-Semitism and Racism." *Trouble and Strife* (Winter 1983). Reprint, in *Sweeping Statements: Writings from the Women's Liberation Movement, 1981–83*, ed. Hannah Kanter et al., 268–73. London: The Women's Press, 1984.

Atwood, Margaret. *The Handmaid's Tale*. London: Jonathan Cape, 1986.

Austin, Frances. "Letter Writing in a Cornish Community in the 1790s." In *Letter Writing as a Social Practice*, ed. David Barton and Nigel Hall, 43–62. Amsterdam: John Benjamins, 2000.

Bâ, Mariama. *So Long a Letter*. 1980. Trans. Modupe Bode-Thomas. London: Virago, 1992.

Balsamo, Anne Marie. *Technologies of the Gendered Body: Reading Cyborg Women.* Durham, N.C.: Duke University Press, 1996.

Barker, Pat. *Union Street*. 1982. London: Virago, 1997.

Barnes, Julian. *Flaubert's Parrot*. London: Picador, 1985.

Barreno, Maria Isabel, Maria Teresa Horta, and Maria Velho da Costa. *The Three Marias: New Portuguese Letters*. Trans. Donald E. Ericson. 1972. St Albans, U.K.: Paladin, 1975.

Barton, David, and Nigel Hall. "Introduction." In *Letter Writing as a Social Practice*, ed. David Barton and Nigel Hall, 1–14. Amsterdam: John Benjamins, 2000.

——, eds. *Letter Writing as a Social Practice*. Amsterdam: John Benjamins, 2000.

Bawden, Nina. *Family Money*. New York: St. Martin's Press, 1991.

Baxandall, Rosalyn Fraad. "Catching the Fire." In *The Feminist Memoir Project: Voices from Women's Liberation*, ed. Rachel Blau DuPlessis and Ann Barr Snitow, 208–24. New York: Three Rivers Press, 1998.

Bazerman, Charles. "Letters and the Social Grounding of Differentiated Genres." In *Letter Writing as a Social Practice*, ed. David Barton and Nigel Hall, 15–30. Amsterdam: John Benjamins, 2000.

Beauchamp, Virginia Walcott, ed. *A Private War: Letters and Diaries of Madge Preston, 1862–67*. New Brunswick, N.J.: Rutgers University Press, 1987.

Behe, Regis. "Love Letter Collection Gives Good Read on Subjects' Feelings." *Pittsburgh Tribune-Review*, 9 February, 2003. http://www.pittsburghlive.com/x/pittsburghtrib/s_117268.html.

Belfrage, Sally. "Down Among the 'Wimmin.'" *The Nation*, June 30 1984, 793–96.

Bellow, Saul. *Herzog*. New York: Viking Press, 1964.

Bensen, Richard. "The Joy of Text." *The Guardian*, 3 June 2000. http://www.guardian.co.uk/Archive/Article/0,4273,4024760,00.html.

Berry, Jeffery M. *The Interest Group Society*. Boston: Little, Brown, 1984.

Bertholf, Robert J., and Albert Gelpi, eds. *The Letters of Robert Duncan and Denise Levertov*. Stanford, Calif.: Stanford University Press, 2004.

Black Women's Liberation Group, Mount Vernon, New York. "Statement on Birth Control." In *Sisterhood Is Powerful: An Anthology of Writings from the Women's Liberation Movement*, ed. Robin Morgan, 360–61. New York: Random House, 1970.

Blackwood, Caroline. *On the Perimeter*. London: Heinemann, 1984.

Blythe, Ronald, ed. *Private Words: Letters and Diaries from the Second World War*. 1991. 2nd ed. London: Penguin, 1993.

Bogus, SDiane. "Mom De Plume." In *Double Stitch: Black Women Write About Mothers and Daughters*, ed. Patricia Bell-Scott, 67–70. New York: HarperPerennial, 1993.

Bohlin-Davis, Odell, ed. *Breaking Silence: Coming-Out Letters*. New York: Xanthus Press, 1995.

Bondoc, Anna, and Meg Daly. *Letters of Intent: Women Cross the Generations to Talk About Family, Work, Sex, Love, and the Future of Feminism*. New York: Free Press, 1999.

Bowden, Peta. *Caring: Gender-Sensitive Ethics*. London: Routledge, 1997.

Bower, Anne L. "Dear ——: In Search of New (Old) Forms of Critical Address." In *Epistolary Histories: Letters, Fiction, Culture*, ed. Amanda Gilroy and W. M. Verhoeven, 155–75. Charlottesville: University Press of Virginia, 2000.

Brant, Clare. "Love Stories? Epistolary Histories of Mary Queen of Scots." In *Epistolary Histories: Letters, Fiction, Culture*, ed. Amanda Gilroy and W. M. Verhoeven, 74–92. Charlottesville: University Press of Virginia, 2000.

Bray, Bernard. "Quelques aspects du systeme epistolaire de Mme De Sévigné." *Revue d'Histoire Litteraire de la France* 69 (1969): 491–505.

Bray-Crawford, Kekula P. "The Ho'okele Netwarriors in the Liquid Continent." In *Women@Internet: Creating New Cultures in Cyberspace*, ed. Wendy Harcourt, 162–72. London: Zed Books, 1999.

Breaching the Peace. London: Onlywomen Press, 1983.

Breckenridge, Keith. "Love Letters and Amanuenses: Beginning the Cultural History of the Working Class Private Sphere in South Africa, 1900–1933." *Journal of Southern African Studies* 26, no. 2 (2000): 337–48.

Broughton, Trev Lynn. *Men of Letters, Writing Lives: Masculinity and Literary Auto/Biography in the Late-Victorian Period*. London: Routledge, 1999.

Brown, Wilmette. *Black Women and the Peace Movement*. First published by the International Women's Day Convention 1983. Reprint, Bristol: Falling Wall Press, 1990.

Buss, Helen M. "Introduction." In *Working in Women's Archives: Researching Women's Private Literature and Archival Documents*, ed. Helen M. Buss and Marlene Kadar, 1–5. Waterloo, Ont.: Wilfrid Laurier University Press, 2001.

Byatt, A. S. *Possession*. London: Vintage, 1991.

Byrne, Paul. "Nuclear Weapons and CND." In *Protest Politics: Cause Groups and Campaigns*, ed. F. F. Ridley and Grant Jordan, 116–26. Oxford: Oxford University Press, 1998.

Card, Claudia. *Lesbian Choices.* Between Men–Between Women. New York: Columbia University Press, 1995.

Carmichael, Stokely, and Charles V. Hamilton. *Black Power: The Politics of Liberation in America.* 1967. London: Jonathan Cape, 1968.

Carroll, Andrew. *War Letters: Extraordinary Correspondence from American Wars.* New York: Washington Square Press, 2002.

Carlyle, Thomas. *The Collected Letters of Thomas and Jane Welsh Carlyle.* Ed. Ian Campbell et al. 34 vols. Duke-Edinburgh edition. Durham, N.C.: Duke University Press, 1970–.

Castle, Terry. "Was Jane Austen Gay?" In *Boss Ladies, Watch Out! Essays on Women, Sex, and Writing,* ed. Terry Castle, 125–36. New York: Routledge, 2002.

Carter, April. *Peace Movements: International Protest and World Politics Since 1945.* London: Longman, 1992.

Castells, Manuel. *End of Millennium.* Malden, Mass.: Blackwell, 1997.

——. *The Rise of the Network Society.* Cambridge, Mass.: Blackwell Publishers, 1996.

Cerne, Adriana. "Writing in Tongues: Chantal Ackerman's *News from Home.*" *Journal of European Studies* 32, nos. 2–3 (2002): 235–47.

(Charles), Helen. "The Language of Womanism: Rethinking Difference." In *Black British Feminism: A Reader,* ed. Heidi Safia Mirza, 278–97. London: Routledge, 1997.

Chesler, Phyllis. *Letters to a Young Feminist.* New York: Four Walls Eight Windows, 1997.

——. *Women and Madness.* Garden City, N.Y.: Doubleday, 1972.

Chodorow, Nancy. *The Reproduction of Mothering: Psychoanalysis and the Sociology of Gender.* 2nd ed. Berkeley: University of California Press, 1999.

Civin, Michael A. *Male, Female, Email: The Struggle for Relatedness in a Paranoid Society.* New York: Other Press, 2000.

Clarke, Norma. *Ambitious Heights: Writing, Friendship, Love: The Jewsbury Sisters, Felicia Hemans, and Jane Welsh Carlyle.* London: Routledge, 1990.

Clarke, Patricia, and Dale Spender. *Life Lines: Australian Women's Letters and Diaries, 1788–1840.* St. Leonards, NSW: Allen & Unwin, 1992.

Clay, Catherine. *British Women Writers, 1914–1945: Professional Work and Friendship.* Aldershot: Ashgate, 2006.

Collins, Patricia Hill. *Black Feminist Thought: Knowledge, Consciousness, and the Politics of Empowerment.* 2nd rev. ed. New York: Routledge, 2000.

Collins, William Wilkie. *The Haunted Hotel: A Mystery of Modern Venice, to Which Is Added, My Lady's Money.* Illus. Arthur Hopkins. 2 vols. London: Chatto & Windus, 1879.

Cook, Alice, and Gwyn Kirk. *Greenham Women Everywhere: Dreams, Ideas, and Actions from the Women's Peace Movement*. London: Pluto Press, 1983.

Cook, Elizabeth Heckendorn. *Epistolary Bodies: Gender and Genre in the Eighteenth-Century Republic of Letters*. Stanford, Calif.: Stanford University Press, 1996.

Corcoran, Marlena G. "Male and F:\Email: Report from Cyberspace." *Soundings: A Journal of Politics and Culture* 78, no. 2 (1995): 339–53.

Couser, G. Thomas. *Vulnerable Subjects: Ethics and Life Writing*. Ithaca, N.Y.: Cornell University Press, 2004.

Curtiss, Mina. *Other People's Letters: A Memoir*. 1978. New York: Helen Marx Books, 2005.

Daly, Mary. *Outercourse: The Be-Dazzling Voyage*. 1992. London: The Women's Press, 1993.

Danahay, Martin A. *A Community of One: Masculine Autobiography and Autonomy in Nineteenth-Century Britain*. SUNY Series, the Margins of Literature. Albany: State University of New York Press, 1993.

Dandekar, Natalie. "International Justice." Trans. Christian Hunold. In *A Companion to Feminist Philosophy*, ed. Alison M. Jaggar and Iris Marion Young, 550–58. Malden, Mass.: Blackwell, 1998.

Davey, Janet. *English Correspondence*. London: Chatto & Windus, 2003.

Davies, Margaret Llewelyn. *Life as We Have Known It*. 1931. Reprint, intro. Anna Davin. London: Virago, 1977.

Davis, Adrienne D., and Robert S. Chang. "The Adventure(S) of Blackness in Western Culture: An Epistolary Exchange on Old and New Identity Wars." *UC Davis Law Review*. Forthcoming. Available at SSRN: http://ssrn.com/abstract=874752.

Davis, Lennard J. *My Sense of Silence: Memoirs of a Childhood with Deafness*. Urbana: University of Illinois Press, 2000.

Davis, Morris Joseph, and Eva Weintrobe Davis. *Shall I Say a Kiss? The Courtship Letters of a Deaf Couple, 1936–1938*. Ed. Lennard J. Davis. Washington, D.C.: Gallaudet University Press, 1999.

Dawson, Jill. *The Virago Book of Love Letters*. London: Virago, 1994.

de la tierra, tatiana. *For the Hard Ones: A Lesbian Phenomenology*. San Diego, Calif.: Calaca Press, 2002; Buffalo, N.Y.: Chibcha Press, 2002.

Dell'Olio, Anselma. "Home Before Sundown." In *The Feminist Memoir Project: Voices from Women's Liberation*, ed. Rachel Blau DuPlessis and Ann Barr Snitow, 149–70. New York: Three Rivers Press, 1998.

Derrida, Jacques. "The Purveyor of Truth." In *The Purloined Poe*, ed. John P. Muller and William J. Richardson, 173–212. Baltimore, Md.: Johns Hopkins University Press, 1988.

Dinnerstein, Dorothy. *The Mermaid and the Minotaur: Sexual Arrangements and Human Malaise*. New York: Harper & Row, 1977.

Donnelly, Daria. "The Power to Die: Emily Dickinson's Letters of Consolation." In *Epistolary Selves: Letters and Letter-Writers, 1600–1945*, ed. Rebecca Earle, 134–51. Aldershot: Ashgate, 1999.

Doubrovsky, Serge. *Un Amour de soi: Roman*. Paris: Hachette litterature generale, 1982.

Douglas, Kate. "Witnessing on the Web: Asylum Seekers and Letter-Writing Projects on Australian Activist Websites." *Auto/biography Studies* 21, nos. 1–2 (2006): 44–57.

Eagleton, Terry. *The Rape of Clarissa: Writing, Sexuality, and Class Struggle in Samuel Richardson*. Oxford: Blackwell, 1982.

Eakin, Paul John. *How Our Lives Become Stories: Making Selves*. Ithaca, N.Y.: Cornell University Press, 1999.

Echols, Alice. *Daring to Be Bad: Radical Feminism in America, 1967–1975*. Minneapolis: University of Minnesota Press, 1989.

Edwards, Nicky. *Mud*. London: The Women's Press, 1986.

Eglin, Josephine. "Women and Peace: From the Suffragists to the Greenham Women." In *Campaigns for Peace: British Peace Movements in the Twentieth Century*, ed. Richard Taylor and Nigel Young, 221–59. Manchester: Manchester University Press, 1987.

Eichberg, Rob. *Coming Out: An Act of Love*. New York: Penguin, Plume, 1991.

Eisenberg, Anne. "E-Mail and the Epistolary Age." *Scientific American*, April 1994, 128.

Ellison, Michael. "Salinger's Letters Sold by Ex-Lover." *The Guardian*, 23 June 1999, International section, 10.

Emberley, Julia, and Donna Landry. "Coverage of Greenham and Greenham as 'Coverage.'" *Feminist Studies* 15, no. 5 (1989): 485–98.

Escobar, Arturo. "Gender, Place, and Networks: A Political Ecology of Cyberculture." In *Women@Internet: Creating New Cultures in Cyberspace*, ed. Wendy Harcourt, 31–54. London: Zed Books, 1999.

Faderman, Lillian. *Surpassing the Love of Men: Romantic Friendship and Love Between Women from the Renaissance to the Present*. New York: Morrow, 1981.

Farrell, Amy Erdman. *Yours in Sisterhood: Ms. Magazine and the Promise of Popular Feminism*. Gender and American Culture. Chapel Hill: University of North Carolina Press, 1998.

Farrell, Michèle Longino. *Performing Motherhood: The Sévigné Correspondence*. Hanover, N.H.: University Press of New England, 1991.

Favret, Mary A. *Romantic Correspondence: Women, Politics, and the Fiction of Letters.* Cambridge Studies in Romanticism. Cambridge: Cambridge University Press, 1993.

Felski, Rita. *Beyond Feminist Aesthetics: Feminist Literature and Social Change.* Cambridge, Mass.: Harvard University Press, 1989.

Ferguson, Frances. "Interpreting the Self Through Letters." *Centrum* 1, no. 2 (1981): 107–12.

Ferrante, Tony, and Paulette Jacobson. *Letters from the Closet.* Sacramento, Calif.: Tzedakah Publications, 1994.

Fischer, Erica. *Aimée and Jaguar: A Love Story, Berlin 1943.* New York: HarperCollins, 1995.

Fletcher, Stephanie D. *E-Mail: A Love Story.* New York: Donald I. Fine Books/Dutton, 1996.

France, Kim. "Passing the Torch: Review of *Letters to a Young Feminist* by Phyllis Chesler." *New York Times Book Review*, 26 April 1998, 10.

Freedman, Estelle. "'The Burning of Letters Continues': Elusive Identities and the Historical Construction of Sexuality." In *Modern American Queer History*, ed. Allida Black, 51–68. Philadelphia: Temple University Press, 2001.

Freeman, Jo. "On the Origins of the Women's Liberation Movement from a Strictly Personal Perspective." In *The Feminist Memoir Project: Voices from Women's Liberation*, ed. Rachel Blau DuPlessis and Ann Barr Snitow, 171–96. New York: Three Rivers Press, 1998.

——. "The Tyranny of Structurelessness." *Berkeley Journal of Sociology* 17 (1972–73): 151–65.

Friedman, Susan Stanford. "Women's Autobiographical Selves: Theory and Practice." In *The Private Self: Theory and Practice of Women's Autobiographical Writings*, ed. Shari Benstock, 34–62. Chapel Hill: University of North Carolina Press, 1988.

Frye, Marilyn. "Some Reflections on Separatism and Power." *Sinister Wisdom* no. 6 (Summer 1978). Also in *The Politics of Reality: Essays in Feminist Theory*, ed. Sarah Lucia Hoagland and Julia Penelope, 62–72. The Crossing Press, 1983; reprint, London: Onlywomen, 1988. Also reprinted in *For Lesbians Only: A Separatist Anthology*. 1977 (presented at a meeting of the Society for Women in Philosophy, Eastern Division, December).

Fussell, Paul. *Wartime: Understanding and Behaviour in the Second World War.* New York: Oxford University Press, 1989.

Gallop, Jane. "Annie Leclerc Writing a Letter, with Vermeer." *October* 33 (1985): 103–18.

Gaskell, Elizabeth Cleghorn. *Cranford/Cousin Phillis*. Ed. and intro. P. J. Keating. Penguin English Library. Harmondsworth: Penguin, 1976.

Gelb, Joyce, and Marian Lief Palley. *Women and Public Policies: Reassessing Gender Politics*. 1987. Charlottesville: University Press of Virginia, 1996.

Geok-Lin Lim, Shirley. "'Ain't I a Feminist?' Re-Forming the Circle." In *The Feminist Memoir Project: Voices from Women's Liberation*, ed. Rachel Blau DuPlessis and Ann Barr Snitow, 450–66. New York: Three Rivers Press, 1998.

Gergen, Kenneth J. *The Saturated Self: Dilemmas of Identity in Contemporary Life*. New York: Basic Books, 1991.

Gerson, Carole. "Locating Female Subjects in the Archives." In *Working in Women's Archives: Researching Women's Private Literature and Archival Documents*, ed. Helen M. Buss and Marlene Kadar, 7–22. Waterloo, Ont.: Wilfrid Laurier University Press, 2001.

Geser, Hans. "Towards a Sociological Theory of the Mobile Phone." Institute of Sociology, University of Zurich, 2004.

Gilbert, Michael C. "The Gilbert Email Manifesto." 2001. *Nonprofit Online News*. http://news.gilbert.org/gem.

Gillespie, Faith. "The Women's Liberation Context." *Index on Censorship* 3, no. 2 (1974): 22–26.

Gilligan, Carol. *In a Different Voice: Psychological Theory and Women's Development*. Cambridge, Mass.: Harvard University Press, 1982.

Gilroy, Amanda, and W.M. Verhoeven, eds. *Epistolary Histories: Letters, Fiction, Culture*. Charlottesville: University Press of Virginia, 2000.

Gittler, Alice Mastrangelo. "Mapping Women's Global Communications and Networking." In *Women@Internet: Creating New Cultures in Cyberspace*, ed. Wendy Harcourt, 91–101. London: Zed Books, 1999.

Gladney, Margaret Rose. "Personalizing the Political, Politicizing the Personal: Reflections on Editing the Letters of Lillian Smith." In *Carryin' on in the Lesbian and Gay South*, ed. John Howard, 93–106. New York: New York University Press, 1997.

Goldsmith, Elizabeth. "Authority, Authenticity, and the Publication of Letters by Women." In *Writing the Female Voice: Essays on Epistolary Literature*, ed. Elizabeth Goldsmith, 46–59. Boston: Northeastern University Press, 1988.

——, ed. *Writing the Female Voice: Essays on Epistolary Literature*. Boston: Northeastern University Press, 1988.

Goodman, Dena. *The Republic of Letters: A Cultural History of the French Enlightenment*. Ithaca, N.Y.: Cornell University Press, 1994.

Gordon, Lyndall. *Charlotte Brontë: A Passionate Life*. London: Vintage, 1995.

Gorris, Marleen. *Broken Mirrors*. Film. 1984. Matthijs van Heijningen.

Green, Sarah F. *Urban Amazons: Lesbian Feminism and Beyond in the Gender, Sexuality, and Identity Battles of London*. New York: St. Martin's Press, 1997.

Grossman, David, Vered Almog, and Maya Gurantz. *Be My Knife*. New York: Farrar, Straus and Giroux, 2001.

Gurumurthy, Anita, et al. "Gender and ICTs." Ed. BRIDGE: Institute for Development Studies, University of Sussex, 2004.

Gusdorf, Georges. "Conditions et limites de l'autobiographie." 1956. In *Autobiography: Essays Theoretical and Critical*, ed. James Olney, 28–48. Princeton, N.J.: Princeton University Press, 1980.

Habermas, Jürgen. *Between Facts and Norms: Contributions to a Discourse Theory of Law and Democracy*. Studies in Contemporary German Social Thought. Cambridge, Mass.: MIT Press, 1996.

Hall, Kira. "Cyberfeminism." In *Computer-Mediated Communication: Linguistic, Social, and Cross-Cultural Perspectives*, ed. Susan C Herring, 147–70. Amsterdam: John Benjamins, 1996.

Hallett, Nicky. "'Anxiously Yours': The Epistolary Self and the Culture of Concern." *Journal of European Studies* 32, nos. 2–3 (2002): 107–20.

——. *Lesbian Lives: Identity and Auto/Biography in the Twentieth Century*. London: Pluto, 1999.

Hamilton, Ian. *In Search of J. D. Salinger*. London: Minerva, 1989.

Hanisch, Carol. "Two Letters from the Women's Liberation Movement." In *The Feminist Memoir Project: Voices from Women's Liberation*, ed. Rachel Blau DuPlessis and Ann Barr Snitow, 197–207. New York: Three Rivers Press, 1998.

Hanscombe, Gillian E. *Between Friends*. Boston: Alyson Publications, 1982. Reprint, London: Sheba Feminist Publishers, 1983; London: Women's Press, 1990.

Hanscombe, Gillian E., and Virginia L. Smyers. *Writing for Their Lives: The Modernist Women, 1900–1940*. London: Women's Press, 1987.

Hansen, Karen V. "'No Kisses Is Like Youres': An Erotic Friendship Between Two African-American Women During the Mid-Nineteenth Century." *Gender and History* 7, no. 2 (1995): 153–82.

Harcourt, Wendy. "Cyborg Melody: An Introduction to Women on the Net (Won)." In *Women@Internet: Creating New Cultures in Cyberspace*, ed. Wendy Harcourt, 1–20. London and New York: Zed Books, 1999.

——, ed. *Women@Internet: Creating New Cultures in Cyberspace*. London: Zed Books, 1999.

——. "World Wide Women and the Web." In *Web.Studies: Rewiring Media Studies for the Digital Age*, ed. David Gauntlett and Ross Horsley, 150–58. 2000. 2nd ed. London: Arnold, 2004.

Harcourt, Wendy, and Arturo Escobar. *Women and the Politics of Place*. Bloomfield, Conn.: Kumarian Press, 2005.

Hardy, Lorna. "Exposure." In *Out the Other Side: Contemporary Lesbian Writing*, ed. Christine McEwen and Sue O'Sullivan, 76–93. London: Virago Press, 1988.

Harpham, Geoffrey Galt. "Ethics." In *Critical Terms for Literary Study*, ed. Frank Lentricchia and Thomas McLaughlin, 387–405. 2nd ed. Chicago: University of Chicago Press, 1995.

Harris, Duchess. "'All of Who I Am in the Same Place': The Combahee River Collective." *Womanist Theory and Research: A Journal of Womanist and Feminist-of-Color Scholarship and Art* 3, no. 1 (1999): unpaginated.

Hartley, Jenny. "'Letters Are *Everything* These Days': Mothers and Letters in the Second World War." In *Epistolary Selves: Letters and Letter-Writers, 1600–1945*, ed. Rebecca Earle, 183–95. Aldershot: Ashgate, 1999.

Hassett, Chris, and Tom Owen-Toole. *Friendship Chronicles: Letters Between a Gay and a Straight Man*. San Diego: Bald Eagle Mountain Press, 1994.

Havel, Vaclav. "The Anatomy of Reticence." 1985. In *Open Letters: Selected Prose, 1965–1990*, ed. Paul Wilson, 291–322. London: Faber and Faber, 1991.

Heilbrun, Carolyn G. *The Last Gift of Time: Life Beyond Sixty*. New York: Dial Press, 1997.

Held, Virginia. *Feminist Morality: Transforming Culture, Society, and Politics*. Women in Culture and Society. Chicago: University of Chicago Press, 1993.

——. "Rights." Trans. Christian Hunold. In *A Companion to Feminist Philosophy*, ed. Alison M. Jaggar and Iris Marion Young, 500–510. Malden, Mass.: Blackwell, 1998.

Herrmann, Anne. *The Dialogic and Difference: "an/Other Woman" in Virginia Woolf and Christa Wolf*. New York: Columbia University Press, 1989.

Hilaire, Patricia. "An Open Letter." In *Black Women Talk Poetry*, ed. Da Choong, 62–64. London: Black Womantalk, 1987.

Hirsch, Marianne. *The Mother/Daughter Plot: Narrative, Psychoanalysis, Feminism*. A Midland Book. Bloomington: Indiana University Press, 1989.

Hoagland, Sarah Lucia. *Lesbian Ethics: Toward New Value*. Palo Alto, Calif.: Institute of Lesbian Studies, 1988.

Hocking, Mary. *Letters from Constance*. London: Virago, 1992.

Holmes, Anna. *Hell Hath No Fury: Women's Letters from the End of the Affair*. New York: Carroll & Graf, 2002.

hooks, bell. *Communion: The Female Search for Love*. New York: W. Morrow, 2002.

——. *Remembered Rapture: The Writer at Work*. New York: Henry Holt, 1999.

Hopkins, Sarah, and Barbara Harford. *Greenham Common: Women at the Wire.* London: Women's Press, 1984.

Jacobus, Mary. "Reading Correspondences." In *Reading Woman: Essays in Feminist Criticism*, 277–310. London: Methuen, 1986.

James, Henry. *Selected Letters of Henry James.* Ed. and intro. Leon Edel. London: Rupert Hart-Davis, 1956.

Jastrzebska, Maria. "Sto Lat Zdrowia." In *Knowing Me: Women Speak About Myalgic Encephalomyelitis and Chronic Fatigue Syndrome*, ed. Caeia March, 110–19. London: The Women's Press, 1998.

Jensen, Katharine Ann. *Writing Love: Letters, Women, and the Novel in France, 1605–1776.* Carbondale: Southern Illinois University Press, 1995.

Joannou, Maroula, and Imelda Whelehan. "This Book Changes Lives: The 'Consciousness-Raising Novel' and Its Legacy." In *The Feminist Seventies*, ed. Helen Graham, 125–40. York: Raw Nerve Books, 2003.

Johnson, Barbara. "Apostrophe, Animation, and Abortion." *Diacritics* 16, no. 1 (1986): 29–47.

——. "The Frame of Reference: Poe, Lacan, Derrida." In *The Purloined Poe*, ed. John P. Muller and William J. Richardson, 213–51. Baltimore, Md.: Johns Hopkins Press, 1988.

Johnson, Deborah G. *Computer Ethics.* 3rd ed. International ed. Harlow, U.K.: Pearson Education International, 2001.

Jolly, James, and Estelle Kohler. *Gay Letters.* London: Marginalia Press, 1995.

Jolly, Margaretta, ed. *Dear Laughing Motorbyke: Letters from Women Welders in the Second World War.* London: Scarlet Press, 1997.

——, ed. *The Encyclopedia of Life Writing.* London and Chicago: Fitzroy Dearborn, 2001.

——. "Myths of Unity: Remembering the Second World War Through Letters and Their Editing." In *Arms and the Self*, ed. Alex Vernon, 144–70. Kent, Ohio: Kent State University Press, 2005.

Jolly, Margaretta, and Liz Stanley. "Letters as/Not a Genre." *LifeWriting* (2006): 75–101.

Jones, Constance, ed. *The Love of Friends: An Anthology of Gay and Lesbian Letters to Friends and Lovers.* New York: Simon & Schuster, 1997.

Jones, Lynne. *Keeping the Peace.* A Women's Peace Handbook 1. London: Women's Press, 1983.

Junor, Beth, and Katrina Howse. *Greenham Common Women's Peace Camp: A History of Non-Violent Resistance, 1984–1995.* London: Working Press, 1995.

Kadar, Marlene. "An Epistolary Constellation: Trotsky, Kahlo, Birney." In *Working in Women's Archives: Researching Women's Private Literature and Archival Docu-*

ments, ed. Helen M. Buss and Marlene Kadar, 103–14. Waterloo, Ont.: Wilfrid Laurier University Press, 2001.

Kahn, Esther Y. "Letters Long Distance to a Lover." In *Serious Pleasure: Lesbian Erotic Stories and Poetry*, ed. Sheba Collective, 71–79. London: Sheba Feminist Publishers, 1989.

Kamuf, Peggy, and Nancy K. Miller. "Parisian Letters: Between Feminism and Deconstruction." In *Conflicts in Feminism*, ed. Marilyn Hirsch and Evelyn Fox Keller, 121–33. London: Routledge, 1990.

Kanneh, Kadiatu. "Sisters Under the Skin: A Politics of Heterosexuality." In *Feminism and Sexuality: A Reader*, ed. Stevi Jackson and Sue Scott, 172–74. New York: Columbia University Pres, 1996.

Kanter, Hannah, et al., eds. *Sweeping Statements: Writings from the Women's Liberation Movement, 1981–83*. London: The Women's Press, 1984.

Katherine, Amber. "'A Too-Early Morning': Audre Lorde's 'An Open Letter to Mary Daly' and Daly's Decision Not to Respond in Kind." In *Feminist Interpretations of Mary Daly*, ed. Sarah Lucia Hoagland and Marilyn Frye, 266–97. University Park: Penn State University Press, 2000.

Kauffman, Linda. *Discourses of Desire: Gender, Genre, and Epistolary Fictions*. Ithaca, N.Y.: Cornell University Press, 1986.

——. "Not a Love Story: Retrospective and Prospective Epistolary Directions." In *Epistolary Histories: Letters, Fiction, Culture*, ed. Amanda Gilroy and W. M. Verhoeven, 198–224. Charlottesville: University Press of Virginia, 2000.

——. *Special Delivery: Epistolary Modes in Modern Fiction*. Women in Culture and Society. Chicago: University of Chicago Press, 1992.

Kenyon, Olga, ed. *Eight Hundred Years of Women's Letters*. Phoenix Mill, U.K.: Alan Sutton, 1992.

Keshen, David, and Jeff Mills. "'Ich bereite mich auf den Tag vor, da es zu Ende geht!' Briefwechsel von Kanadierinnen und Kanadiern im Krieg." In *Andere Helme—Andere Menschen? Heimaterfahrung und Frontalltag im zweiten Weltkreig*, ed. Detlef Vogel and Wolfram Wette, 257–82. Tubingen: Klartext, 1995.

King, Katie. *Theory in Its Feminist Travels: Conversations in U.S. Women's Movements*. Bloomington: Indiana University Press, 1994.

King, Ynestra. "All Is Connectedness: Scenes from the Women's Pentagon Action USA." In *Keeping the Peace: A Women's Peace Handbook 1*, ed. Lynne Jones, 40–63. London: Women's Press, 1983.

Koppelman, Susan. "Excerpts from Letters to Friends." In *The Intimate Critique: Autobiographical Literary Criticism*, ed. Diane P. Freedman, Olivia Frey, and Frances Murphy Zauhar, 75–80. Durham, N.C.: Duke University Press, 1993.

Krasniewicz, Louise. *Nuclear Summer: The Clash of Communities at the Seneca Women's Peace Encampment*. Ithaca, N.Y.: Cornell University Press, 1992.

kris. "Ain't We Wimmin Too?" *Lysistrata*, no. 2 (Winter 1983). Reprint, in *Sweeping Statements: Writings from the Women's Liberation Movement 1981–83*, ed. Hannah Kanter, et al., 107–9. London: The Women's Press, 1984.

Lacan, Jacques. "The Purloined Poe." In *The Purloined Poe*, ed. John P. Muller and William J. Richardson, 28–54. Baltimore, Md.: Johns Hopkins University Press, 1988.

Laclos, Choderlos de. *Les Liaisons dangereuses*. Trans. and ed. Richard Aldington London: Ark, 1987.

Laws, Sophie. "An Open Letter to Women in Wont and the Women's Peace Alliance." *Catcall* (December 1981). Reprint, in *Sweeping Statements: Writings from the Women's Liberation Movement 1981–83*, ed. Hannah Kanter et al., 121–23. London: The Women's Press, 1984.

Leclerc, Annie. "La Lettre d'amour." In *La Venue a l'écriture*, ed. Hélène Cixous, Madeleine Gagnon, and Annie Leclerc, 117–40. Paris: Union Générale d'Editions, 1977.

Lelland, Stephanie. "Greenham Women Are Everywhere." In *Feminist Action I*, ed. Joy Holland, 110–24. London: Battle Axe Books, 1983.

Lennon, J. Robert. *Mailman: A Novel*. New York: Norton, 2003.

Letherby, Gayle, and Dawn Zdrodowski. "'Dear Researcher': The Use of Correspondence as a Method Within Feminist Qualitative Research." *Gender and Society* 9, no. 5 (1995): 576–93.

Levinas, Emmanuel. *Totality and Infinity: An Essay on Exteriority*. Pittsburgh: Duquesne University Press, 1969.

Lister, Anne, and Jill Liddington. *Female Fortune: Land, Gender, and Authority: The Anne Lister Diaries and Other Writings, 1833–36*. London: Rivers Oram Press, 1998.

Lister, Ruth. "Dialectics of Citizenship." *Hypatia* 12, no. 4 (1997): 6–26.

Lorde, Audre. "Eye to Eye: Black Women, Hatred, and Anger." In *Sister Outsider: Essays and Speeches*, 145–75. Trumansburg, N.Y.: Crossing Press, 1984.

——. "An Open Letter to Mary Daly." In *This Bridge Called My Back: Writing by Radical Women of Colour*, ed. Cherríe Moraga and Gloria Anzaldúa, 94–97. Watertown, Mass.: Persephone Press, 1981.

——. "An Open Letter to Mary Daly." In *Sister Outsider: Essays and Speeches*, 66–71. Freedom, Calif.: The Crossing Press, 1984.

——. *Sister Outsider: Essays and Speeches*. Trumansburg, N.Y.: Crossing Press, 1984.

MacArthur, Elizabeth Jane. *Extravagant Narratives: Closure and Dynamics in the Epistolary Form*. Princeton, N.J.: Princeton University Press, 1992.

MacLean, Gerald. "Postscript." In *Epistolary Histories: Letters, Fiction, Culture*, ed. Amanda Gilroy and W. M. Verhoeven, 170–72, 175. Charlottesville: University Press of Virginia, 2000.

Maihofer, Andrea. "Care." Trans. Christian Hunold. In *A Companion to Feminist Philosophy*, ed. Alison M. Jaggar and Iris Marion Young, 383–92. Malden, Mass.: Blackwell, 1998.

Maraini, Dacia. *Letters to Marina*. Trans. Dick Kitto and Elspeth Spottiswood. 1981. London: Camden Press, 1987.

Marcus, Laura. *Auto/Biographical Discourses: Theory, Criticism, Practice*. Manchester: Manchester University Press, 1994.

Marks, Shula. "The Context of Personal Narrative: Reflections on 'Not Either an Experimental Doll—the Separate Worlds of Three South African Women.'" In *Interpreting Women's Lives: Feminist Theory and Personal Narratives*, ed. Personal Narratives Group, 39–58. Bloomington: Indiana University Press, 1989.

——, ed. *Not Either an Experimental Doll: The Separate Worlds of Three South African Women*. 2nd ed. London: Women's Press, 1987. Durban and Pietermaritzburg, South Africa: Killie Campbell Africana Library and The University of Natal Press, 1987 (1st printing).

Martindale, Kathleen, and Martha Saunders. "Realising Love and Justice: Lesbian Ethics in the Upper and Lower Case." *Hypatia* 7, no. 4 (Fall 1992). Reprint, in *Adventures in Lesbian Philosophy*, ed. Claudia Card, 163–85. Bloomington: Indiana University Press, 1994.

Mason, Mary G. "The Other Voice: Autobiographies of Women Writers." In *Autobiography: Essays Theoretical and Critical*, ed. James Olney, 207–35. Princeton, N.J.: Princeton University Press, 1980.

Mason, Mary Grimley, and Carol Hurd Green. *Journeys: Autobiographical Writings by Women*. Boston: G. K. Hall, 1979.

Matthews, Carol, and Marilyn Callahan. "Wilderness Stationery: Women's Letters and Women's Research." *Affilia* 11, no. 3 (1996): 338–55.

Maybin, Janet. "Death Row Penfriends: Some Effects of Letter Writing on Identity and Relationships." In *Letter Writing as a Social Practice*, ed. David Barton and Nigel Hall, 151–78. Amsterdam: John Benjamins, 2000.

Mayer, Bernadette. *The Desires of Mothers to Please Others in Letters*. West Stockbridge, Mass.: Hard Press, 1994.

McAlpin, Mary. "Poststructuralist Feminism and the Imaginary Woman Writer: The Lettres Portugaises." *The Romanic Review* (1999): 27–44.

Meese, Elizabeth. *(Sem)Erotics: Theorising Lesbian Writing*. New York: New York University Press, 1992.

Meigs, Mary. *Lily Briscoe, a Self-Portrait: An Autobiography.* Vancouver: Talonbooks, 1981.

——. *The Time Being.* Burnaby, B.C.: Talonbooks, 1997.

——. "To 'R': Extracts." In *The Virago Book of Love Letters*, ed. Jill Dawson, 35–36. London: Virago, 1994.

Melucci, Alberto, John Keane, and Paul Mier. *Nomads of the Present: Social Movements and Individual Needs in Contemporary Society.* London: Hutchinson Radius, 1989.

Mercer, Gina. *Parachute Silk: Friends, Food, Passion: A Novel in Letters.* North Melbourne, Vic.: Spinifex, 2001.

Meyers, Diana Tietjens. "Agency." In *A Companion to Feminist Philosophy*, ed. Alison M. Jaggar and Iris Marion Young, 372–82. Malden, Mass.: Blackwell, 1998.

Middlebrook, Diane. "Arguing with Stories: Misremembering Ted Hughes." In *The Ethics of Life Writing*, ed. Paul John Eakin, 40–50. Ithaca, N.Y.: Cornell University Press, 2004.

——. "'Fair Use' in Theory and Practice." Discussion at Salon of Women Writers, London, 2003.

Miller, Nancy K. *Bequest and Betrayal: Memoirs of a Parent's Death.* New York: Oxford University Press, 1996.

——. *But Enough About Me: Why We Read Other People's Lives.* Gender and Culture. New York: Columbia University Press, 2002.

——. "The Ethics of Betrayal: Diary of a Memoirist." In *The Ethics of Life Writing*, ed. Paul John Eakin, 148–60. Ithaca, N.Y.: Cornell University Press, 2004.

——. *Getting Personal: Feminist Occasions and Other Autobiographical Acts.* New York: Routledge, 1991.

——. "Representing Others: Gender and the Subjects of Autobiography." *differences: a Journal of Feminist Cultural Studies* 6, no. 1 (1994): 1–27.

——. "Writing Fictions: Women's Autobiography in France." In *Life/Lines: Theorizing Women's Autobiography*, ed. Bella Brodzki and Celeste Schenk, 45–61. Ithaca, N.Y.: Cornell University Press, 1988.

Mooney, Bel. *Intimate Letters.* London: Warner, 1997.

Morgan, Robin. *Going Too Far: The Personal Chronicle of a Feminist.* New York: Random House, 1977.

——. "Letter to a Sister Underground." In *Sisterhood Is Powerful: An Anthology of Writings from the Women's Liberation Movement*, ed. Robin Morgan, xxxvi–xl. New York: Random House, 1970.

Mueller, Carol. "Recognition Struggles and Process Theories of Social Movements." 2001. 18 July 2003. http://www.sociology.su.se/cgs/Conference/Mueller%20Paper.pdf.

Muller, John P., and William J. Richardson. *The Purloined Poe: Lacan, Derrida, and Psychoanalytic Reading.* Baltimore, Md.: Johns Hopkins University Press, 1988.

Namjoshi, Suniti, and Gillian E. Hanscombe. *Flesh and Paper.* Seaton, Devon: Jezebel, 1986.

Namjoshi, Suniti, Gillian E. Hanscombe, et al. *Flesh and Paper.* Videocassette. 26 min. Women Make Movies, New York, N.Y., 1990.

Nash, Kate. "A Movement Moves: Is There a Women's Movement in England Today?" *The European Journal of Women's Studies* 9, no. 3 (2002): 311–28.

Nestle, Joan, and John Preston. *Sister and Brother: Lesbians and Gay Men Write About Their Lives Together.* San Francisco: HarperSanFrancisco, 1994.

Noddings, Nel. "Caring." In *Justice and Care: Essential Readings in Feminist Ethics*, ed. Virginia Held, 7–30. Boulder, Colo.: Westview Press, 1995.

——. *Caring: A Feminine Approach to Ethics and Moral Education.* 1984. 2nd ed. Berkeley: University of California Press, 2003.

Norton, Rictor, ed. *My Dear Boy: Gay Love Letters Through the Centuries.* San Francisco: Leyland, 1998.

Nussbaum, Martha, and Amartya Sen. "Internal Criticism and Indian Rationalist Tradition." In *Relativism: Interpretation and Confrontation*, ed. Michael Krausz, 299–325. Notre Dame, Ind.: University of Notre Dame Press, 1989.

Omolade, Barbara. "Sisterhood in Black and White." In *The Feminist Memoir Project: Voices from Women's Liberation*, ed. Rachel Blau DuPlessis and Ann Barr Snitow, 377–408. New York: Three Rivers Press, 1998.

Owen, Hilary. "Exiled in Its Own Land." *Index on Censorship* 28, no. 1 (1999): 57–60.

——. *Portuguese Women's Writing, 1972 to 1986: Reincarnations of a Revolution.* Women's Studies 29. Lewiston, N.Y.; Lampeter: Edwin Mellen Press, 2000.

Page, Kathy. *Back in the First Person.* London: Virago, 1986.

Palmer, Paulina. *Contemporary Women's Fiction: Narrative Practice and Theory.* Hemel Hempstead: Harvester, 1989.

Payne, Karen, ed. *Between Ourselves: Letters Between Mothers and Daughters 1750–1982.* London: Picador, 1984.

Picardie, Ruth. *Before I Say Goodbye.* Ed. Matt Seaton and Justine Picardie. London: Penguin, 1998.

Plath, Sylvia. *Collected Poems.* Ed. Ted Hughes. London: Faber and Faber, 1981.

Plath, Sylvia, and Aurelia Schober Plath. *Letters Home: Correspondence, 1950–1963.* New York: Harper & Row, 1975.

Plummer, Ken. *Telling Sexual Stories: Power, Change, and Social Worlds.* London: Routledge, 1995.

Pool, Gail. *Other People's Mail: An Anthology of Letter Stories.* Columbia: University of Missouri Press, 2000.

Poster, Mark. *Information Please: Culture and Politics in the Age of Digital Machines.* Durham, N.C.: Duke University Press, 2006.

Preston, Morag. "Are You Fully Prepared for Ditigal Posterity?" *The Times* (London), 28 October 1998, Compact Disc Edition ed.: 12.

Prince, Brenda. "A Letter to My Mother." In *What Can a Woman Do with a Camera?*, ed. Jo Spence and Joan Solomon, 75–76. London: Scarlet Press, 1995.

Redstockings, The. "The Redstockings Manifesto." In *Sisterhood Is Powerful: An Anthology of Writings from the Women's Liberation Movement*, ed. Robin Morgan, 533–36. New York: Random House, 1970.

Republican Women POWs, Armagh Jail. "Letter to the Women's Movement." *London Women's Liberation Newsletter* 199 (1980). Reprint, in *Sweeping Statements: Writings from the Women's Liberation Movement 1981–83*, ed. Hannah Kanter et al, 261–262. London: The Women's Press, 1984.

Rheingold, Howard. *The Virtual Community: Homesteading on the Electronic Frontier.* Rev. ed. Cambridge, Mass.: MIT Press, 2000.

Rhys-Thomas, Deirdre, and Janice Owens. *Letters for My Children: One Mother's Quest for Answers About the Nuclear Threat.* London: Pandora, 1987.

Ribeiro, Alvaro, S.J. "Real Business, Elegant Civility, and Rhetorical Structure in Two Letters by Charles Burney." In *Sent as a Gift: Eight Correspondents from the Eighteenth Century*, ed. Alan T. Mckenzie, 90–108. Athens: University of Georgia Press, 1993.

Rich, Adrienne. *Of Woman Born: Motherhood as Experience and Institution.* 1976. London: Virago, 1977.

Rochon, Thomas R. "The West European Peace Movement and the Theory of New Social Movements." In *Challenging the Political Order: New Social and Political Movements in Western Democracies*, ed. Russell J. Dalton and Manfred Kuechler, 105–21. New York: Oxford University Press, 1990.

Rosen, Ruth, and Sue Davidson, eds. *The Maimie Papers.* London: Virago, 1979.

Roseneil, Sasha. *Common Women, Uncommon Practices: The Queer Feminisms of Greenham.* London: Cassell, 2000.

——. *Disarming Patriarchy: Feminism and Political Action at Greenham.* Buckingham: Open University Press, 1995.

Royle, Nicholas. "What Is Deconstruction?" In *Deconstructions: A User's Guide*, ed. Nicholas Royle, 1–13. Houndmills: Palgrave, 2000.

Ruddick, Sara. "Maternal Thinking." *Feminist Studies* 6, no. 2 (1980): 342–67.

——. *Maternal Thinking: Toward a Politics of Peace.* With a new preface. Boston: Beacon Press, 1995.

Ruddick, Sara, and Pamela Daniels. *Working It Out: Twenty-three Women Writers, Artists, Scientists, and Scholars Talk About Their Lives and Work*. New York: Pantheon Books, 1977.

Sackville-West, Vita, et al. *The Letters of Vita Sackville-West to Virginia Woolf*. London: Hutchinson, 1984.

Sandford, John. *The Sword and the Ploughshare: Autonomous Peace Initiatives in East Germany*. London: Merlin, 1983.

Schaffer, Kay, and Sidonie Smith. *Human Rights and Narrated Lives: The Ethics of Recognition*. New York: Palgrave Macmillan, 2004.

Schneider, Robert L., and Lori Lester. *Social Work Advocacy: A New Framework for Action*. Belmont, Calif.: Brooks/Cole, 2000.

Scott, Gavin. *How to Get Rid of the Bomb: A Peace Action Handbook*. London: Fontana, 1982.

Scott, Manda. "feMail." In *The New English Library Book of Internet Stories*, ed. Maxim Jakubowski, 295–308. London: New English Library, 2000.

Scott, Tim, et al. *I on the Mouse, ICTs for Women's Advocacies and Networking in Asia and the Pacific*. Manila, Philippines: Asian Women's Resource Exchange, Isis International–Manila, Association for Progressive Communications, Women's Networking Support Programme, 2001.

Segal, Lynne. *Is the Future Female? Troubled Thoughts on Contemporary Feminism*. London: Virago, 1987.

Seidler, Victor. "Embodied Knowledge and Virtual Space." In *The Virtual Embodied: Presence/Practice/Technology*, ed. John Wood, 15–29. London: Routledge, 1998.

Sexton, Anne. *Anne Sexton: A Self-Portrait in Letters*. Ed. Linda Gray Sexton and Lois Ames Boston: Houghton Mifflin, 1977.

Shade, Leslie Regan. *Gender and Community in the Social Construction of the Internet*. Digital Formations vol. 1. New York: P. Lang, 2002.

Sharp, Ann Margaret. "Letter-Writing: A Tool in Feminist Inquiry." *Inquiry: Critical Thinking Across the Disciplines* 14, no. 3 (1995). http://www.chss.montclair.edu/inquiry/spr95/sharp.html.

Silverstone, Roger. "Complicity and Collusion in the Mediation of Everyday Life." *New Literary History* 33 (2002): 761–80.

Simon, Sunka. *Mail-Orders: The Fiction of Letters in Postmodern Culture*. The Suny Series in Postmodern Culture. Albany: State University of New York Press, 2002.

Smith, Sidonie, and Julia Watson. "Introduction: Situating Subjectivity in Women's Autobiographical Practices." In *Women, Autobiography, Theory: A Reader*, ed. Sidonie Smith and Julia Watson, 3–52. Madison: University of Wisconsin Press, 1998.

——. *Reading Autobiography: A Guide for Interpreting Life Narratives*. Minneapolis: University of Minnesota Press, 2001.

Slevin, James. *The Internet and Society*. Cambridge: Polity Press/Blackwell Publishers, 2000.

Smith-Rosenberg, Caroll. "The Female World of Love and Ritual: Relations Between Women in Nineteenth-Century America." In *Feminism and History*, ed. Joan Wallach Scott, 366–97. 1975. Rev. ed. Oxford: Oxford University Press, 1996.

Snitow, Ann. "Holding the Line at Greenham: Being Joyously Political in Dangerous Times." *Mother Jones* (February–March 1985): 30–47.

Spacks, Patricia. *Imagining a Self: Autobiography and Novel in Eighteenth-Century England*. Cambridge, Mass.: Harvard University Press, 1976.

Spooner, M., and K. Yancey. "Postings on a Genre of Email." *College Composition and Communication* 47, no. 2 (1996): 252–78.

Starhawk. *Truth or Dare: Encounters with Power, Authority, and Mystery*. 1987, Miriam Simos. Reprint, San Francisco: HarperCollins, 1990.

Steedman, Carolyn. "A Woman Writing a Letter." In *Epistolary Selves: Letters and Letter-Writers, 1600–1945*, ed. Rebecca Earle, 111–33. Aldershot: Ashgate, 1999.

Steinem, Gloria. "Networking." In *Outrageous Acts and Everyday Rebellions*, 214–23. 1983. 2nd ed. New York: H. Holt, 1995.

Stockton, Christine Heron. *Lesbian Letters*. San Francisco: Heron Press, 1986.

Stone, Allucquère Rosanne. *The War of Desire and Technology at the Close of the Mechanical Age*. Cambridge, Mass.: MIT Press, 1995.

Stotsky, Sandra. "Writing in a Political Context: The Value of Letters to Legislators." *Written Communication* 9, no. 9 (1987): 394–410.

Teller, Astro. *Exegesis*. New York: Vintage Contemporaries, 1997.

Thom, Mary. *Letters to Ms., 1972–1987*. New York: H. Holt, 1987.

Thompson, Tierl, ed. *Dear Girl: The Diaries and Letters of Two Working Women, 1897–1917*. London: Women's Press, 1987.

Truss, Lynne. *Eats, Shoots and Leaves: The Zero Tolerance Approach to Punctuation*. New York: Gotham Books, 2004.

Tunde, Carmen. "An Open Letter." In *Black Women Talk Poetry*, ed. Da Choong, 87–91. London: Black Womantalk, 1987.

Turkle, Sherry. *Life on the Screen: Identity in the Age of the Internet*. New York: Simon & Schuster, 1997.

Turner, Kay., ed. *Baby Precious Always Shines: Selected Love Notes Between Gertrude Stein and Alice B. Toklas*. New York: St. Martin's Press, 1999.

——. *Between Us: A Legacy of Lesbian Love Letters*. San Francisco: Chronicle Books, 1996.

Turner, Victor Witter. *The Ritual Process: Structure and Anti-Structure.* The Lewis Henry Morgan Lectures, 1966. Chicago: Aldine, 1969.

Tweedie, Jill. *Letters from a Fainthearted Feminist.* London: Robson Books, 1982.

——. *More from Martha: Further Letters from a Fainthearted Feminist.* London: Robson Books, 1983.

Umans, Meg. *Like Coming Home: Coming-Out Letters.* Austin, Tex.: Banned Books, 1988.

Versini, Laurent. *Le Roman épistolaire.* Paris: PUF, 1979.

Walker, Alice. *The Color Purple: A Novel.* New York: Harcourt Brace Jovanovich, 1982.

——. *In Search of Our Mothers' Gardens: Womanist Prose.* San Diego: Harcourt Brace Jovanovich, 1983.

Wallace, Michele. "To Hell and Back: On the Road with Black Feminism in the 1960s and 1970s." In *The Feminist Memoir Project: Voices from Women's Liberation,* ed. Rachel Blau DuPlessis and Ann Barr Snitow, 426–42. New York: Three Rivers Press, 1998.

Williams, Carolyn. "'Trying to Do Without God': The Revision of Epistolary Address in the Color Purple." In *Writing the Female Voice: Essays on Epistolary Literature,* ed. Elizabeth Goldsmith, 273–85. Boston: Northeastern University Press, 1988.

Williams, Patricia J. *The Alchemy of Race and Rights.* Cambridge, Mass.: Harvard University Press, 1991.

Winterson, Jeanette. *The PowerBook.* New York: Knopf, 2000.

Wittig, Monique, and Evelyne Le Garrec. "Note pour l'edition francaise." In *Nouvelles lettres Portugaises,* by Maria Isabel Barreno, Maria Teresa Horta and Maria Velho da Costa, ed. and trans. Monique Wittig and Evelyne Le Gerrec, 7–11. 1972. Paris: Seuil, 1974.

Women at Greenham Common, The. "Open Letter." In *My Country Is the Whole World: An Anthology of Women's Work on Peace and War,* ed. Cambridge Women's Peace Collective, 262–63. London: Pandora, 1984.

Women of the American Revolution (WAR). "Letter to Our Sisters in Social Work." In *Sisterhood Is Powerful: An Anthology of Writings from the Women's Liberation Movement,* ed. Robin Morgan, 524–26. New York: Random House, 1970.

Woo, Merle. "Letter to Ma." In *This Bridge Called My Back: Writings by Radical Women of Color,* ed. Cherríe Moraga and Gloria Anzaldúa, 140–47. Watertown, Mass.: Persephone Press, 1981.

Woolf, Virginia. "Dorothy Osborne's Letters." In *A Woman's Essays,* ed. Rachel Bowlby, 126–32. London: Penguin, 1992.

——. "The Humane Art." *New Statesman and Nation,* 8 June 1940, 726.

Xiao, Hong. "Class, Gender, and Parental Values in the 1990s." *Gender and Society* 14, no. 6 (2000): 785–803.

Yates, Simeon. "Computer-Mediated Communication: The Future of the Letter?" In *Letter Writing as a Social Practice*, ed. David Barton and Nigel Hall, 233–54. Amsterdam: John Benjamins, 2000.

Young, Alison. *Femininity in Dissent.* Sociology of Law and Crime. London: Routledge, 1990.

Youngs, Gillian. "Virtual Voices: Real Lives." In *Women@Internet: Creating New Cultures in Cyberspace*, ed. Wendy Harcourt, 55–68. London: Zed Books, 1999.

——. "Closing the Gaps: Women, Communications and Technology." *Development* 45, no. 4 (2002): 23–28.

Yue Mei. "To My Friends in the Chinese Society for Women's Studies." In *Reflections and Resonance: Stories of Chinese Women Involved in International Preparatory Activities for the 1995 Ngo Forum on Women*, ed. Lisa Stearns, Mary Anna Burris, and Yuen Ling Wong, 54–60. Beijing: The Ford Foundation, 1995.

Zilcosky, John. "Kafka's Remains." In *Lost in the Archives*, ed. Rebecca Comay, 631–43. Toronto: Alphabet City Media, 2002.

Zuern, John. "Online Lives." *Biography* 26, no. 1 (2003): v–xxv.

Acknowledgments

The correspondences I enjoyed in researching this book were an education of their own in helping me to understand just how complex and sensitive the world of letter-writing can be. I thank all the women and men who were so generously willing to share their accounts of the life of political change. Some I only know by first name and others have wished to remain anonymous. I particularly thank "S," Lise, Kevin Littlewood, Carole Harwood, Karen Payne, "Kate," and Wendy Harcourt for their dialogues with me and for their permission to share their dialogues with others. Others who were especially helpful were Eileen Bower, Sasha Roseneil, Sabine Erika, Charlotte Bunch, Lee Waldorf, Roxanna Carillo, Noeleen Heyzer, Fatma Alloo, Gillian Youngs, David Morgan, Alice Cook, Juley Howard, Ginette Leach, Millie Oliver, Elizabeth Barakah Hodges, and Ann Pettit.

The following people were also important in offering sources and ideas: Penny Lowery, Julia Watson, Caiea March, Gill Branston, Melissa Hardie, Di Parkin, Claire Grey, Daphne Kingdom, Jill Golden, Laura Potts, Jill Dawson, Jan Montefiore, Anna Holmes, Margery Lewis, Nicky Hallett, Charmion Cannon, Sarah Hipperson, Carole Stibbs, Ilona Singer, Ann Kalowsi-Naylor, Diane Middlebrook, Laura Gowing, Ra'ida Al-Zu'bi, Odine de Guzman, Cynthia Huff, Zohl de Ishtar,

Jenny Maxwell, Helen Buss, Gwyn Kirk, Laura Ahearn, Louise Krasniewicz, Nicole Constable, Kay Turner, Jana Runnalls, Helen John, Joan Nestle, Ruth Rosen, and Clare Brant. Members of the International Auto/Biography Association, Women's Studies Network UK, and Older Feminists Network also kindly gave time and effort to help my research. My apologies to any I may have forgotten and my thanks to some very helpful people who have chosen to remain anonymous.

I should like to thank several librarians and archivists for their care. The staff at the Lesbian Herstory Archives were wonderfully generous and I especially acknowledge Deborah Edel for her kindness. Jane Hargreaves at the Feminist Archive (South) has been keeping the place alive and kept me so, too. The Schlesinger Library at Radcliffe College provided a fabulously organized atmosphere. Kathryn Jacob, assistant curator at the Schlesinger Library, kindly let me interview her about the problems of donors. Jacalyn R. Blume was very helpful in guiding me through the papers of the Women's Encampment for a Future of Peace and Justice, and Sarah Hutcheon, in advising on my visit generally. Amy Hague, curator of manuscripts at the Sophia Smith Collection at Smith College and Susan Edwards at the Glamorgan Records Office in Cardiff, were also welcoming. The Women's Library at London Metropolitan University was a treat, and Teresa Doherty's comments as head of Special Collections eye-opening. Dorothy Sheridan at the Mass-Observation Archive remains an archivist friend of distinction. Jessica Gardner, head of Special Collections at the University of Exeter, I cannot thank enough for her professional help as well as loveliness as a friend.

I thank members of the Department of English, University of Exeter, for general support: Ashley Tauchert and Helen Hanson offered stimulating comments on drafts; Tony Da Silva was a kindred spirit in life writing; and Helen Taylor was quietly encouraging throughout. Teachers and colleagues who have been formative in my thinking about letters and life history include Janet Gurkin Altman, Philippe Lejeune, Dorothy Sheridan, Laura Marcus, Treva Broughton, Julia Swindells, Tom Couser, Paul John Eakin, Liz Stanley, Terry Castle, Jenny Bourne Taylor, and Jenny Shaw.

Nancy Miller and Victoria Rosner, editors of the Columbia University Press Gender and Culture series, were fantastically inspirational and stylish guides, who saw what I was trying to do and made me do it better. I also warmly thank Jennifer Crewe, Michael Haskell, Clare Wellnitz, and Afua Adusei at the Press, as well as the anonymous readers of the manuscript, for such careful suggestions.

I give special thanks to friends: Jay Prosser for loving and inspirational conversations, Niamh Moore for ecofeminism and reading drafts, Jacquetta Morris for making me laugh and write better, Clare Benjamin for thinking so interestingly about relationships, Sheila Hamilton for her encyclopedic memory, Anna T for talking politics with me, Anne Nyssen for being more revolutionary than I could ever be, Gwyn Lewis and Shau Lan Chan for their loyalty, Lisa Freedman for her eloquence, Christine Edwards, Faith Mosley, Isanna Curwen, Brenda Whisker, and Xiao Pe He for women's love, Margaret Nairn for being such a faithful correspondent, Sue Teddern for being able to write situation comedy, and Craig Howes for making conferences such fun. Nick Fairclough has been a sparkling joy in life as well as writing.

My thanks, finally, go to my family, especially my parents, Richard and Alison Jolly, for always being there, for keeping me strong, not to mention reading more drafts than I could dare to expect.

This research was funded in part by the Arts and Humanities Research Council, the British Academy, and the Department of English, University of Exeter, for which I am deeply grateful.

I have tried assiduously to contact every source, and to obtain copyright permission. If at the time of publication it has not been possible to trace any authors cited, I would be pleased to hear from them. I very gratefully acknowledge permission to include brief extracts from the following people:

Laura Agustín, for permission to quote from an e-mail to Women on the Net, quoted in Wendy Harcourt, "Cyborg Melody: An Introduction to Women on the Net (Won)," in *Women@Internet: Creating New Cultures in Cyberspace*, ed. Wendy Harcourt (London: Zed Books, 1999), 1–20.

Fatma Alloo, for permission to quote from an e-mail to Women on the Net, quoted in Wendy Harcourt, "Cyborg Melody: An Introduction to Women on the Net (Won)," in *Women@Internet: Creating New Cultures in Cyberspace*, ed. Wendy Harcourt (London: Zed Books, 1999), 1–20.

Eileen Bonner, for permission to quote from personal interview, September 2002, and from an unpublished letter to lover, August 1982, Bonner's personal collection.

Alison Burns, for permission to quote from an unpublished letter to Nan Talese, 9 November 1982, Karen Payne personal papers.

tatiana de la tierra, for permission to quote from a letter dated 6 March 1994, published in Kay Turner, *Between Us: A Legacy of Lesbian Love Letters* (San Francisco: Chronicle Books, 1996).

John Wenger Berquist DeHority, for permission to quote from an unpublished "Epistle to the Peace Encampment," 15 July 1983, Women's Encampment for Peace and Justice Collection, box no. 4, folder 107, Schlesinger Library, Radcliffe Institute, Harvard University, Cambridge, Mass.

Sabina Erika, for permission to quote from personal interview, September 2002.

Roy Fuller, for permission to quote from "War Letters," quoted in Ronald Blythe, ed., *Private Words: Letters and Diaries from the Second World War* (1991), 2nd ed. (London: Penguin, 1993).

Gillian E. Hanscombe, for permission to quote from *Between Friends* (Boston: Alyson, 1982; London: Sheba Feminist Publishers, 1983; London: Women's Press, 1990).

Wendy Harcourt, for permission to quote from "Cyborg Melody: An Introduction to Women on the Net (Won)," in *Women@Internet: Creating New Cultures in Cyberspace*, ed. Wendy Harcourt (London: Zed Books, 1999), 1–20.

Wendy Harcourt, for permission to quote from an unpublished e-mail to Kekula Bray-Crawford, 6 February 1998, personal archives of Wendy Harcourt.

Carole Harwood, for permission to quote from personal interview, 20 May 2003; from an unpublished letter to the author, 21 January 2003.

Xiao Pei He, for permission to quote from an unpublished e-mail to Susan Jolly, 18 March 2004.

Noeleen Heyzer, for permission to quote from an unpublished e-mail to the author, 16 December 2002.

Maria Jastrebska, for permission to quote from "Sto Lat Zdrowia," in *Knowing Me: Women Speak About Myalgic Encephalomyelitis and Chronic Fatigue Syndrome*, ed. Caeia March (London: The Women's Press, 1998), 110–19.

Susan Jolly, for permission to quote from an unpublished e-mail to He Xiao Pei, 18 March 2004.

Kate, for permission to quote from a letter to Teresa, 5 May 1975, and from a letter to Teresa, 14 October 1977. Also from editorial notes to her correspondence with Teresa, published in Karen Payne, *Between Ourselves: Letters between Mothers and Daughters, 1750–1982* (Boston: Houghton Mifflin, 1983). Also for permission to quote from an unpublished letter to Karen Payne, 7 May 1983, Karen Payne personal papers.

Gwyn Kirk, for permission to quote from Alice Cook and Gwyn Kirk, *Greenham Women Everywhere: Dreams, Ideas, and Actions from the Women's Peace Movement* (London: Pluto Press, 1983).

Ginette Leach, for permission to quote from the unpublished diary of Ginette Leach, 30 May–2 June 1984, personal collection of Ginette Leach.

Lise, for permission to quote from her letters to Joan Nestle. For more information, contact the Lesbian Herstory Archives, New York.

Elizabeth Meese, for permission to quote from *(Sem)Erotics: Theorising Lesbian: Writing* (New York: New York University Press, 1992). Also for permission to quote from a letter to Sandy, 14 July 1989, published in Kay Turner, ed.,

Between Us: A Legacy of Lesbian Love Letters (San Francisco: Chronicle Books, 1996).

Nancy Miller, for permission to quote from "The Ethics of Betrayal: Diary of a Memoirist," in *The Ethics of Life Writing*, ed. Paul John Eakin (Ithaca, N.Y.: Cornell University Press, 2004), 148–60.

Robin Morgan, for permission to quote from "Letter to a Sister Underground," in *Sisterhood Is Powerful: An Anthology of Writings from the Women's Liberation Movement*, ed. Robin Morgan (New York: Random House, 1970), xxxvi–xl. Also, for permission to quote from Black Women's Liberation Group, Mount Vernon, New York, "Statement on Birth Control," in *Sisterhood Is Powerful: An Anthology of Writings from the Women's Liberation Movement*, ed. Robin Morgan (New York: Random House, 1970), 360–61.

Suniti Namjoshi and Gillian E. Hanscombe, for permission to quote from *Flesh and Paper* (Seaton, Devon: Jezebel, 1986).

Joan Nestle, for permission to quote from Authors' note to letters, published in Kay Turner, ed., *Between Us: A Legacy of Lesbian Love Letters* (San Francisco: Chronicle Books, 1996). Also for permission to quote from an unpublished letter to Beth Hodges, 3 January 1977, and for permission to quote from an unpublished e-mail to the author, 9 July 2005.

Karen Payne, for permission to quote from draft notes to *Between Ourselves: Letters Between Mothers and Daughters 1750–1982*, Karen Payne personal papers.

Ann Pettitt, for permission to quote from an unpublished article sent to *The Guardian*, September 1981, Glamorgan Record Office, Cardiff, Wales, GB 214 DWLE/3/7. And for permission to quote from Chain letter from Pettitt and others, Glamorgan Record Office, Cardiff, Wales, GB 214 DWLE/6/11.

Marisa Belausteguigoitia Rius, for permission to quote from an e-mail to Women on the Net, published in Wendy Harcourt, "Cyborg Melody: An Introduction to Women on the Net (Won)," in *Women@Internet: Creating New Cultures in Cyberspace*, ed. Wendy Harcourt (London: Zed Books, 1999), 1–20.

Jana Runnalls, for permission to quote from an unpublished letter to S, 10 September 1982, personal collection of S. Also, for permission to quote from Letter to S. 17 December 1982, personal collection of S.

S, for permission to quote from unpublished interviews, written and taped, between September 2001 and August 2005.

Schlesinger library, Radcliffe Institute for Advanced Study, Harvard University, for permission to quote from Minutes from Brainstorming, Heartsearching Meeting, Part 2, October 11–12, 1986, Minutes, Agendas, Etc., Women's Encampment for Peace and Justice collection, Schlesinger Library, Radcliffe Institute, Harvard

University, Cambridge, Mass., box 1, file 10 and the Terms of Use of the Records of, Women's Encampment for Peace and Justice collection, box 4, folder no. 116.

The Sophia Smith Archives for permission to quote from Audio letter, Noel Phyllis Birkby to Bertha Harris, undated, Noel Phyllis Birkby Papers, Sophia Smith Collection, Northampton, Mass.

The Sophia Smith Archives for permission to quote from "Love Letter," Appendix: Descriptive List of Films, Finding Aid to the Noel Phyllis Birkby Papers, Sophia Smith Collection, Northampton, Mass.

Carol Ann Stibbs, for permission to quote from "Beyond the Pale: Representations of the Greenham Women" (master's diss., Sheffield City Polytechnic, 1987).

Kay Turner, for permission to quote from *Between Us: A Legacy of Lesbian Love Letters* (San Francisco: Chronicle Books, 1996).

Lise Weil, for permission to quote from a letter by Mary Meigs to R, 2 August 1992, published in Jill Dawson, *The Virago Book of Love Letters* (London: Virago, 1994).

Gillian Youngs, for permission to quote from an e-mail quoted in Harcourt, Wendy. "Cyborg Melody: An Introduction to Women on the Net (Won)," in *Women@Internet: Creating New Cultures in Cyberspace*, ed. Wendy Harcourt (London: Zed Books, 1999), 1–20.

Gillian Youngs, "Virtual Voices: Real Lives," in *Women@Internet: Creating New Cultures in Cyberspace*, ed. Wendy Harcourt (London: Zed Books, 1999), 55–68.

For images reproduced, I thank the following:

Barbara Hammer, for permission to reproduce letter photocollage to Florrie Burke. Published in Kay Turner, *Between Us: A Legacy of Lesbian Love Letters* (San Francisco: Chronicle Books, 1996).

David Legge, for permission to reproduce cover illustration of *Life Lines: Australian Women's Letters and Diaries, 1788–1840*, ed. Patricia Clarke and Dale Spender (St Leonards, NSW: Allen & Unwin, 1992).

Christine McCauley, for permission to reproduce cover illustration of *Spare Rib* (December 1980)

The Spare Rib Collective, for permission to reproduce "Letters Page" of *Spare Rib* (December 1980)

Ed Barber and Random House Group Ltd., for permission to reproduce "Greenham women reading letters," originally titled "Greenham Common October 1981." Published in *Peace Moves: Nuclear Protest in the 1980s* (London; Chatto & Windus, Hogarth Press, 1984), 32–33. Photograph by Ed Barber, text by Zoe Fairburns and James Cameron.

Merrily Harpur, for permission to reproduce cover illustration of *Letters from a Fainthearted Feminist*, by Jill Tweedie (London: Robson Books, 1982).

Greenham chain letter, reproduced from Alice Cook and Gwyn Kirk, *Greenham Women Everywhere: Dreams, Ideas, and Actions from the Women's Peace Movement* (London: Pluto Press, 1983).

H, for permission to reproduce a letter to the author, 1987.

Elizabeth Barakah Hodges, for permission to reproduce *Ghosts*, 1996, and for permission to reproduce *Jan and Me*, 1996, as the cover illustration.

All copyright rests with the owners.

I also thank the following for permission to reprint excerpts from articles that have constituted earlier expressions of portions of this book:

Sage Publications, for "Confidantes, Co-Workers, and Correspondents: Feminist Discourses of Letter-Writing from 1970–Present," *Journal of European Studies* 32, nos. 2–3 (2002): 267–82.

Taylor & Francis, for "We Are the Web: Letter-Writing and the 1980s Women's Peace Movement," *Prose Studies* 26, nos. 1–2 (2003): 196–218. Also published in *Women's Life Writing and Imagined Communities*, ed. Cynthia Huff (London: Routledge, 2005)

Ashgate Publishers, for "Corresponding in the Sex and Gender Revolution: Desire, Education, and Feminist Letters, 1970–2000," in *Gender and Politics in the Age of Letter-Writing, 1750–2000*, eds. Caroline Bland and Máire Cross (Aldershot: Ashgate, 2004), 253–70.

Arnold Journals, Hodder Headline Group, for "Censored/Uncensored: Lovers in Dialogue," *Auto/Biography* 12, no. 2 (2004): 165–84.

Center for Biographical Research, University of Hawai'i, for "E-Mail in a Global Age: The Ethical Story of 'Women on the Net.'" *Biography* 28, no. 1 (2004): 152–65.

Index

Page locators in italics refer to figures

Seaton, Matt, 210

second-wave feminism, 3; decline of, 243–244, 247; as literary, 5, 79–80; third wave, dialogue with, 4, 18, 171–177, 180; Victorian women writers, view of, 80–81

seduction, literary, 23, 27–28, 57, 155

Segal, Lynne, 131

self, relational, 16, 80–85, 81–85, 229; e-mail and, 194–195

self-care, 87, 111, 166–171, 247. *See also* autonomy

(Sem)erotics: Theorising Lesbian Writing (Meese), 56–58

Seneca Women's Encampment for Peace and Justice, 3, 17, 117, 129, 254–255n. 6, 255n. 9, 256n. 13, 261–262n. 13; as liminal world, 133–134; open letters, 131, 137–138, 140; public response to, 136–138, 148–149; rituals of community at, 133–140

separatism, 9–10, 14, 149–152; ethics of care and, 168; individual, needs of, 159–161; preservation of cultural purity, 158–159

Sepâulveda-Pulvirenti, Emma, 46

Serious Pleasure: Lesbian Erotic Stories and Poetry (Sheba Collective), 46

Sévigné, Madame de, 11, 39, 83, 100, 173

Sexton, Anne, 98

sexual epistolary, 207–209

sexuality, 58, 209, 216–217

sex workers, 199

Shade, Leslie, 198

Shall I Say a Kiss? Courtship Letters of a Deaf Couple (Davis and Davis), 232

Shange, Ntozake, 18, 174–175

Sharp, Ann Margaret, 54, 89

Sheba Collective, 46

signature, 63, 85, 207

silence, 112

Si longue lettre, Une (Bâ), 46

Silvia, M.T., 31

Simon, Sunka, 183

Sister and Brother: Lesbians and Gay Men Write About Their Lives Together (Nestle and Preston), 162

Sisterhood is Powerful, 67

"S" (letter writer), 30–31, 156–161, 164, 228

Smith, Barbara, 41

Smith, Lillian, 216–217, 226

Smith, Sidonie, 81, 82–83, 212–213, 224–225

Smith College, 213

Smith-Rosenberg, Caroll, 9–10, 13, 81, 97, 100, 244

Smyers, Virginia L., 48

Snelling, Paula, 216

sociability, privatization of, 197

social codes, 3, 6, 28–29

socialist feminism, 41, 61

social movements, life cycle of, 12–14, 18, 20; separatism, 158–159

Society for International Development, 186, 187

socio-anthropological theories, 6

Solomon, Joan, 112

Sommer, Doris, 224

South African letters, 91, 220–222

Spare Rib, 49–51, 63, 109, 219

Special Delivery (Kauffman), 83

Spence, Jo, 112

Spender, Dale, 38

Spinsters, the, 118

spontaneity, lack of, 28–29

Stanford University, 217

Starhawk, 138

"Statement on Birth Control" (Black Women's Liberation Group), 67–68

stealing letters, 224–239; justification for, 226, 229–230, 237

Steedman, Carolyn, 70

Steinem, Gloria, 18, 37, 175–176, 185

Stibbs, Carol, 123–124

Stone, Allucquere Rosanne, 181

style, 41, 56, 60–61, 88–89, 118, 123, 125, 135, 184, 188, 217, 219, 233, 260n. 5

Sue (Acorn, Flame), 28

Surpassing the Love of Men: Romantic Friendship and Love Between Women from the Renaissance to the Present (Faderman), 97

Sweeping Statements (ed. Kanter et al.), 67

Talese, Nan, 218–219

Tanzania Media Women's Association, 187

GENDER AND CULTURE
A Series of Columbia University Press
Nancy K. Miller and Victoria Rosner, Series Editors

Unbecoming Women: British Women Writers and the Novel of Development
Susan Fraiman

The Apparitional Lesbian: Female Homosexuality and Modern Culture
Terry Castle

George Sand and Idealism
Naomi Schor

Becoming a Heroine: Reading About Women in Novels
Rachel M. Brownstein

Nomadic Subjects: Embodiment and Sexual Difference in Contemporary Feminist Theory
Rosi Braidotti

Engaging with Irigaray: Feminist Philosophy and Modern European Thought
Edited by Carolyn Burke, Naomi Schor, and Margaret Whitford

Second Skins: The Body Narratives of Transsexuality
Jay Prosser

A Certain Age: Reflecting on Menopause
Edited by Joanna Goldsworthy

Mothers in Law: Feminist Theory and the Legal Regulation of Motherhood
Edited by Martha Albertson Fineman and Isabelle Karpin

Critical Condition: Feminism at the Turn of the Century
Susan Gubar

Feminist Consequences: Theory for the New Century
Edited by Elisabeth Bronfen and Misha Kavka

Simone de Beauvoir, Philosophy, and Feminism
Nancy Bauer

Pursuing Privacy in Cold War America
Deborah Nelson

But Enough About Me: Why We Read Other People's Lives
Nancy K. Miller

Palatable Poison: Critical Perspectives on The Well of Loneliness
Edited by Laura Doan and Jay Prosser

Cool Men and the Second Sex
Susan Fraiman

Modernism and the Architecture of Private Life
Victoria Rosner

Virginia Woolf and the Bloomsbury Avant-Garde: War, Civilization, Modernity
Christine Froula

Gender and Culture Readers

Modern Feminisms: Political, Literary, Cultural
Edited by Maggie Humm

Feminism and Sexuality: A Reader
Edited by Stevi Jackson and Sue Scott

Writing on the Body: Female Embodiment and Feminist Theory
Edited by Katie Conboy, Nadia Medina, and Sarah Stanbury